PROFESSIONAL RESPONSIBILITY
A Problem Approach

LITTLE, BROWN AND COMPANY

Law Book Division

Editorial Advisory Board

A. James Casner, CHAIRMAN
Austin Wakeman Scott Professor of Law, Harvard University

Francis A. Allen
*Edson R. Sunderland Professor of Law,
University of Michigan*

Clark Byse
Bussey Professor of Law, Harvard University

Thomas Ehrlich
*Professor of Law, Stanford University (on leave)
President, Legal Services Corporation*

Geoffrey C. Hazard, Jr.
Professor of Law, Yale University

Frank C. Newman
*Jackson H. Ralston Professor of International Law,
University of California at Berkeley*

Willis L. M. Reese
*Charles Evans Hughes Professor of Law and Director,
Parker School of Foreign and Comparative Law,
Columbia University*

Bernard Wolfman
Fessenden Professor of Law, Harvard University

PROFESSIONAL RESPONSIBILITY
A Problem Approach

Norman Redlich
Dean, New York University School of Law

Little, Brown and Company
Boston and Toronto
1976

COPYRIGHT © 1976 BY LITTLE, BROWN AND COMPANY (INC.)

ALL RIGHTS RESERVED. NO PART OF THIS BOOK MAY BE REPRODUCED IN ANY FORM OR BY ANY ELECTRONIC OR MECHANICAL MEANS INCLUDING INFORMATION STORAGE AND RETRIEVAL SYSTEMS WITHOUT PERMISSION IN WRITING FROM THE PUBLISHER, EXCEPT BY A REVIEWER WHO MAY QUOTE BRIEF PASSAGES IN A REVIEW.

LIBRARY OF CONGRESS CATALOG CARD NO. 76-7646

PUBLISHED SIMULTANEOUSLY IN CANADA
BY LITTLE, BROWN & COMPANY (CANADA) LIMITED

PRINTED IN THE UNITED STATES OF AMERICA

To
J. Lee Rankin

Preface

When I returned to full-time law teaching in 1974 after several years of service as a government lawyer, Watergate was causing the practicing bar and the law schools to question seriously the adequacy of training for lawyers in the area of legal ethics and professional responsibility. For many years the prevailing attitude among law teachers toward this subject was typically expressed by such comments as: "Ethics can't be taught," or "If they don't know right from wrong by the time they reach law school, nothing we do will make any difference," or "How can you teach someone to be honest?"

My own experience in government convinced me that the problems of professional responsibility were interesting and that they could be taught, but not from the customary teaching tools such as cases, codes, and bar association opinions. The important issues derive from an attempt to define the lawyer's role in a variety of situations — in the creation of the attorney-client relationship, as advocate, as advisor, as lawyer for the government, and where conflicts of interest arise. The hard questions growing out of these role-definition problems are rarely decided in court cases or bar association opinions. And while the Code of Professional Responsibility provides valuable guidance for the resolution of these questions, the Code itself is not, and never was intended to be, a useful teaching tool.

I decided, therefore, to prepare a set of problems designed to raise, in a two- or three-hour course, what I consider to be the most important questions which lawyers must face in order to understand the nature of their roles and responsibilities. These problems may not have clear answers, and teachers and students will undoubtedly differ with my selection of the issues. But the problems should provoke discussion, raise the student's level of awareness of the issues, and familiarize the student with the most important provisions of the Code of Professional Responsibility. The quizzes in Part V are intended to cover some areas where, it is hoped, the answers are clearer than in the problems.

This book was prepared neither as a treatise nor as an all-encompassing study of the area of legal ethics and professional responsibility. The aim of the book is quite limited: to be a helpful and manageable teaching tool for students and professors as they wrestle with the difficult, and interesting, issues which lawyers face in defining their responsibilities to clients, courts, and consciences.

I would like to thank Thomas M. Fitzpatrick, a member of the class of 1976 at the New York University School of Law, for his assistance in reviewing the manuscript, checking sources, citations, and proofs, and performing invaluable services far beyond a research assistant's normal duties. I am also indebted to Helen Oless, Valerie Ribaudo, and Ellen Katz Cooperman who accepted competently and cheerfully the tasks of typing, proofreading, and guiding the manuscript to publishable form.

I have used a preliminary version of this book in the Professional Responsibility course at this law school. I am especially grateful to the students in those classes for their helpful suggestions and their perceptive classroom observations.

The quizzes in Part V have been reproduced with

Preface

permission of the New York State Bar Association, for whom they were originally prepared. The Code of Professional Responsibility is reproduced with permission of the American Bar Association. I also acknowledge permission to reprint the following from copyrighted sources: Slayer's 2 Lawyers Kept Secret of 2 More Killings, The New York Times, June 20, 1974, Copyright © 1974 by the New York Times Company, reprinted by permission; Did Jaffurs Represent Liquor Control Board Clients or Public?, The Philadelphia Evening and Sunday Bulletin, August 26, 1973, Copyright © 1973 by the Philadelphia Evening and Sunday Bulletin, reprinted by permission.

N. R.

New York, New York
May, 1976

Contents

Preface, vii
Table of Cases, xv

PART I
The Lawyer and the Client: Defining the Relationship, 1

    Problem 1   The Unpopular Client and the Lawyer with a Conscience, 3
    Problem 2   Identifying the Client, 7
    Garner v. Wolfinbarger, 9
    Problem 3   Whose Client Is It?, 22
    Problem 4   Identifying with the Client, 26
    Problem 5   Involvement in Business Affairs of Client, 28

Part II
The Lawyer as Advocate, 33

    Problem 6   Who Controls the Case?, 35
    Problem 7   The Use of False or Perjured Testimony, 40
    In re Metzger, 44
    Problem 8   Cross-Examining the Truthful Witness, 54
    Problem 9   The Requirement of Candor, 57
    Slayer's 2 Lawyers Kept Secret of 2 More Killings, 60

Problem 10   Advocacy Outside the Courtroom, 65
   In re Sawyer, 67
   A.B.A. Formal Opinion 336, 86

PART III
Conflicts of Interest, 89

Problem 11   Representing Both Sides: When Is It Permissible?, 91
Problem 12   Opposing a Former Client, 94
   T.C. Theatre Corp. v. Warner Bros., 95
Problem 13   Disqualifying a Lawyer Because of What His Law Firm (Past or Present) Knew, Knows, or Is Assumed to Know, 106
   Laskey Bros. v. Warner Bros. Pictures, Inc., 108

PART IV
Special Problems of Government Lawyers, 121

Problem 14   Client Identification in a Government Context, 123
   Did Jaffurs Represent Liquor Control Board Clients or Public?, 125
   The Government Client and Confidentiality, 128
Problem 15   Lawyer or Policymaker?, 138
   Matter of Kay v. Board of Higher Education, N.Y. City, 142
Problem 16   The Prosecutor's Decision to Prosecute, 145
Problem 17   The Standard of Prosecution, 149
Problem 18   The Former Government Lawyer, 152
   United States v. Standard Oil Co., 155
   General Motors Corp. v. City of New York, 178

Contents

    Problem 19   Structuring the Facts, 190
    Problem 20   Responsibilities of Advisors
                         to Non-clients, 193
      A.B.A. Formal Opinion 341, 197
      SEC v. Spectrum, 204
      SEC v. National Student Marketing Corp., 215
      ABA Statement of Policy, 222

PART V
Testing Your Ethics: Five Self-Administered Quizzes, 231

    Quiz 1   General, 232
    Quiz 2   Criminal Defense, 235
    Quiz 3   Conduct of Public Officials, 237
    Quiz 4   General, 239
    Quiz 5   Disclosure and Suppression
              of Evidence, 242

APPENDIX
The ABA Code of Professional Responsibility, 247

Table of References to the ABA Code, 327

Table of Cases

Italics indicate principal cases.

Adams, In re, 88
Allied Realty of St. Paul v. Exchange Nat. Bank of Chicago, 185
Belanger v. Alton Box Board Co., 11
Bridges v. California, 70, 85
Brown v. Miller, 163
Buck v. City of New York, 143
Buckley, In re, 88
Chernoff, In re, 87
Chicago Council of Lawyers v. Bauer, 88
Committee on Legal Ethics v. Scherr, 87
Coniglio v. Highwood Serivces, Inc., 186
Consolidated Theatres v. Warner Bros. Circuit Management Corp., 109, 163
Craig v. Harney, 70
Dennis v. United States, 73
Dennis, W., & Sons, Ltd. v. West Norfolk Farmers' Manure & Chem. Co., 17
8 in 1 Pet Products, Inc. v. Swift & Co., 10
Emle Industries, Inc. v. Patentex, Inc., 119, 184, 187
Ernst & Ernst v. Hochfelder, 229
Federal Trust Co. v. Damron, 168
Fellner v. Bar Association of Baltimore, 87
Fleischmann, Matter of v. Graves, 144

Forty-first and Park Avenue Corp., People ex rel. v. Walsh, 144
Garner v. Wolfinbarger, 9
Garrison v. Louisiana, 88
General Motors Corp. v. City of New York, 178
Glasser v. United States, 93
Goldfarb v. Virginia State Bar, 242
Gould, In re, 87
Gouraud v. Edison Gower Bell Telephone Co., 17
Halvorsen v. Halvorsen, 93
Hearn v. Rhay, 137
Howell, In re, 86
Judson v. City of Niagara Falls, 144
Justices of Appellate Div. v. Erdman, 88
Kay, Matter of v. Board of Higher Education, N.Y. City, 142
Kentucky State Bar Association v. Martin, 87
Kirtz, In re, 87
Krulewitch v. United States, 74
Laskey Bros. v. Warner Bros. Pictures, Inc., 108, 169, 175
Lowber v. Mayor, etc., of N.Y., 143
Metzger, In re, 44
Milliken v. Bradley, 153, 155
Murphy v. Erie County Bar Association, 87
New York Times Co. v. Sullivan, 88
Pennekamp v. Florida, 70
People ex rel. Forty-first and Park Avenue Corp. v. Walsh, 144
People ex rel. Sherrill v. Guggenheimer, 144
Polk v. State Bar of Texas, 88
Prudence Bonds Corp., In re, 17
Radiant Burners, Inc. v. American Gas Ass'n, 11
Ramson v. Mayor, etc., of N.Y., 143
Rotante v. Lawrence Hospital, 119

Sawyer, In re, 67, 88
Schwimmer v. United States, 11
SEC v. Spectrum, Ltd., 194, *204*
Sharp v. Mayor, etc., of N.Y., 143
Sherrill, People ex rel. v. Guggenheimer, 144
Silver Chrysler Plymouth, Inc. v. Chrysler Motors Corp., 119
T.C. Theatre Corp. v. Warner Bros. Pictures, Inc., 95, 163, 164, 175
Thatcher v. United States, 168
United States v. Aluminum Co. of America, 186
United States v. Fujimoto, 67
United States v. General Motors, 180 et seq.
United States v. Grinnell Corp., 186
United States v. Louisville & N. R.R., 11
United States v. Peoni, 214
United States v. Standard Oil Co., 108, *155*, 188
W. Dennis & Sons, Ltd. v. West Norfolk Farmers' Manure & Chem. Co., 17
Watson v. Watson, 163
Wilson, In re (Ind. 1966), 87
Wilson, In re (Mo. 1965), 87
Wood v. Strickland, 58, 59

PROFESSIONAL RESPONSIBILITY
A Problem Approach

PART I
The Lawyer and the Client: Defining the Relationship

PROBLEM 1

The Unpopular Client and the Lawyer with a Conscience

What are the permissible limits of discretion in accepting or rejecting a client?
Should the lawyer consider the merits of the client's case only in legal terms?
Should the lawyer pass judgment on the societal objectives of the client?
Should it matter whether the unpopular client is poor or rich?

Richard St. John and Alan Charles are two partners in the Washington, D.C. law firm of St. John and Charles, which consists of six partners and fifteen associates. One day Mr. St. John receives a call from the president of United Motors, a major automobile manufacturer, who says: "Your firm has a reputation for knowing its way around the Washington bureaucracy and for handling certain types of antitrust cases. We, and several other auto makers, have been sued by the Department of Justice and by several state and municipal governments for conspiring to delay technological development in the production of automobile antipollution devices. In addition, the Federal Environmental Protection Agency is trying to compel us to install these devices on the 1978 models and we want the EPA to approve our request that compliance be delayed until the 1981 model year. We need your help."

Assume that the firm could use the new business and there are no intra-firm conflicts of interest that would prevent the firm from handling the case.

1. Would it be proper for St. John and Charles to decline to handle the case solely because they did not want the firm to be less attractive to the bright "public interest type" law students which the firm interviews each year?

2. Would it be proper for the firm to refuse to take the case on grounds that, while they would undertake the antitrust defense, they did not want to be a party to any proceeding which would delay the installation of antipollution devices on autos, since the partners were strong believers in tough enforcement of pollution control laws?

3. Suppose Mr. Charles says to Mr. St. John, "We can't take this case. I'm considering a race for Congress in Maryland, where I live, and identification with these polluters and monopolists, even if they're innocent, would kill me politically." Is this a valid basis for sending United Motors elsewhere?

4. Would the law firm's responsibilities be different if United had been a client of the firm for the past five years?

ASSIGNMENT

Canon 2; EC2-1, EC2-26, EC2-27, EC2-28, EC2-29, EC2-30; DR2-109, DR2-110(B) and (C).

Problem 1. The Unpopular Client and the Lawyer

BACKGROUND READING

Compare these provisions of the Code with Canon 31 of the old A.B.A. Canons of Professional Ethics: "No lawyer is obliged to act either as adviser or advocate for every person who may wish to become his client. He has the right to decline employment. Every lawyer upon his own responsibility must decide what employment he will accept as counsel, what causes he will bring into Court for plaintiffs, what cases he will contest in Court for defendants. The responsibility for advising as to questionable transactions, for bringing questionable suits, for urging questionable defenses, is the lawyer's responsibility. He cannot escape it by urging as an excuse that he is only following his client's instructions."

The issues involved in the lawyer's becoming identified with the client are discussed in Rostow, The Lawyer and His Client, 44 A.B.A. Journal 25, 146 (1962); Thode, The Ethical Standard for the Advocate, 39 Texas L. Rev. 575 (1961); Symposium: The Right to Counsel and the "Unpopular Cause," 20 U. Pitt. L. Rev. 725 (1959); Seasongood, What Employments Must a Lawyer Accept?, 2 Prac. Law., No. 5 at 43 (1956); Stone, Legal Education on the Couch, 85 Harv. L. Rev. 392 (1971).

Compare these American views with the frequently quoted statement of the famous English barrister, Thomas Erskine, who defended Thomas Paine when he was prosecuted for the publication of The Rights of Man: "From the moment that any advocate can be permitted to say that he will or will not stand between the Crown and the subject arraigned in the court where he daily sits to practice, from that moment the liberties of England are at an end. If the advocate refuses to defend, from what he may think of the charge or of the defence, he assumes the character of the judge; nay, he assumes it before the hour of judgment; and in proportion to his rank and reputation, puts the heavy influence of perhaps a mistaken opinion into the scale against the accused . . ." See I Erskine, Speeches 474 (High ed. 1876).

PROBLEM 2

Identifying the Client

Whom does the lawyer represent when the "client" is an association or corporation?
Who defines the "client's" interest?
Should the lawyer respect confidences as between different parts of a client entity?

Linda Jeffries is the attorney for a labor union whose members are employees of the major retail department stores in New York City. She was retained by the president of the union, Mr. John Sanford. Her retention was approved by the executive committee of the union which consists of elected representatives from each of the locals in the individual stores.

Negotiations for a new contract have gone on for several months. In fact, the old agreement expired one month ago and the employees have continued working while mediation efforts have gone forward, thus far to no avail. Finally, the union leadership calls for a strike authorization vote among the union's 10,000 members. On August 1 Mr. Sanford announces to a press conference that the members have "overwhelmingly approved the strike," which he announces will commence at ten a.m. on August 15 if the union's executive committee approves. On August 2 Mr. Sanford confers with Ms. Jeffries and informs her that the vote was actually 51 percent against the strike and 49 percent in favor of it, but that he had to make the public statement about overwhelming approval in order to strengthen his position at the bargaining table. He informs her that he has scheduled a meeting of the union's executive committee for that afternoon at which he will ask for approval of his strike call. He intends to repeat yesterday's statement about "overwhelming" membership approval of the strike.

"You can't lie to the executive committee," she says. "I have to keep the strike threat alive," he replies. "It's the only way we'll get a fair settlement."

Assume that the strike (apart from any question of the false statement about the membership vote) would be perfectly legal and that there has never been an instance where a union leader has been subject to either criminal or civil liability for engaging in the conduct which Mr. Sanford has practiced.

1. What advice should Ms. Jeffries give to Mr. Sanford?

2. Should Ms. Jeffries take any action with regard to the meeting of the executive committee?

3. Assuming the committee meets, knowing nothing about the correct vote count, and approves the strike, what should Ms. Jeffries do, if anything?

4. Would your answers differ if the union were a union of police officers, strikes by public employees were unlawful, and the union, as well as each member who went on strike, could be subject to heavy fines, the loss of pay and possibly dismissal if the strike takes place?

Problem 2. Identifying the Client

ASSIGNMENT

Canon 4; EC4-1, EC4-5, EC4-6; DR4-101.
Canon 5; EC5-18.
Canon 7; EC7-3, EC7-4, EC7-5, EC7-8, EC7-9, EC7-12, EC7-27; DR7-102(B)(1).
Also read the following case: *Garner v. Wolfinbarger.*

Garner v. Wolfinbarger
430 F.2d 1093 (5th Cir. 1973)

GODBOLD, Cir. J. This case presents the important question of the availability to a corporation of the privilege against disclosure of communications between it and its attorney, when access to the communications is sought by stockholders of the corporation in litigation brought by them against the corporation charging the corporation and its officers with acts injurious to their interests as stockholder. . . .

The District Court in an order reported at 280 F.Supp. 1018 (N.D. Ala. 1968), held the privilege was not available as against the stockholders as plaintiffs. . . .

Stockholders of First American Life Insurance Company of Alabama (FAL) brought, in the Northern District of Alabama, a class action alleging violations of the Securities Act of 1933, the Securities Exchange Act of 1934, SEC Rule 10(b)(5), the Investment Company Act of 1940, the Alabama Securities Act and common law fraud, seeking to recover the purchase price which they and others similarly situated paid for their stock in FAL. The defendants are FAL and various of its directors, officers and controlling persons. The plaintiffs also claim that FAL was itself damaged by alleged fraud in the purchase and sale of securities, and they assert against various individual defendants a derivative action on behalf of the corporation.

FAL filed a cross-claim against all other defendants, asserting in its own behalf the rights the plaintiff shareholders had claimed in the derivative aspect of their complaint.

R. Richard Schweitzer served as attorney for the corporation in connection with the issuance of the FAL stock here involved. After the transactions sued upon were complete he became its president. On deposition Schweitzer was asked numerous questions concerning advice given by him to the corporation about various aspects of the issuance and sale of the stock and related matters. Other questions went into the content of discussions at meetings attended by him and company officials and information furnished to him by the corporation. All questions related to times at which Schweitzer acted solely as attorney, before he became an officer of the company and before the filing of suit. Objections were made by counsel for the corporation and by Schweitzer himself that the attorney-client privilege barred his revealing both communications to him by the corporation and the advice which he gave to the corporation.[7]

The plaintiffs had served a subpoena duces tecum on Schweitzer to bring various documents to the taking of his

---

7. The objection is the client's to invoke, not the attorney's. Since FAL counsel objected we need not inquire into the effectiveness of Schweitzer's objection. The parties make no distinction between the client's communications to the attorney and the attorney's communications to the client, and it is not necessary that we do so. See, e.g., 8 in 1 Pet Products, Inc. v. Swift & Co., 218 F.Supp. 253 (S.D.N.Y. 1963); 8 Wigmore, Evidence, §2320 at 628 (McNaughton rev. 1961).

Problem 2. Identifying the Client 11

deposition. Both he and the corporation claimed the privilege with respect to some of the documents. . . .

The District Judge held that the privilege is not available to the corporation as against these plaintiff stockholders. . . .

Turning to the merits, there is no contention by plaintiffs that FAL is outside the ambit of the attorney-client privilege because a corporation is not a client.[10] Their argument is that the privilege is not available to FAL in the circumstances of this case against the demands of the corporate stockholders for access to the communications. The corporation says that its right to assert the privilege is absolute and of special importance where disclosure is sought in a suit brought by the shareholders against the corporation. The American Bar Association appears as amicus curiae and supports the view of an absolute privilege.

The privilege does not arise from the position of the corporation as a party but its status as a client. However, in this instance plaintiffs deny the availability to the corporation of the otherwise existent privilege because of the role of the corporation as a party defending against claims of its stockholders.

We do not consider the privilege to be so inflexibly absolute as contended by the corporation, nor to be so totally

---

10. Numerous cases sustain the proposition that a corporation is a client for the purpose of invoking the privilege. E.g., United States v. Louisville & N. R.R., 236 U.S. 318, 35 S. Ct. 363, 59 L. Ed. 598 (1915); Schwimmer v. United States, 232 F.2d 855 (8th Cir.), cert. denied, 352 U.S. 833, 77 S. Ct. 48, 1 L. Ed. 2d 52 (1956); Belanger v. Alton Box Board Co., 180 F.2d 87 (7th Cir. 1950). A decision to the contrary, Radiant Burners, Inc. v. American Gas Ass'n, 207 F.Supp. 771 (N.D. Ill. 1962) was reversed by the Seventh Circuit, 320 F.2d 314 (7th Cir.), cert. denied, 375 U.S. 929, 84 S. Ct. 330, 11 L. Ed. 2d 262 (1963).

unavailable against the stockholders as thought by the District Court. We conclude that the correct rule is between these two extreme positions.

The availability *vel non* of the privilege involves a complex problem of choice of law. 2B Barron & Holtzoff, Federal Practice & Procedure, §967 at 241-44 (Wright ed. 1961). The order of the District Court appears to treat Alabama standards as controlling. We conclude that the choice of law cannot be settled by reference to any simple talisman, but can be arrived at only after a consideration of state and federal interests that are inseparable from the factors bearing on the availability of the privilege itself.

Our starting point is Rule 43(a), Fed. R. Civ. P.:

> All evidence shall be admitted which is admissible under the statutes of the United States, or under the rules of evidence heretofore applied in the courts of the United States on the hearing of suits in equity, or under the rules of evidence applied in the courts of general jurisdiction of the state in which the United States court is held. In any case, the statute or rule which favors the reception of the evidence governs. . . .

Since this is a case of first impression at the court of appeals level, neither the law of Alabama nor federal law offers many guideposts. Alabama has codified its common law attorney-client privilege, Tit. 7, §438, Code of Ala. (1958 Recomp.), and apparently affords it to corporations . . . as does federal decisional law. Alabama follows the exceptions discussed *infra* for consultations concerning contemplated crimes . . . and for communications to a joint attorney, as between joint clients. . . . There is no comprehensive federal body of law surrounding the attorney-client privilege, and no opinion of the circuit courts of appeals discussing the precise issue at

Problem 2. Identifying the Client

hand. There is then no direct conflict between state and federal rules of privilege and nonprivilege in this case.

This is a federal question case (with ancillary state aspects) rather than a diversity case. Such actions are predicated on federal law, embodying federal policies. Enforcement of those policies demands that the federal courts apply their own rules of privilege where substantial state interests are not infringed. See Comment, Evidentiary Privileges in the Federal Courts, 52 Calif. L. Rev. 640 (1964), 2B Barron & Holtzoff, Federal Practice & Procedure, §967 at 243-44 (Wright ed. 1961), cf. 4 Moore, Federal Practice, ¶26.23[9] at 1481-85 (1969)....

This is not to say that state interests play no part. Our discussion below points up that many of the factors to be weighed in the consideration of federal and state interests are predicated on values long embodied in policies of the states rather than federal law. And it goes without saying that a federal court must take full account of the reasons for any asserted privilege including any especially strong policies of the state in which the court sits. But it must take account of federal interests as well.

The competing interests in disclosure on the one hand and confidentiality on the other, neither of which lies exclusively within the state or federal realm, are the subject of the next part of our discussion.

The privilege must be placed in perspective. The beginning point is the fundamental principle that the public has the right to every man's evidence, and exemptions from the general duty to give testimony that one is capable of giving are distinctly exceptional. 8 Wigmore, Evidence, §2192 at 70. An exception is justified if — and only if — policy requires it be recognized when measured against the fundamental responsibility of every person to give testimony. *Id.*,

§2285 at 527. Professor Wigmore describes four conditions, the existence of all of which is prerequisite to the establishment of a privilege of any kind against the disclosure of communications:

> §2285. *General principle of privileged communications.* Looking back upon the principle of privilege, as an exception to the general liability of every person to give testimony upon all facts inquired of in a court of justice, and keeping in view that preponderance of extrinsic policy which alone can justify the recognition of any such exception (§§2192 and 2197 *supra*), four fundamental conditions are recognized as necessary to the establishment of a privilege against the disclosure of communications:
>
> (1) The communications must originate in a *confidence* that they will not be disclosed.
>
> (2) This element of *confidentiality* must be *essential* to the full and satisfactory maintenance of the relation between the parties.
>
> (3) The *relation* must be one which in the opinion of the community ought to be sedulously *fostered.*
>
> (4) The *injury* that would inure to the relation by the disclosure of the communications must be *greater than the benefit* thereby gained for the correct disposal of litigation.
>
> Only if these four conditions are present should a privilege be recognized.

Id., §2285 at 527. And he points out that in the case of communications between attorney and client all four conditions are present, with the only condition open to dispute being the fourth. *Id.*, §2285 at 528.

As to this particular type of privileged communication:

Problem 2. Identifying the Client

> [T]he privilege remains an exception to the general duty to disclose. Its benefits are all indirect and speculative; its obstruction is plain and concrete.... It is worth preserving for the sake of a general policy, but is nonetheless an obstacle to the investigation of the truth. It ought to be strictly confined within the narrowest possible limits, consistent with the logic of its principle.

Id., §2291 at 554.

> The policy of the privilege has been plainly grounded since the latter part of the 1700s on subjective considerations. In order to promote freedom of consultation of legal advisers by clients, the apprehension of compelled disclosure by the legal advisers must be removed; hence the law must prohibit such disclosure except on the client's consent. Such is the modern theory.

Id., §2291 at 545.

The problem before us concerns Wigmore's fourth condition, a balancing of interests between injury resulting from disclosure and the benefit gained in the correct disposal of litigation. We consider it in a particularized context: where the client asserting the privilege is an entity which in the performance of its functions acts wholly or partly in the interests of others, and those others, or some of them, seek access to the subject matter of the communications.

It is urged that disclosure is injurious to both the corporation and the attorney. Corporate management must manage. It has the duty to do so and requires the tools to do so. Part of the managerial task is to seek legal counsel when desirable, and, obviously, management prefers that it confer with counsel without the risk of having the communications revealed at the instance of one or more dissatisfied stockholders. The managerial preference is a rational one, because it is difficult to envision the management of any sizeable corporation pleasing all of its stockholders all of the time, and management desires protection from those who might second-guess or even harass in matters purely of judgment.

But in assessing management assertions of injury to the corporation it must be borne in mind that management does not manage for itself and that the beneficiaries of its action are the stockholders. Conceptualistic phrases describing the corporation as an entity separate from its stockholders are not useful tools of analysis. They serve only to obscure the fact that management has duties which run to the benefit ultimately of the stockholders. For example, it is difficult to rationally defend the assertion of the privilege if all, or substantially all, stockholders desire to inquire into the attorney's communications with corporate representatives who have only nominal ownership interests, or even none at all.[17] There may be reasonable differences over the manner of characterizing in legal terminology the duties of management, and over the extent to which corporate management is less of a fiduciary than the common law trustee. There may be many situations in which the corporate entity or its management, or both, have interests adverse to those of some or all stockholders. But when all is said and done management is not managing for itself.

17. Due regard must be paid to the interests of nonparty stockholders, which may be affected by impinging on the privilege, sometimes injuriously (though not necessarily so — in some situations shareholders who are not plaintiffs may benefit). The corporation is vulnerable to suit by shareholders whose interests or intention may be inconsistent with those of other shareholders, even others constituting a majority.

Problem 2. Identifying the Client

The representative and the represented have a mutuality of interest in the representative's freely seeking advice when needed and putting it to use when received. This is not to say that management does not have allowable judgment in putting advice to use. But management judgment must stand on its merits, not behind an ironclad veil of secrecy which under all circumstances preserves it from being questioned by those for whom it is, at least in part, exercised.

The District Court relied upon two English cases, *Gouraud v. Edison Gower Bell Telephone Co.*, 57 L.T.Ch. 498, 59 L. T. 813 (1888) and *W. Dennis & Sons, Ltd. v. West Norfolk Farmers' Manure & Chem. Co.*, 2 All E.R. 94, 112 L.J. Ch. 239, 169 L.T. 74, 59 TLR 298, 87 Sol. Jo. 211 (1943). Both cases treat the relationship between shareholder and company as analogous to that between beneficiaries and trustees, a basis which the defendants in the present case say has no viability for American corporations. Though not binding precedents, these English cases are persuasive recognition that there are obligations, however characterized, that run from corporation to shareholder and must be given recognition in determining the applicability of the privilege.

Apart from the conceptualism that surrounds the management-stockholder relationship, the ABA alternatively contends, implicitly within the framework of Wigmore's fourth condition, that the benefits of disclosure are outweighed by the harm done to both client and attorney. In support of this policy argument, the ABA relies heavily upon *In re Prudence Bonds Corp.*, 76 F.Supp. 643 (E.D.N.Y. 1948), which held that a trustee for bondholders in an action for an accounting brought by the bondholders would not be required to produce opinions of counsel rendered to the trustee over a period of eighteen years. That case in turn distinguished the English cases cited above, speculating that the unavailability of the privilege might ultimately harm both attorneys and bondholders.

The ABA urges that the privilege is most necessary where the corporation has sought advice about a prospective transaction, where counsel in good faith has stated his opinion that it is not lawful, but the corporation has proceeded in total or partial disregard of counsel's advice. The ABA urges that the cause of justice requires that counsel be free to state his opinion as fully and forthrightly as possible without fear of later disclosure to persons who might attack the transaction, and that without the cloak of the privilege counsel may be "required by the threat of future discovery to hedge or soften their opinions."

The ABA brief does not always distinguish clearly between the separate interests of the corporate client and of the attorney in freedom from disclosure, nor is it possible always to do so. The privilege's exemptions from the broad duty to divulge are designed not only to protect the individual client who may assert the privilege but also to promote free and open communication between clients and attorneys in all matters. All these interests should properly be taken into account in any decision on the privilege. However, we reject the idea that the prospective decision of the client on whether to abide by advice or disregard it, or the guarantee of a veil of secrecy, either establishes or narrows the attorney's obligation in the giving of advice. And to grant to corporate management plenary assurance of secrecy for opinions received is to encourage it to disregard with impunity the advice sought.[18]

18. We do not consider it determinative whether the attorney consulted is corporated or house counsel, or whether his fees are paid for by the corporation or by management on its own account.

Problem 2. Identifying the Client 19

Two traditional exceptions are also persuasive in negativing any absolute privilege in a corporation in the circumstances of this case. These are the exceptions for communications in contemplation of a crime or fraud, and for communications to a joint attorney.

Communications made by a client to his attorney during or before the commission of a crime or fraud for the purpose of being guided or assisted in its commission are not privileged. . . . The stockholders claim to have been the victims of improprieties in the issuance and sale of FAL's stock. The questions, and the documents sought, concerned those alleged improprieties, with particular regard to whether the attorney advised the corporation that proposals it had in mind were not legal and that statements to be put in its prospectus were misleading.

The plaintiffs say that some of the matter claimed to be privileged concerned prospective criminal transactions, including issuance by FAL of a misleading prospectus, the circulation of which it is said was a criminal offense under federal securities law, and the granting of options (allegedly as bribes) for securing state registrations of FAL's stock and of its broker-dealer and salesmen. In considering the interplay of interest of management, of stockholders, and of the lawsuit, it must be recognized that management has an obligation to the corporation, to the stockholders and to the public to do what is lawful. But we do not consider unavailability of the privilege to be confined to the narrow ground of prospective criminal transactions. The differences between prospective crime and prospective action of questionable legality, or prospective fraud, are differences of degree, not of principle.[20]

20. The crime-fraud exception is particularly instructive because it covers advice concerning prospective action. We recognize the much

A second exception is also instructive. In many situations in which the same attorney acts for two or more parties having a common interest, neither party may exercise the privilege in a subsequent controversy with the other. This is true even where the attorney acts jointly for two or more persons having no formalized business arrangement between them. . . .

In summary, we say this. The attorney-client privilege still has viability for the corporate client. The corporation is not barred from asserting it merely because those demanding information enjoy the status of stockholders. But where the corporation is in suit against its stockholders on charges of acting inimically to stockholder interests, protection of those interests as well as those of the corporation and of the public require that the availability of the privilege be subject to the right of the stockholders to show cause why it should not be invoked in the particular instance.[21]

There are many indicia that may contribute to a deci-

---

stronger policy justifications behind the confidentiality of communications with one who is already a wrongdoer and seeks legal advice appropriate to his plight as opposed to one who seeks advice concerning proposed future conduct and, having later acted, seeks to maintain the secrecy. See 8 Wigmore, §2298 at 573. FAL does not recognize the unavailability of the privilege even as to communications about transactions wholly prospective (except, possibly, where relating to commission of a proposed crime).

21. This approach is neither new nor world-shaking. At common law the stockholder has the right to see corporate books and records but it is not unlimited. His demand must be germane to his interest as stockholder, and the interests of the corporation and other shareholders may control to deny inspection. 5 Fletcher, Corporations, §2218 at 799 (1967). The existent Alabama statute, which follows the Model Business Corporation Act, allows shareholder examination of books and records of account, minutes and record of stockholders, upon written demand and "for any proper purpose." Tit. 10, §21(46), Code of Ala. (Supp. 1969).

sion of presence or absence of good cause, among them the number of shareholders and the percentage of stock they represent; the bona fides of the shareholders; the nature of the shareholders' claim and whether it is obviously colorable; the apparent necessity or desirability of the shareholders having the information and the availability of it from other sources; whether, if the shareholders' claim is of wrongful action by the corporation, it is of action criminal, or illegal but not criminal, or of doubtful legality; whether the communication related to past or to prospective actions; whether the communication is of advice concerning the litigation itself; the extent to which the communication is identified versus the extent to which the shareholders are blindly fishing; the risk of revelation of trade secrets or other information in whose confidentiality the corporation has an interest for independent reasons. The court can freely use *in camera* inspection or oral examination and freely avail itself of protective orders, a familiar device to preserve confidentiality in trade secret and other cases where the impact of revelation may be as great as in revealing a communication with counsel.

The order relating to availability of the attorney-client privilege is Vacated. The cause is Remanded for further proceedings not inconsistent with this opinion.

BACKGROUND READING

McDaniel, Ethical Problems of Counsel for Big Business, 38 A.B.A. Journal 205 (1952).

PROBLEM 3

Whose Client Is It?

The law firm's?
The partner's?
The associate's?
Associates in law firms: Are they professionals or are they employees?

Clark Chemicals is a large producer of drug products including the well-known mouthwash — Rinse Kleen. For several years the Federal Trade Commission has been trying to force Clark to discontinue the claim that Rinse Kleen "helps destroy cold-causing germs." The product is actually a harmless mouthwash which produces a pleasant-tasting fresh sensation, but which has no provable germ-killing qualities. Before an FTC hearing officer and before the commission itself Clark has argued that anything which encourages people to rinse their mouths will help prevent the formation of germs. This argument has been unsuccessful, and the commission has ordered the advertising claim to be discontinued in the future and has also ordered that all existing stocks of Rinse Kleen be relabelled to remove the allegedly false claim.

The law firm of Kincaid, Gold and Clarendon has been

Problem 3. Whose Client Is It?   23

representing Clark Chemicals before the commission. Two associates, Joan Watson and Harry Michaelson, have been working on the case under the direction of one of the partners, James Clarendon. A few days after the FTC order has been issued, there is a conference in the firm's offices attended by Clarendon, Watson and Michaelson, as well as by several officers of Clark Chemicals, including Janet Sibley, the vice-president for marketing.

Mr. Clarendon opens the meeting: "We've reviewed the record and the commission's order, and we don't think we have any chance at all of winning a reversal if we appeal to the courts. Do you agree?"

Ms. Watson and Mr. Michaelson nod in agreement. Ms. Sibley and her colleagues from Clark look glum and impassive.

"How much time can we get by appealing?" asks Ms. Sibley.

"As much as two years," replies Mr. Clarendon.

"Good. Let's appeal. We have several million bottles in inventory and the cost of relabelling and repackaging would be prohibitive."

"Okay," says Mr. Clarendon, and the conference adjourns after a few more pleasantries.

Ms. Watson and Mr. Michaelson are both strong believers in consumer protection laws and have had misgivings about this case from the start, but they have worked on it because they were satisfied that, while the advertising claim may have been "puffed up," the product itself was harmless. Now, however, they have had enough of the case and they decide to discuss it with Mr. Clarendon.

"This would be a frivolous appeal," argues Ms. Watson. "And Harry agrees with me."

"Well, I don't," replies Mr. Clarendon.

"But you, yourself, said we couldn't win."

"I know, but you never know what happens in a law suit. And besides, we'll be making the same arguments we made before the commission. That didn't seem to bother you."

"It's different now," says Mr. Michaelson. "The only purpose of this appeal is delay."

"Not as far as I'm concerned," says Mr. Clarendon. "I hope to win."

"Have you discussed this with any of your partners? Or any of the associates?" asks Ms. Watson.

"No, and I don't intend to. Let's meet tomorrow morning at ten to plan our appeal strategy. See you then."

1. Would it be proper for Ms. Watson and Mr. Michaelson to refuse to do any more work on the case?

2. Would it be proper for them to raise with partners or associates the propriety of the firm's prosecuting the appeal?

3. Should Mr. Clarendon discuss the matter with his partners or with other associates?

4. If Ms. Watson and Mr. Michaelson refuse to work on the case, would it be proper for the firm to fire them?

ASSIGNMENT

Canon 2; EC2-30, EC2-31, EC2-32; DR2-109, DR2-110.
Canon 7; EC7-1, EC7-3, EC7-4, EC7-5, EC7-7, EC7-8; DR7-101(A)(1), DR7-101(B)(1), DR7-102(A)(1).

Problem 3. Whose Client Is It?

BACKGROUND READING

See the discussion of the work of the partners and associates in Wall Street firms in Smigel, The Wall Street Lawyer 141-170 (The Free Press of Glencoe, 1964).

For a discussion of these issues in the context of a government law office see Weinstein, Some Ethical and Political Problems of a Government Attorney, 18 Maine L. Rev. 155 at 165-166 (1966).

PROBLEM 4

Identifying with the Client

Is the lawyer free to oppose the client's interests on public issues?
Do lawyers sell their services or themselves?
Should lawyers identify with particular types of clients?

Kenneth Roberts represents a large public utility that is seeking to locate a new power plant in a town in Westchester County in New York State. Mr. Roberts has been appearing before the New York State Public Service Commission and is optimistic that the commission will approve, thus removing the last legal obstacle to the start of construction.

Mr. Roberts also serves on the Environmental Law Committee of the Association of the Bar of the City of New York. The committee is about to publish a report which will urge the New York State Legislature, which is now in session, to pass a pending bill creating a new state agency which would have final approval power for new power plant locations in the state. If the bill passes, it would prevent the client's plant from being started unless approval of the new agency is obtained. Mr. Roberts' client is vigorously opposed to the bill and has retained an Albany law firm to lobby against its

Problem 4. Identifying with the Client

passage. Mr. Roberts has not been involved in the lobbying activity, and he agrees with the forthcoming Bar Association committee report.

As a result of his service on the committee, Mr. Roberts has been asked to represent a citizens group which is trying to prevent a public utility in upstate New York (an area not served by Mr. Roberts' client) from building an atomic power plant. Mr. Roberts' client has no plans to construct an atomic power plant.

1. Should Roberts ask his client's permission before signing the report?

2. If the client directs him not to sign the report, what should he do?

3. Was it proper for Roberts to serve on a committee and assert, during such service, a position which he knew to be contrary to the interests of his client?

4. Should Roberts obtain the permission of the public utility he represents before accepting the new employment? Should he accept the new employment at all?

ASSIGNMENT

EC6-2, EC7-17, EC9-6.

BACKGROUND READING

The conflicting roles of the private and public lawyer are discussed in Paul, The Lawyer as a Tax Adviser, 25 Rocky Mt. L. Rev. 412 (1953).

PROBLEM 5

Involvement in Business Affairs of Client

Should a lawyer accept a "piece of the action" in lieu of cash fee?
What is a "speculative" interest in litigation?
What is a contingent fee?
Should a lawyer serve on the board of directors of a corporate client?

James Leeds is a partner in a major Chicago law firm. He specializes in real estate work and one of his principal clients is the Starr Construction Corporation whose president is Robert Starr. Mr. Leeds has been asked to handle the legal work for Mr. Starr's proposal to the city government for the development of a new housing project alongside Lake Michigan. City approval for the project is required because it will be built under a program which provides for abatement of city real estate taxes and for a low-interest mortgage loan from the city.

The owner of the project will be the Lakeside Housing Company, a partnership which will be owned by Mr. Starr and a few of his wealthy friends, none of whom is known to

Problem 5. Involvement in Business Affairs of Client 29

Mr. Leeds. The project will cost fifty million dollars and the partnership will invest five million dollars, with the balance coming from the mortgage loan.

One day Mr. Starr drops in to see Mr. Leeds and asks, "How much do you estimate your fees will come to for the Lakeside housing project?"

"About half a million dollars," replies Mr. Leeds.

"That's a lot."

"It's a complicated deal."

"I have an idea. The equity contribution of the partners will be five million. Instead of your fee, why not take a ten percent interest in the project."

"Not a bad idea," replies Mr. Leeds. There is a moment of silence as he quickly calculates the tax advantage of being able to take a large depreciation deduction based on the full value of the project, including the mortgage.

"What happens if, for some reason, the deal doesn't go through?" asks Mr. Leeds.

"Then bill me for the time you've put into it," replies Mr. Starr. "Besides, with the friends we have in this town, the deal can't miss."

"Do you want me to continue representing Starr Construction?" asks Mr. Leeds.

"Of course. The construction corporation will be the prime contractor on the job. And, by the way, I think it would be a good idea for you to be on the board of Starr Construction. We sure could use your good advice and sound judgment."

1. Should Mr. Leeds accept the ownership interest as a fee?

2. If he accepts the interest, should he advise the public authorities with whom he may deal that he possesses such an interest in the project?

3. Should Mr. Leeds agree to join the board of Starr Construction?
4. Should Mr. Leeds agree to represent Lakeside Housing and Starr Construction?

ASSIGNMENT

EC2-20.
Canon 5; EC5-1, EC5-2, EC5-3, EC5-7, EC5-14, EC5-15, EC5-16, EC5-19; DR5-103(A).

BACKGROUND READING

The assigned provisions in the Code of Professional Responsibility are derived from Canon 10 of the ABA Canons of Professional Ethics, which reads as follows: "The lawyer should not purchase any interest in the subject matter of the litigation which he is conducting." Formal Opinion 279 (1949) of the ABA Committee on Professional Ethics disapproves an attorney's accepting stock in a corporation organized by him for the purpose of prosecuting an application for a radio station license before the FCC. Most of the discussion in this area is concerned with the lawyer stirring up litigation by acquiring an interest in the outcome. See Drinker, Legal Ethics 99-101 (Columbia University Press, 1953).

See the discussion on contingent fees in Countryman, Finman, and Schneyer, The Lawyer in Modern Society 193-205 (Little, Brown and Company, 2d ed., 1976).

That a lawyer remains subject to the Code of Professional Responsibility even when he is acting in a non-legal

Problem 5. Involvement in Business Affairs of Client

capacity, such as a member of a board of a corporation, was emphasized in A.B.A. Formal Opinion 336 of June 3, 1974, which stated: "It is recognized that lawyers are subject to discipline for improper conduct in connection with business activities, individual or personal activities, and activities as a judicial, governmental, or public official."

For a discussion of the propriety of a lawyer serving on a board of a client corporation see Lawyers As Directors, 30 Bus. Law. 41 (Special Issue — Advisors to Management: Responsibilities and Liabilities of Lawyers and Accountants, 1975); Folk, Civil Liabilities under the Federal Securities Acts: The BarChris Case, 55 Va. L. Rev. 1, 199 (1969); Hudson, Outside Counsel: Inside Director (Law Journal Press, 1973).

PART II
The Lawyer as Advocate

PROBLEM 6

Who Controls the Case?

May the client decide the arguments the lawyer should and should not assert?
Can an argument be called frivolous until a judge says it is?
Does the client have the right to make the lawyer look bad?
Responsibility as advocate v. responsibility to court.

Clarence David is a wealthy real estate developer and he has been represented for years by the prestigious law firm of Cabot and Clark. One day Mr. David tells Mr. Cabot of the following problem.

It appears that the city has enacted a law authorizing the owners of buildings which have been designated as landmarks by the City Landmarks Commission to transfer air rights above the landmark buildings to another property owner in the same zoning district. The transfer must, however, be approved by the City Planning Commission which, according to the law, must schedule a hearing on the transfer with five days notice to the public. The purpose of the law was to provide some form of compensation to owners of buildings which have been designated as landmarks and which, as a result of such designation, cannot be demolished or converted to more profitable uses.

Recently the Planning Commission approved the sale of air rights by a church, whose building has been designated a landmark, to a piece of land adjacent to a luxury apartment owned by Mr. David. As a result the owner of the land will be able to build an apartment house which will completely block out the view of the East River now enjoyed by Mr. David's building. This would not have been possible without the additional development space made available by the transfer of the air rights. Mr. David wants the Cabot and Clark firm to take legal steps to prevent the transfer from going forward.

Mr. Cabot has been working on the problem for a few days when he receives a call from Mr. David.

"How are things going on the case?" he asks.

"Okay, we have a top-flight team researching the issues."

"Good . . . Oh, by the way, I was discussing this case with a lawyer friend of mine at my country club . . ."

"Oh, no . . ." thought Mr. Cabot to himself. "Not another golf course opinion."

"Well, she was wondering whether the chairman of the Planning Commission was presiding at the meeting of the commission when they held the hearing on the transfer of the air rights. My friend says that the city charter provides that the chairman shall preside and there is no provision in the charter allowing the chairman to delegate this function."

"He did vote on the matter," says Mr. Cabot.

"I know," replies Mr. David, now more intrigued by his own argument, "but if he wasn't presiding at the hearing, that makes his vote uninformed."

Problem 6. Who Controls the Case?

"I'll look into it and get back to you."

After a few weeks of research, Mr. Cabot invites Mr. David to the firm's office and, with guarded optimism, says, "We have three good arguments to raise in our suit against the city and the developer to prevent the sale of air rights. First, in counting the five days notice, the Planning Commission counted the day of the hearing itself, and we believe that the hearing date must be excluded. Therefore, notice was not legally adequate. Second, the view which your building has of the East River is such a valuable property right that we feel we can argue that the blocking of the view constitutes a "taking" of property by the city without compensation. Third, we think that the legislation permitting transfer of air rights is unconstitutional under the state constitution because this is a subject specifically pre-empted by prior state legislation, and the city, therefore, had no power to pass the law without state authorization."

"Forget about the third argument," says Mr. David. "I've got several deals pending myself for the purchase of air rights, and I don't want to kill them. Besides, I think this is a good way to help preserve landmarks, and I'm in favor of that sort of thing. It's good for the city."

"But the third argument is the strongest one we've got," says Mr. Cabot, "and our firm doesn't like to go into a major case like this, and then lose because we haven't fired all our guns. We have to think of our reputation."

"I pay the bills," says Mr. David, "and that's the way it is going to be. I won't go along with the third argument."

There is a silence in the room which is finally broken when Mr. David asks, "By the way, what about the idea suggested by my lawyer friend?"

"We checked that out and, frankly, we'd be ashamed to assert it."

"Why? It made sense to me."

"Look, for the past twenty years, ever since the Planning Commission was established, the chairman has authorized the assistant chairman, who is also a member of the commission, to preside over hearings when the chairman was too busy with other matters to attend himself. A court simply would not invalidate an administrative practice of such long standing. It could make hundreds, perhaps thousands, of Planning Commission actions illegal."

"I'm not persuaded," says Mr. David. "Has the issue ever been decided by a court?"

"No, probably because no one would raise such a silly point."

"Well, I don't think it's silly. Besides, who are you, the lawyer or the judge?"

"We have a duty to the court," replies Mr. Cabot.

"And you also have one to me. Okay, we make my friend's argument and forget about that final one of yours."

What is Mr. Cabot's proper course of action?

ASSIGNMENT

EC2-30; DR2-110(C)(1)(a), (c), (d), and (e).
Canon 7; EC7-3, EC7-4, EC7-7, EC7-8, EC7-9, EC7-19, EC7-23; DR7-101(A)(1) and (B)(1), DR7-102(A)(2).

BACKGROUND READING

Debates about the ethics of advocacy generally discuss the limitations which ethical considerations impose on the lawyer's pursuit of a client's cause, an issue more fully

Problem 6. Who Controls the Case?

raised in the remaining problems in this Part. See, generally, Thode, The Ethical Standard for the Advocate, 39 Texas L. Rev. 575 (1961); Curtis, The Ethics of Advocacy, 4 Stan. L. Rev. 3 (1951); Drinker, Some Remarks on Mr. Curtis' "The Ethics of Advocacy," 4 Stan. L. Rev. 349 (1952); Freedman, Lawyers' Ethics in an Adversary System (Bobbs-Merrill, 1975).

The problem of control of the case may be particularly acute in "public interest" litigation, where the interests of the individual client and those of the organization which employs the lawyer may diverge. The individual client, for example, may be interested only in obtaining a permit to speak in a park, or in securing welfare benefits. The organization, on the other hand, may want a regulation of the parks department, or a welfare statute, declared unconstitutional. See Council on Legal Education for Professional Responsibility, Inc., Lawyers, Clients & Ethics (M.T. Bloom, ed. 1974), particularly problem 9.

PROBLEM 7

The Use of False or Perjured Testimony

Is deception permissible — even to prove the truth? Can a lawyer be effective and truthful at the same time?

Harry Knowles owns a small hardware store in Tulsa, Oklahoma. The store has not been doing too well and on December 29, 1975 it burned to the ground under conditions which the local fire department has described as "suspicious". After an investigation by police and fire officials, and by the district attorney, Mr. Knowles has been indicted for arson. His son Jerry, who helps out in the store during school vacations, has also been indicted. Harry Knowles has retained Charles Golden, a lawyer who specializes in criminal defense work. Their first conversation was as follows:

Golden: "Well, Mr. Knowles, if I'm going to defend you properly, the first thing I need is a complete statement of what happened."

Knowles: "Complete?"

Golden: "Complete."

Knowles: "Is it true that you're not allowed to repeat what I tell you?"

Golden: "That's right. This is privileged commu-

Problem 7. The Use of False or Perjured Testimony

nication which means that I could be disbarred for revealing it and, what's more, the government can't compel me to reveal it. And I can't use this information to your disadvantage in any way. It says so right here in the Code of Professional Responsibility."

Knowles: "Okay, I set the fire."

Golden: "Why?"

Knowles: "Business was bad. I had some loans coming due. And I wanted to collect on the insurance. I made sure that no one could get hurt."

Golden: "Anyone else involved?"

Knowles: "No . . . if you mean my son, he had absolutely nothing to do with it."

Jerry Knowles, meanwhile, has retained Louise Spencer, another criminal lawyer, for his defense. Their first conversation was as follows:

After assuring her client that she has to know all the facts, and after telling him about the attorney-client privilege, Ms. Spencer asks:

Spencer: "Did you have anything to do with this fire?"

Knowles: "No. I only work in the store during vacations, and I really don't know anything about Dad's business."

Spencer: "Were you anywhere near the store on the night of the fire?"

Knowles: "Do you really want to know the truth?"

Spencer: "Sure."

Knowles: "Well, I know it sounds bad, but I returned to the store after it closed on the night of the fire to pick up a bottle of whiskey I had left under a counter by mistake. I saw that Dad was still there and he doesn't like me to drink, so I just left without going in."

Spencer: "Did anyone see you?"

Knowles: "Absolutely not. I'm sure."

At the trial the prosecution's principal witness, a fire department expert, testifies as to his observations and conclusions as to the cause of the fire. His testimony is damaging to Harry Knowles, but Mr. Golden believes that the jury is not fully convinced. Harry wants to testify on his own behalf. Mr. Golden is convinced that Mr. Knowles will make an excellent witness. He is forceful, composed, and has had an unblemished business and civic record in the community. Mr. Golden also knows that, in response to the question, "Were you responsible in any way for the fire which occurred on your premises?" Mr. Knowles will reply with a firm and convincing "No."

Louise Spencer is having her problems with her client, Jerry Knowles. He, too, is most anxious to testify.

"When the D.A. cross-examines you," she explains, "he'll ask you whether you were in the vicinity of the store after it closed on the night of the fire. A truthful answer will really hurt you and your Dad."

"Don't worry about that," replies Jerry. "I'll deny I was there. I'll say I went to a movie. I know what was playing. They'll never know."

"That's perjury."

"But I'm innocent. I had nothing to do with the fire."

1. Should Mr. Golden and Ms. Spencer allow their clients to testify?

2. Should Mr. Golden ask his client the question which he has good reason to believe will be answered untruthfully?

3. If Harry and Jerry Knowles answer untruthfully, what should Mr. Golden and Ms. Spencer do, if anything?

Problem 7. The Use of False or Perjured Testimony

ASSIGNMENT

Canon 4; EC4-1, EC4-4, EC4-5; DR4-101(A) and (B), DR4-101(C)(3).
Canon 7; EC7-9, EC7-26; DR7-102(A)(4), (5) and (6), DR7-102(B)(1).

Consider the standard of conduct set forth in the ABA's Standards Relating to the Defense Function, Section 7.7:

>Testimony by the defendant.
>
>(a) If the defendant has admitted to his lawyer facts which establish guilt and the lawyer's independent investigation establishes that the admissions are true but the defendant insists on his right to trial, the lawyer must advise his client against taking the witness stand to testify falsely.
>
>(b) If, before trial, the defendant insists that he will take the stand to testify falsely, the lawyer must withdraw from the case, if that is feasible, seeking leave of the court if necessary.
>
>(c) If withdrawal from the case is not feasible or is not permitted by the court, or if the situation arises during the trial and the defendant insists upon testifying falsely in his own behalf, the lawyer may not lend his aid to the perjury. Before the defendant takes the stand in these circumstances, the lawyer should make a record of the fact that the defendant is taking the stand against the advice of counsel in some appropriate manner without revealing the fact to the court. The lawyer must confine his examination to identifying the witness as the defendant and permitting him to make his statement to the trier or the triers of the facts; the lawyer may not engage in direct examination of the defendant

as a witness in the conventional manner and may not later argue the defendant's known false version of facts to the jury as worthy of belief and he may not recite or rely upon the false testimony in his closing argument.

Also consider the *Metzger* case, which follows.

In re Metzger
31 Hawaii 929 (1931)

PERRY, C.J. This is an information by the attorney general charging the respondent, an attorney duly licensed to practice in all the courts of this Territory, with misconduct. The facts are as follows:

In the course of the trial, before a jury, of a case wherein the indictment charged the two defendants, William Poai and William Spalding, with the crime of murder in the first degree, the prosecution examined a witness by the name of Bailey who testified, as an expert on handwriting, that a certain letter (exhibit "G") and an envelope (exhibit "F") were written by the same hand that had filled in the handwritten portions of a card (exhibit "E"), the handwriting upon which (the card) was admittedly that of the defendant Spalding. The present respondent was the attorney for the two defendants at that trial. He cross-examined Bailey for two and one-half hours and then, at 4 p.m. on Thursday, May 29, 1930, expressing surprise at the introduction by the prosecution of the testimony of Bailey and unpreparedness to conduct what he deemed to be further necessary cross-examination, requested an adjournment for the day and a postponement of the trial until the following Monday morn-

Problem 7. The Use of False or Perjured Testimony 45

ing, — the next day (Friday) being Decoration Day and Saturday being at best a short day for judicial business. The presiding judge granted the request.

On the Saturday morning, with the leave of the court, the respondent, giving to the clerk a receipt for the three papers, withdrew the letter, the envelope and the card and retained them in his possession until the Monday morning shortly before the opening of the trial. Exhibit "E" was a card bearing some typewritten matter and some penciled handwriting. It had come originally from the office of the sheriff. The respondent procured from one of the clerks in the sheriff's office a few blank cards of the same size and nature of exhibit "E" and taking them to his office fabricated there, with a typewriting machine and by his hand, a facsimile of exhibit "E," duplicating the typewritten matter and the handwritten matter as closely as he could. He was possessed, apparently, of considerable skill in that respect. He duplicated also the notation which had been made on exhibit "E" by the clerk of the court showing the filing of the paper as an exhibit and duplicated also in that connection the clerk's signed initials "B.H.K." Before making the fabrication the respondent consulted at his office two other members of the bar of this court, the late J.W. Russell and Mr. T.E.M. Osorio. The fabrication was approved by these attorneys as a probably successful device for testing the ability and the credibility of Bailey as a handwriting expert and no doubt was expressed by them concerning the ethical quality of the trick.

One Flanary, called in by the respondent for the purpose, was present during all of the time that the respondent made the spurious exhibit "E" and made certain concealed marks upon the paper which would enable him to identify it beyond doubt at the trial, at the proper time.

As stated by Osorio in an affidavit filed in the case at bar, at the conference with the two attorneys prior to the fabrication, "Russell again asked Metzger" (the respondent) "as to his plan for getting it" (the spurious exhibit "E") "into the witness's hand without arousing his suspicions and Metzger again stated his plan, which was the one followed by him." Mr. Osorio was present at the proceedings on Monday and personally saw the method and plan which was followed by the respondent in getting the false card into the hands of the witness Bailey.

On Monday morning, shortly before the resumption of the trial, the respondent, retaining the genuine exhibit "E" in his custody, handed to the clerk of the court the letter and the envelope which he had received from the clerk and the spurious exhibit "E." The clerk thereupon offered to return to the respondent his receipt for the papers, but the respondent asked him to keep it for the time being, with a statement to the effect that there would be further transactions in the matter. Respondent at the same time asked the clerk to be extremely careful not to permit any of the three papers just handed to him to leave his custody until the respondent should call for them. This the clerk agreed to do.

On the Thursday a very large part of the two and a half hours of cross-examination by the respondent of the witness Bailey had been devoted to minute inquiries and details of similarities and dissimilarities of the writings on the letter and the envelope on the one hand and the genuine exhibit "E" on the other. No other writings were produced in that connection or were involved or referred to in either the direct examination, which in itself had been detailed in its nature, or in the cross-examination of Thursday. When Bailey took the stand on Monday morning his cross-examination, by the respondent, was resumed in the following

Problem 7. The Use of False or Perjured Testimony

words: "Q: After — when Mr. Mills came back after being two or three days down there" (the reference was to a visit by Mills to Bailey at Honolulu for the purpose of securing Bailey's examination of the handwritings) "did he bring this letter and card back with him, the writing that you examined?" . . . "A: Yes. Q: And did you tell him before he left that you would be willing to testify that these were written, those three pieces were written by the same person? A: Yes. Q: Then did he engage you at that time to come up here? A: I don't believe there was any discussion as to whether I was going to testify; he just asked me for my opinion at that time. Q: Were arrangements made later? A: There were no arrangements made; I received a wire that I was to be subpoenaed." Then followed a brief examination as to the nature and extent of the witness' study and experience as an expert on handwriting, followed still later by cross-examination as to characteristic similarities and dissimilarities in general and similarities and dissimilarities in particular in the handwritings then immediately under consideration. In the midst of this latter cross-examination the respondent said to the clerk of the court: "You got that exhibit there, so that Mr. Bailey may see it?" When this was said the clerk was at his desk and the respondent was standing near the witness and the witness saw and heard what was being said and done. In answer to the question or request the clerk handed to the respondent and the respondent handed to the witness the letter (exhibit "G") and the spurious exhibit "E" which latter at the time was the only exhibit "E" in the possession of the clerk. Upon handing these two papers to the witness the respondent immediately resumed his cross-examination as to the peculiarities of the handwritings, saying to the witness: "Then on the card the 'g' seems to have a characteristic something like this (drawing on blackboard); had you not noticed that?" Lengthy and detailed cross-examination followed, relating to the peculiarities, similarities and dissimilarities of the writings on the letter and on the spurious exhibit "E." . . . The plan had been carefully devised. His express purpose, as he admitted at the hearing in this court in answer to a question by a member of the court, was, in saying what he said and in doing what he did, to deceive the witness into thinking that he was handing him the genuine exhibit "E." The plan devised and followed was well calculated to accomplish that purpose; and succeeded. The respondent first deceived the clerk by failing to return to him, as was his duty, the precise paper (exhibit "E") which he had received from him and for which he had given him a receipt and by the method pursued made the clerk an innocent and unwitting participant in the misrepresentation and deception, to the witness, which followed. When, after a lengthy examination and a lengthy cross-examination upon the handwriting of the letter, the envelope and the genuine card, the clerk, in answer to the cross-examining attorney's request, produced the letter and a card, the witness had a right to believe, and could only believe, that the card was the genuine exhibit "E." The presentation by the respondent to the witness of a card as exhibit "E" was a deliberate misrepresentation. If the representation had been made in words, e.g., "this is exhibit 'E,' " instead of by acts, it would have been a deliberate falsehood. So, also, forgery of the clerk's signature (by initials), for the purpose of conveying to the witness the clerk's apparent certification of the genuineness of the card, was in itself an offense which cannot be ignored.

There can be no doubt that it was the right and the duty of the respondent, who was entrusted with the defense of two men who were on trial for their lives, to expose if he

Problem 7. The Use of False or Perjured Testimony

could what he believed to be a lack of ability and a lack of credibility or accuracy on the part of the witness who had testified as an expert on handwriting; but there was a limitation upon that right and that duty and the limitation was that the test and the exposure must be accomplished by fair and lawful means, free from falsehood and misrepresentation. The so-called "necessities of the case," the keenness of the desire of the attorney to defend the accused to the best of his ability, cannot in our judgment justify falsehood or misrepresentation by the attorney to a witness or to the clerk of the court, whether that falsehood or misrepresentation be expressed in direct language or be conveyed by artful subterfuge. We are unwilling to certify to the younger attorneys who are beginning their experience at the bar of this court, or to any of the attorneys of this Territory, that it is lawful and proper for them to defend men, even though on trial for their lives, by the use of falsehood and misrepresentation, direct or indirect. The conduct of the respondent was unethical and unprofessional.

With reference to the action to be taken in consequence of this finding and this ruling, it is proper to consider the surrounding circumstances. The responsibility of an attorney who is defending men in a capital case is a serious one. Right and justice require that he should be zealous and active in securing all proper evidence in behalf of the accused and in cross-examining as effectively as may be the witnesses produced by the prosecution. The respondent testifies that when he devised and executed his plan he was not conscious of the fact that it might be deemed unethical or unprofessional. We accept his statement. The two attorneys whom he consulted as to the probable success of the plan did not utter any caution as to its possible impropriety. . . . In order to give emphasis to our disapproval of the respondent's conduct, we feel that it is our duty to suspend his license for a brief period of time.

A judgment of suspension for ten days will be signed upon presentation.

BANKS, J. (dissenting). Metzger's right to impeach by every proper means Bailey's opinion that the letter, envelope and card were written by the same hand it seems to me must be conceded. Indeed it was not only his right to do this but his duty to do so — his duty to his clients, to the jury and to the court. Of course if he had known that the letter and the envelope were in the handwriting of one of his clients, as he knew that the writing on the card was, the situation would be quite different. Under such circumstances his effort would have been not to destroy what he believed to be false but to destroy what he knew to be true. I think a lawyer, even in his zeal to extricate his client from a serious position, may not ethically go so far. This, however, was not the case. At the hearing of the instant proceeding Metzger testified that having had considerable experience in chirography he believed that the writing on the card was not by the same person as the writing on the envelope and in the letter. There is no apparent reason for disbelieving him. His purpose therefore was not the evil one of misleading the jury as to a fact which he knew existed but the laudable one of exposing what he believed to be an erroneous opinion. This was in the interest of justice and not against it. Metzger also testified that he had been unable after a long cross-examination of Bailey to discredit his opinion and that there was no other handwriting expert available whom he could consult or to whose opinion he could submit the writings. His only alternative therefore was in some way to lead Bailey to disclose his own fallibility. The question that remains is whether the means he used to accomplish his purpose were unethical.

Problem 7. The Use of False or Perjured Testimony

I do not think that his treatment of the witness was unfair. A cross-examiner is certainly under no professional obligation to warn an expert witness, whose opinion he wishes to test, of the pit which has been dug for him and into which he will fall unless he has sufficient technical learning to discover and avoid it. Nor do I think it a violation of legal ethics to withhold from such witness a fact which, if he knew it, would enable him to discover the pit independently of his technical knowledge. It is a principle peculiar to the cross-examination of expert witnesses that in order to evaluate their opinions things may be assumed as facts which are not facts. This is all that Metzger really did. He in effect assumed, in the presence of the witness, the court and the jury, that the fabricated card was the real exhibit about which the witness had already testified and proceeded to ascertain by cross-examination whether he was capable of discovering that the assumption was false. In doing this he was entirely fair to the witness. According to his testimony he required Bailey to subject the fabricated card to the same tests to which he had subjected the real exhibit and to compare it with the writing on the envelope and the letter just as he had compared the real exhibit. It was an acid test of the value of Bailey's opinion, but no more severe than that to which a handwriting expert may properly be put.

Under the evidence in this proceeding I likewise see no disregard of legal ethics on Metzger's part in delivering to the clerk the fabricated card instead of the original exhibit, without informing him of the substitution. I think the ethical quality of everything that Metzger did in carrying out the plan he devised for testing the accuracy of Bailey's opinion must be judged by the motive that actuated him to make the test, *unless what he did was otherwise inherently wrong*. His motive in making the test was to discredit an opinion that had been given by a putative expert, which opinion he believed to be erroneous. I see nothing *inherently* wrong in his temporarily withholding from the clerk the fact that the fabricated card which he delivered was not the original exhibit. That he only intended to temporarily withhold this fact from the clerk is shown by Metzger's testimony that when he handed the clerk the simulated card together with two of the exhibits he had withdrawn the clerk said to him, "I will destroy your receipt," and that he told the clerk not to do this because there would be further transactions with respect to these papers. He did in fact return the original exhibit to the clerk after he had concluded his cross-examination of Bailey. His purpose in withholding the fact from the clerk was to guard against the danger of having his plan for testing the value of Bailey's opinion frustrated by a premature exposure. This was not in my opinion a fraud on the clerk nor was it a fraud on the court nor was it inimical to the cause of justice. It was done not to defeat a fair trial but to promote it. If it had not been done the weakness of Bailey's opinion might not have been revealed and men whom the jury found to be innocent might have been found guilty and sent to the gallows.

I cannot agree that Metzger did anything wrong and I therefore most respectfully dissent from the majority opinion.

BACKGROUND READING

Dean Monroe Freedman discusses the question of perjured testimony in a chapter entitled, "Perjury: The Criminal Defense Lawyer's Trilemma," in his book, Lawyers' Ethics in an Adversary System (Bobbs-Merrill, 1975). He concludes:

Problem 7. The Use of False or Perjured Testimony

"In my opinion, the attorney's obligation in such a situation would be to advise the client that the proposed testimony is unlawful, but to proceed in the normal fashion in presenting the testimony and arguing the case to the jury if the client makes the decision to go forward. Any other course would be a betrayal of the assurances of confidentiality given by the attorney in order to induce the client to reveal everything, however damaging it might appear." *Id.* at 31.

See also A.B.A. Formal Opinion 287 (1953), which deals with the question of how the lawyer should act when he learns that his client has committed perjury. (Issued under the old Canons of Professional Ethics.)

Consider whether different rules should apply in civil and criminal cases. In an informal opinion issued under the new Code, the ABA Committee on Ethics and Professional Responsibility has reaffirmed "A lawyer may never countenance the use of perjured testimony or a willful misstatement of fact in a pleading." A.B.A. Informal Opinion 1271 (1973).

PROBLEM 8

Cross-Examining the Truthful Witness

Do lawyers pursue the truth or is that someone else's business?
How can the adversary system achieve truth by subverting it?

Dr. Harold Crimmins is a respected plastic surgeon who is a defendant in a one million dollar malpractice suit. The incident which gave rise to the lawsuit occurred in the office which Dr. Crimmins maintains in his home, where he performs minor surgery that does not require hospital facilities. One such operation involved the removal of a minor tumor from the nose of a young television actress. According to the plaintiff's complaint the operation was performed negligently, leaving the actress with a permanent scar.

Dr. Crimmins is being represented by Richard Cowans, who has built his proposed defense on the theory that the scar resulted from a subsequent infection, which the patient failed to report to a physician.

During one of his conferences with his client Mr. Cowans brings up an unpleasant subject.

"Do you remember your former nurse, Sarah Wimberly?"

Problem 8. Cross-Examining the Truthful Witness

"Yes," replies the Doctor. "She was awful. I'm glad I fired her. But what does she have to do with this case?"

"She was on duty on the morning of the operation, wasn't she?"

"She is going to be a plaintiff's witness and I took her examination before trial yesterday. She claims that you used to drink during working hours, and that she thought she saw you walking toward the room in the house where the bar is located on the morning of the operation. Is that true?"

"Frankly, I don't remember. I occasionally take something before a minor operation. It calms my nerves."

"Well," says Mr. Cowans. "I checked up on her story. I asked your cleaning woman, who happened to be working in your home that morning because it was a Tuesday, and she comes in on Tuesdays. And she says that she did see you take a drink that morning."

"Maybe," replies Dr. Crimmins, "but I don't remember it and, besides, I'm sure that the operation had nothing to do with that woman's scar."

Cowans now starts to look into the background of Ms. Wimberly. She has held 10 jobs in the last two years, and was once charged with embezzlement, although never brought to trial. She was fired by Dr. Crimmins two months after the incident involved in this case, and has expressed great bitterness about the fact that Dr. Crimmins has not given her favorable references.

"I think we have enough to destroy her credibility," Cowans confidently advises Dr. Crimmins.

"But the woman is probably telling the truth," Dr. Crimmins replies.

"You said you didn't remember."

"But what about the cleaning woman?"

"She hasn't been questioned and I doubt that the plaintiff's lawyers know about her. Remember, this is an important case."

When Ms. Wimberly testifies, should Mr. Cowans use the information he has uncovered to destroy her credibility?

Should he conceal the facts of his conversation with the cleaning woman?

ASSIGNMENT

Canon 4; EC4-1, EC4-4, EC4-5; DR4-101(A) and (B).
Canon 7; EC7-9, EC7-10, EC7-19, EC7-24, EC7-26; DR7-102(A)(4) and (6).

BACKGROUND READING

This issue is discussed in the context of a criminal case in Freedman, Lawyers' Ethics in an Adversary System 43-49 (Bobbs-Merrill, 1975). In his recent Benjamin N. Cardozo Lecture, Judge Marvin Frankel raised serious questions about the adversary system as a method for ascertaining truth. Frankel, The Search For Truth — An Umpireal View, 30 Record 14 (Assn. of the Bar of the City of New York, 1975). See Dean Freedman's Comments on the Frankel lecture, 123 N.Y.L. Journal, January 29, 1975, at 1, col. 1.

See also Report of the Joint Conference of the American Bar Association and the Association of American Law Schools on Professional Responsibility, 44 A.B.A. Journal 1159 (1958); and the provocative book by Curtis, It's Your Law (Harv. University Press, 1954).

PROBLEM 9

The Requirement of Candor

*Concealing evidence and withholding evidence
 — is there a difference?
How much law which is unfavorable to your
 side do you have to tell the judge?
Candor v. confidentiality — which comes first?*

Paula O'Hearn is a general practitioner in Muncie, Indiana and she has been retained by Tom Lockwood, a star forward on the local high school basketball team. Mr. Lockwood has been dropped from the team for two months during the height of the season by William Ackerman, the principal of the school, as a disciplinary measure; allegedly because Mr. Lockwood was found smoking marijuana in the men's room of the school.

Ms. O'Hearn has brought an action against Mr. Ackerman under 42 U.S.C. §1983, alleging a violation by Mr. Ackerman of her client's constitutional rights under the Fourteenth Amendment. The complaint alleges that removal from the basketball team is like a suspension from school, and that the failure to provide a hearing, with a right to counsel, was a violation of Lockwood's constitutional rights. The complaint asks immediate reinstatement to the team and half a million dollars in damages on grounds that Lockwood's inability to play during this period harmed his chances to go to a college with a major basketball program, and may have thwarted a professional basketball career.

Mr. Ackerman's attorney is George Berkow. There has been a trial which established that Mr. Lockwood was called in to Mr. Ackerman's office where he was asked whether he had, in fact, been smoking marijuana, as alleged. He admitted the offense, although there was conflicting testimony as to whether he had admitted prior similar acts.

During the course of the trial Ms. O'Hearn learns, through chatting with a law school classmate who practices law in California and is visiting in Muncie for a few days, that a federal district judge in northern California has handed down a decision, which is unreported, holding that suspension from an athletic team is not the same as suspension from school and can be imposed by school authorities without the type of hearing which would be required in the case of a school suspension.

Ms. O'Hearn is also aware of the U.S. Supreme Court's decision in *Wood v. Strickland,* 420 U.S. 308 (1975), which held that money damages can be obtained in a §1983 case only if the public official knew, or should have known, that his conduct was a violation of the plaintiff's constitutional rights. Neither in the trial nor in any legal memoranda which have been filed with the court has Mr. Berkow asserted the *Wood v. Strickland* defense. Ms. O'Hearn has not mentioned the case.

Mr. Berkow, on the other hand, has learned from his client that prior to the suspension of Mr. Lockwood from the team, Mr. Ackerman had sought advice from another attorney who had advised him that his actions might be a

Problem 9. The Requirement of Candor 59

violation of Mr. Lockwood's constitutional rights unless a hearing was provided. Mr. Ackerman ignored the advice.

The judge decides that: (1) the suspension from the team without a hearing violated Mr. Lockwood's constitutional rights; (2) Mr. Lockwood should be reinstated immediately; and (3) since there was no proof that Mr. Ackerman either knew or had reason to know that there was any violation of Mr. Lockwood's rights, the claim for money damages should be denied, citing *Wood v. Strickland* (and commenting critically on counsel's failure to discuss it).

1. Should Ms. O'Hearn have advised the court of the unreported California case?

2. Should she have raised the *Wood v. Strickland* issue?

3. Should Mr. Berkow have discussed *Wood v. Strickland* (assuming he knew about it)?

4. Did Mr. Berkow act properly in remaining silent when the judge decided the damage question on the erroneous assumption that Mr. Ackerman was ignorant of any possible constitutional violation?

ASSIGNMENT

Canon 4; EC4-1, EC4-4, EC4-5; DR4-101(A) and (B)(1) and (2).

Canon 7; EC7-23, EC7-26, EC7-27; DR7-101(B)(1), DR7-106(B)(1).

This problem has dealt with the responsibility of the advocate to disclose certain facts and legal precedents to the court. Compare your reaction to this problem with the following news story.

Slayer's 2 Lawyers Kept Secret of 2 More Killings
New York Times, June 20, 1974

Lake Pleasant, N.Y., June 19 — Two lawyers for a man on trial here for murder did not disclose for six months that they had seen the bodies of two other people killed by their client because, they said, they were bound by the confidentiality of a lawyer-client relationship.

The court-appointed attorneys said today that their client had told them where to find the bodies of two missing women. They photographed the bodies, they said, but did not report the discoveries to authorities searching for the murder victims.

The lawyers also said they had kept their discovery from the father of one of the women, who had visited them in the hope that they could shed some light on the disappearance of his 20-year-old daughter.

"The information was so privileged — I was bound by my lawyer's oath to keep it confidential after I found the bodies," said Francis Belge, one of the two lawyers representing Robert Garrow. Mr. Garrow, a 38-year-old mechanic for a Syracuse bakery, is accused of fatally stabbing Philip Domblewski, an 18-year-old Schenectady student who was camping in the Adirondacks last July.

From what his lawyers said in a news conference today, as well as from what Mr. Garrow has — sometimes incoherently — blurted out in court, the defendant may be connected to at least four murders.

Mr. Belge and his associate on the case, Frank Armani,

Problem 9. The Requirement of Candor

told of the secret they had kept at a news conference in this Adirondack village. They indicated that they could come forth now, released from their obligation by Mr. Garrow's own testimony yesterday. At that time the defendant implicated himself in Essex County Court.

The Police Chief of Syracuse, where one of the women's bodies was ultimately found, said he would ask the Onondaga District Attorney to bring charges against the lawyers. The prosecutor could not be reached for comment.

[According to a number of legal authorities in New York City, the issue of what a lawyer should do when apprised by his client of criminal action is a gray area.]

According to Mr. Belge, Mr. Garrow told him of raping and killing a woman in an abandoned mine shaft near Mineville, N.Y. The lawyer said this information was provided by Mr. Garrow a few weeks after the suspect was wounded and captured last August 9 following a manhunt involving 200 state troopers and others.

Some three weeks later Mr. Belge said he discovered the body of Susan Petz, a 20-year-old woman from Skokie, Ill. She had been missing since July 20, when the body of her camping companion, Daniel Porter, a Harvard student, was found near Weavertown.

"We passed the shaft 10 times before I found it with a flashlight at twilight," Mr. Belge said. "Frank lowered me into the shaft by my feet and I took pictures."

The finding of Miss Petz's body was reported to the state police four months later by two children who had been playing in the mine.

Meanwhile, Mr. Belge said Miss Petz's father visited him because his client, Mr. Garrow, had been unofficially linked to killings in the area.

"I spent many, many sleepless nights over my inability to reveal the information, especially after Mr. Petz came in from Chicago and talked to me," Mr. Belge said.

The lawyer found the second body at the end of September. He said that while Mr. Garrow provided a rough diagram locating Miss Petz's body, in the second instance he gave only a general description of an area in Syracuse near Syracuse University.

There in Oakwood Cemetery, Mr. Belge said, he found the body of Alicia Hauck, a 16-year-old high school girl who disappeared from her home in Syracuse nearly two months earlier, on July 11.

Miss Hauck's body was ultimately found and reported by a Syracuse University student on December 1. In the intervening months, her father, the owner of a bowling alley in Syracuse, and the police, were treating the case as that of a runaway and were advertising pleas for the girl to come home.

"We both, knowing how the parents must feel, wanted to advise them where the bodies were," Mr. Belge said. "But since it was a privileged communication we could not reveal any information that was given to us in confidence."

Both lawyers had apparently felt the weight of the confidence they honored until today. "Death is difficult enough to accept," Mr. Armani said, "but worrying and wondering, it'll drive you insane."

In his testimony yesterday, Mr. Garrow blurted out that he was "embarrassed" and tearfully said that while he could not remember specific rapes and murders he had pieced together the story of his involvement in the killings from accounts given by authorities and his lawyers. He did not identify the victims by name, but the details and locations he cited coincided with known details of the murders.

Problem 9. The Requirement of Candor

BACKGROUND READING

A.B.A. Formal Opinion 287 (1953) concludes, in a problem which discusses one of the issues raised in the instant problem, that when a judge is imposing a sentence on a defendant based on misinformation that the defendant has no criminal record, there is no duty on the part of the lawyer to correct the misinformation "if the attorney for the defendant learns of the previous record through the client's communications...."

A.B.A. Formal Opinion 280 (1949) discusses the lawyer's duty to disclose adverse precedents. It concludes: "The test in every case should be: Is the decision which opposing counsel has overlooked one which the court should clearly consider in deciding the case? Would a reasonable judge properly feel that a lawyer who advanced, as the law, a proposition adverse to the undisclosed decision, was lacking in candor and fairness to him? Might the judge consider himself misled by an implied representation that the lawyer knew of no adverse authority?"

See also A.B.A. Informal Opinion 1141 (1970), which deals with a lawyer's obligation to reveal the whereabouts of a deserter from the armed forces who has sought advice concerning his rights. The opinion concludes: "Accordingly, if the fugitive comes to see a lawyer concerning his rights, the information given to the lawyer would be privileged. If, on the other hand, the fugitive comes to see the lawyer in order to secure advice as to how he can best remain a fugitive or a deserter in the future, then the lawyer is obliged: (a) To advise him to turn himself in; and (b) To refuse to represent him if he declines to do so; and (c) To advise him that the lawyer will reveal his whereabouts to the authorities if he persists in his illegal conduct and if the matter is brought to his attention again by the client."

The extent of the lawyer's duty to disclose unlawful conduct is discussed more fully in Problem 20. It is raised here because it is related to the lawyer's duty of candor to the court and the conflict with the lawyer's duty to preserve the confidences and secrets of the client.

See also A.B.A. Formal Opinion 341 (1975), which is assigned with Problem 20, *infra*. This opinion appears to limit (even further than the limitation in DR7-102(B)(1)) the lawyer's duty to disclose frauds which have been perpetrated "upon a . . . tribunal" in the course of the lawyer's representation of the client.

PROBLEM 10

Advocacy Outside the Courtroom

How far can the lawyer go in criticizing the judge? Arguing your case in the press — why is it wrong? Should lawyers criticize other lawyers in public? Does the First Amendment apply to lawyers?

Attorney Louise Winters has brought an action in U.S. District Court in Illinois against the Midwestern Telephone Corporation on behalf of Black and Spanish-speaking persons who are challenging Midwestern's procedures for hiring switchboard operators and secretarial personnel. The case has come to trial and has aroused widespread public interest. Sam Harris, an attorney, has been asked by the Chicago Star to cover the trial and to record his comments in a series of columns.

The company uses written examinations as part of its hiring process. On the first day of the trial Ms. Winters tries to introduce into evidence the results of a survey conducted by the Rand Institute showing that a higher proportion of minority group candidates failed the last three examinations than did white candidates. Such evidence has been received in similar cases in federal courts throughout the country. While not conclusive in determining whether the examination is a violation of federal law, such factual discrimination generally has been held to shift the burden to the testing authority to establish that the examination is job related.

Judge Walter Miller, who is presiding at the trial, is not noted for his sympathy with suits of this kind, or for his erudition in civil rights matters. He rules that the results of the Rand survey are inadmissible because such statistical data is irrelevant to the question of discrimination in the examination.

This happens on a Friday. On Sunday Ms. Winters appears on a television program dealing with the general subject of discriminatory testing procedures and, when asked how the case is going, replies, "Very badly. Judge Miller simply is unaware of recent developments in this area, and it is unfortunate that we are going to have to go through the expense and inconvenience of an appeal in order to obtain a reversal of his erroneous rulings."

A few days later Sam Harris, in his Chicago Star column, writes, "The way Judge Miller is conducting this case is a travesty of justice. He is not only woefully ignorant with regard to constitutional matters, but his racial bigotry is permeating his conduct of the entire trial. And the lawyers for Midwestern are just as bad. They shouldn't be lending themselves to the cause of bigotry."

The next day Mr. Harris calls Ms. Winters and says, "I'd like to prepare a list of law firms who are representing companies like Midwestern in these discrimination cases — you're active in this field. Can you help me compile the list?"

"What do you plan to do with it?" she asks.

"I'm doing an article for the Student Law Journal, which is distributed to law students throughout the country, and I want to let them know the names of the law firms that

Problem 10. Advocacy Outside the Courtroom

are helping giant corporations deny employment opportunities to minorities."

1. Were the comments of Ms. Winters proper?
2. Were the comments of Mr. Harris proper?
3. Should Ms. Winters assist in the preparation of Mr. Harris' article?
4. Is it proper for Mr. Harris to write the article?

ASSIGNMENT

Canon 1; DR1-102(A)(5) and (6); EC7-22, EC7-33, EC7-36; DR7-107(G).
Canon 8; EC8-6; DR8-102(B)
Canon 9; EC9-1, EC9-4, EC9-6.
Also the following case, *In re Sawyer,* and A.B.A. Formal Opinion 336 (1974).

In re Sawyer
360 U.S. 622 (1959)

Mr. Justice BRENNAN announced the judgment of the Court, and delivered an opinion, in which The CHIEF JUSTICE, Mr. Justice BLACK, and Mr. Justice DOUGLAS join. . . .

Petitioner has been a member of the Territorial Bar in Hawaii since 1941. For many months beginning in late 1952 she participated, in the United States District Court at Honolulu, as one of the defense counsel in the trial of an indictment against a number of defendants for conspiracy under the Smith Act, 18 U.S.C. §2385, 18 U.S.C.A. §2385. The trial was before Federal District Judge Jon Wiig and a jury. *United*

States v. Fujimoto, D.C., 107 F.Supp. 865. Both disciplinary charges against petitioner had to do with the Smith Act trial. One charge related to a speech she made about six weeks after the trial began. The speech was made on the Island of Hawaii, at Honokaa, a village some 182 miles from Honolulu, Oahu, on a Sunday morning. The other charge related to interviews she had with one of the jurors after the trial concluded.

The Bar Association of Hawaii preferred the charges which were referred by the Territorial Supreme Court to the Association's Legal Ethics Committee for investigation. The prosecutor who represented the Government at the Smith Act trial conducted the investigation and presented the evidence before the Committee. . . . The gist of the Committee's findings was that the petitioner's speech reflected adversely upon Judge Wiig's impartiality and fairness in the conduct of the Smith Act trial and impugned his judicial integrity. The Committee concluded that petitioner "in imputing to the Judge unfairness in the conduct of the trial, in impugning the integrity of the local Federal courts and in other comments made at Honokaa, was guilty of violation of Canons 1 and 22 of the Canons of Professional Ethics of the American Bar Association[3] and should be disciplined for

---

3. Canon 1 is entitled "The Duty of the Lawyer to the Courts." It reads:

"It is the duty of the lawyer to maintain towards the Courts a respectful attitude, not for the sake of the temporary incumbent of the judicial office, but for the maintenance of its supreme importance. Judges, not being wholly free to defend themselves, are peculiarly entitled to receive the support of the Bar against unjust criticism and clamor. Whenever there is proper ground for serious complaint of a judicial officer, it is the right and duty of the lawyer to submit his grievances to the proper authorities. In such cases, but not otherwise, such charges should be encouraged and the person making them should be protected."

Problem 10. Advocacy Outside the Courtroom

the same." The Territorial Supreme Court held that ". . . she engaged and participated in a willful oral attack upon the administration of justice in and by the said United States District Court for the District of Hawaii and by direct statement and implication impugned the integrity of the judge presiding therein . . . and thus tended to also create disrespect for the courts of justice and judicial officers generally. . . . She has thus committed what this court considers gross misconduct." 41 Haw. at pages 422-423.

Canon 22 is entitled "Candor and Fairness." It reads:

"The conduct of the lawyer before the Court and with other lawyers should be characterized by candor and fairness.

"It is not candid or fair for the lawyer knowingly to misquote the contents of a paper, the testimony of a witness, the language or the argument of opposing counsel, or the language of a decision or a text-book; or with knowledge of its invalidity, to cite as authority a decision that has been overruled, or a statute that has been repealed; or in argument to assert as a fact that which has not been proved, or in those jurisdictions where a side has the opening and closing arguments to mislead his opponent by concealing or withholding positions in his opening argument upon which his side then intends to rely.

"It is unprofessional and dishonorable to deal other than candidly with the facts in taking the statements of witnesses, in drawing affidavits and other documents, and in the presentation of causes.

"A lawyer should not offer evidence which he knows the Court should reject, in order to get the same before the jury by argument for its admissibility, nor should he address to the Judge arguments upon any point not properly calling for determination by him. Neither should he introduce into an argument, addressed to the Court, remarks or statements intended to influence the jury or bystanders.

"These and all kindred practices are unprofessional and unworthy of an officer of the law charged, as is the lawyer, with the duty of aiding in the administration of justice."

We do not perceive any specification by the Committee of the respect in which Canon 22 was thought to have been violated by petitioner's speech, and such a violation does not occur to us.

We think that our review may be limited to the narrow question whether the facts adduced are capable of supporting the findings that the petitioner's speech impugned Judge Wiig's impartiality and fairness in conducting the Smith Act trial and thus reflected upon his integrity in the dispensation of justice in that case. We deal with the Court's findings, not with "misconduct" in the abstract. Although the opinions in the Court of Appeals and the argument before us have tended in varying degrees to treat the petitioner's suspension as discipline imposed for obstructing or attempting to obstruct the administration of justice, in a way to embarrass or influence the tribunal trying the case, such was neither the charge nor the finding of professional misconduct upon which the suspension was based. Since no obstruction or attempt at obstruction of the trial was charged, and since it is clear to us that the finding upon which the suspension rests is not supportable by the evidence adduced, we have no occasion to consider the applicability of *Bridges v. California,* 314 U.S. 252, 62 S. Ct. 190, 86 L. Ed. 192; Pennekamp v. Florida, 328 U.S. 331, 66 S. Ct. 1029, 90 L. Ed. 1295; or Craig v. Harney, 331 U.S. 367, 67 S. Ct. 1249, 91 L. Ed. 1546, which have been extensively discussed in the briefs. We do not reach or intimate any conclusion on the constitutional issues presented.

Petitioner's clients included labor unions, among them the International Longshoremen's and Warehousemen's Union. Some of the defendants in the Smith Act trial were officers and members of that union and their defense was being supported by the union. The meeting at Honokaa was sponsored by the ILWU and was attended in large part by its members. The petitioner spoke extemporaneously and no transcript or recording was made of her speech. Precisely what she did say is a matter of dispute. Neither the Territo-

Problem 10. Advocacy Outside the Courtroom 71

rial Supreme Court nor the Court of Appeals saw the witnesses, but both courts, on reading the record, resolved matters of evidentiary conflict in the fashion least favorable to the petitioner. For the purposes of our review here, we may do the same. The version of the petitioner's speech principally relied upon by the Court of Appeals, 260 F.2d at 197-198, is derived from notes made by a newspaper reporter, Matsuoka, who attended the meeting and heard what the petitioner said. These were not Matsuoka's original notes — the originals were lost — but an expanded version prepared by him at the direction of his newspaper superiors after interest in the speech was aroused by Matsuoka's account of it in the newspaper.[4] We set forth the notes in full as an Appendix to this opinion, and summarize them here, as an account of what petitioner said. The summary will illumine the basis of our conclusion that the finding that the petitioner's speech impugned the integrity of Judge Wiig or reflected upon his impartiality and fairness in presiding at the Smith Act trial is without support. The fact finding

---

4. The portion of the article, in the Hilo Tribune-Herald, that deals with petitioner's speech is as follows:

"Mrs. Sawyer, speaking for a half hour, spoke of 'some rather shocking and horrible things that go on at the trial.'

"There's 'no such thing as a fair trial in a Smith act case,' she charged. 'All rules of evidence have to be scrapped or the government can't make a case.'

"They 'just make up the rules as they go along,' she told her listeners.

" 'Unless we stop the Smith act trial in its tracks here' there will be a 'new crime' that of knowing what's in books and will lead to 'dark ages of thought control,' asserted the chic and attractive woman lawyer.

"She referred to reading by the prosecution of books 'supposed to have been in a duffel bag' owned by a witness, Henry Johnson. She urged her listeners to tell others 'what a vicious thing the Smith Act is.' Persons are 'tried for books written years ago' by others, she said."

below does not remove this Court's duty of examining the evidence to see whether it furnishes a rational basis for the characterization put on it by the lower courts. . . . We conclude that there is no support for any further factual inference than that petitioner was voicing strong criticism of Smith Act cases and the Government's manner of proving them, and that her references to the happenings at the Honolulu trial were illustrative of this, and not a reflection in any wise upon Judge Wiig personally or his conduct of the trial.

Petitioner said that the Honolulu trial was really an effort to get at the ILWU. She wanted to tell about some "rather shocking and horrible things that go on at the trial." The defendants, she said, were being tried for reading books written before they were born. Jack Hall, one of the defendants, she said, was on trial because he had read the Communist Manifesto. She spoke of the nature of criminal conspiracy prosecutions, as she saw them, and charged that when the Government did not have enough evidence "it lumps a number together and says they agreed to do something." "Conspiracy means to charge a lot of people for agreeing to do something you have never done." She generally attacked the FBI, saying they spent too much time investigating people's minds, and next dwelt further on the remoteness of the evidence in the case and the extreme youth of some of the defendants at the time to which the evidence directly related. She said "no one has a memory that good, yet they use this kind of testimony. Why? Because they will do anything and everything necessary to convict." Government propaganda carried on for 10 years before the jurors entered the box, she charged, made it "enough to say a person is a communist to cook his goose." She charged that some of the witnesses had given prior inconsistent testimony but that the Government went ahead and had them "say things in

Problem 10. Advocacy Outside the Courtroom 73

order to convict." "Witnesses testify what Government tells them to." The Government, she claimed, read in evidence for two days Communist books because one of the defendants had once seen them in a duffel bag. Unless people informed on such defendants, the FBI would try to make them lose their jobs. "There's no such thing as a fair trial in a Smith Act case. All rules of evidence have to be scrapped or the Government can't make a case." She related how in another case (in the territorial courts) she was not allowed to put in evidence of a hearsay nature to exonerate a criminal defendant she was representing, but in the present case "a federal judge sitting on a federal bench permits Crouch [a witness] to testify about 27 years ago, what was said then . . . here they permit a witness to tell what was said when a defendant was five years old." She then declared, "There's no fair trial in the case. They just make up the rules as they go along." She gave the example of the New York Smith Act trial before Judge Medina, see Dennis v. United States, 341 U.S. 494, 71 S. Ct. 857, 95 L. Ed. 1137, where she claimed "The Government can't make a case if it tells just what they did so they widened the rules and tell what other people did years ago, including everything including the kitchen sink." She declared, "Unless we stop the Smith trial in its tracks here there will be a new crime. People will be charged with knowing what is included in books — ideas." Petitioner said in conclusion that if things went on the freedom to read and freedom of thought and action would be subverted. She urged her auditors to go out and explain what a vicious thing the Smith Act was.

The specific utterances in the speech that the Legal Ethics Committee and the Supreme Court found as furnishing the basis for the findings that petitioner impugned Judge Wiig's integrity were the references (which we have quoted in full above) to "horrible and shocking" things at the trial; the impossibility of a fair trial; the necessity, if the Government's case were to be proved, of scrapping the rules of evidence; and the creation of new crimes unless the trial were stopped at once. We examine these points in particular, though of course we must do so in the context of the whole speech. In so doing we accept as obviously correct the ruling of the courts below that petitioner's remarks were not a mere generalized discourse on Smith Act prosecutions but included particular references to the case going on in Honolulu.

I. We start with the proposition that lawyers are free to criticize the state of the law. Many lawyers say that the rules of evidence relative to the admission of statements by those alleged to be co-conspirators are overbroad or otherwise unfair and unwise; [6] that there are dangers to defendants, of a sort against which trial judges cannot protect them, in the trial of numerous persons jointly for conspiracy; and that a Smith Act trial is apt to become a trial of ideas. Others disagree. But all are free to express their views on these matters, and no one would say that this sort of criticism constituted an improper attack on the judges who enforced such rules and who presided at the trials. This is so, even though the

6. One of the classic statements of this point of view is Mr. Justice Jackson's concurring opinion in Krulewitch v. United States, 336 U.S. 440, 453, 69 S. Ct. 716, 723, 93 L. Ed. 790: "But the order of proof of so sprawling a charge [as conspiracy] is difficult for a judge to control. As a practical matter, the accused often is confronted with a hodgepodge of acts and statements by others which he may never have authorized or intended or even known about, but which help to persuade the jury of the existence of the conspiracy itself. In other words, a conspiracy often is proved by evidence that is admissible only upon assumption that conspiracy existed. The naive assumption that prejudicial effects can be overcome by instructions to the jury . . . all practicing lawyers know to be unmitigated fiction."

Problem 10. Advocacy Outside the Courtroom

existence of questionable rules of law might be said in a sense to produce unfair trials. Such criticism simply cannot be equated with an attack on the motivation or the integrity or the competence of the judges. And surely permissible criticism may as well be made to a lay audience as to a professional; oftentimes the law is modified through popular criticism; Bentham's strictures on the state of the common law and Dickens' novels come to mind.[11] And needless to say, a lawyer may criticize the law-enforcement agencies of the Government, and the prosecution, even to the extent of suggesting wrongdoing on their part, without by that token impugning the judiciary. Simply to charge, for example, the prosecution with the knowing use of perjured testimony in a case is not to imply in the slightest any complicity by the judge in such actions. To charge that the Government makes overmuch use of the conspiracy form of criminal prosecution, and this to bolster weak cases, is not to suggest any unseemly complicity by the judiciary in the practice.

In large part, if not entirely, Matsuoka's notes of petitioner's speech do not reveal her as doing more than this. She dwelt extensively on the nature of Smith Act trials and on conspiracy prosecutions. The Honolulu trial, to be sure, was the setting for her remarks, but they do not indicate more than that she referred to it as a typical, present example of the evils thought to be attendant on such trials. The specific statements found censurable (without which the bringing of the charge would have been inconceivable) are not in the least inconsistent with this, even though they must be taken to relate to the trial in progress. These specific statements are hardly damning by themselves, and clearly

---

11. Both were at the bar. Bentham was of Lincoln's Inn and Dickens of the Middle Temple.

call for the light examination in context may give them; so examined, they do not furnish any basis for a finding of professional misconduct. She said that there were "horrible" and "shocking" things going on at the trial, but this remark, introductory to the speech, of course was in the context of what she further said about conspiracy prosecutions, Smith Act trials, and the prosecution's conduct. Petitioner's statement that a fair trial was impossible in context obviously related to the state of law and to the conduct of the prosecution and the FBI, not to anything that Judge Wiig personally was doing or failing to do. It occurred immediately after an account of the FBI's alleged pressuring of witnesses. The same seems clearly the case with the remark about the necessity of scrapping the rules of evidence. The statement that if the trial went on to a conviction, new crimes — those of thought or ideas — would be created could hardly be thought to reflect on the trial judge's integrity no matter how divorced from context it be considered. How any of this reflected on Judge Wiig, except insofar as he might be thought to lose stature because he was a judge in a legal system said to be full of imperfections, is not shown. To say that "the law is a ass, a idiot" is not to impugn the character of those who must administer it. To say that prosecutors are corrupt is not to impugn the character of judges who might be unaware of it, or be able to find no method under the law of restraining them. Judge Wiig was not by name mentioned in the speech, and there was virtually none of petitioner's complaints that was phrased in terms of what "the judge" was doing. For aught that appears from petitioner's speech, Judge Wiig might have been totally out of sympathy, as a personal matter, with the Smith Act, the practice of trying criminal offenses on a conspiracy basis, and the rules of evi-

Problem 10. Advocacy Outside the Courtroom

dence in conspiracy trials, but felt bound to apply the law as laid down by higher courts.

Even if some passages can be found which go so far as to imply that Judge Wiig was taking an erroneous view of the law . . . we think there was still nothing in the speech warranting the findings. If Judge Wiig was said to be wrong on his law, it is no matter; appellate courts and law reviews say that of judges daily, and it imputes no disgrace. Dissenting opinions in our reports are apt to make petitioner's speech look like tame stuff indeed. Petitioner did not say Judge Wiig was corrupt or venal or stupid or incompetent. The public attribution of honest error to the judiciary is no cause for professional discipline in this country. . . .

But it is said that while it may be proper for an attorney to say the law is unfair or that judges are in error as a general matter, it is wrong for counsel of record to say so during a pending case. The verbalization is that it is impermissible to litigate by day and castigate by night. See 260 F.2d at page 202. This line seems central to the Bar Association's argument, as it appears to have been to the reasoning of the court below,[16] and the dissent here is much informed by it, but to us it seems totally to ignore the charges made and the findings. The findings were that petitioner impugned the integrity of Judge Wiig and made an improper attack on his administration of justice in the Honolulu trial. A lawyer does not acquire any license to do these things by not being

---

16. For example, the petitioner argued in the Court of Appeals that a law professor at Yale had made criticisms in more pungent terms than hers. Said the court: "We would uphold Professor Rodell's right to say from his Yale vantage point just about what he wants to say. But when he speaks he is not simultaneously harassing the very court in which he is trying an unfinished case." 260 F.2d at page 200.

presently engaged in a case. They are equally serious whether he currently is engaged in litigation before the judge or not. We can conceive no ground whereby the pendency of litigation might be thought to make an attorney's out-of-court remarks more censurable, other than that they might tend to obstruct the administration of justice. Remarks made during the course of a trial might tend to such obstruction where remarks made afterwards would not. But this distinction is foreign to this case, because the charges and findings in no way turn on an allegation of obstruction of justice or of an attempt to obstruct justice, in a pending case. To the charges made and found, it is irrelevant whether the Smith Act case was still pending. Judge Wiig remained equally protected from statements impugning him, and petitioner remained equally free to make critical statements that did not cross that line. We find that hers cannot be said to have done so. Accordingly, the suspension order, based on the charge relating to the speech, cannot stand. . . .

Reversed.

[The following are excerpts from Justice FRANKFURTER'S dissenting opinion, with which Justices CLARK, HARLAN, & WHITTAKER concurred.]

Thus, the real issue before us is whether evidence supports the conclusion that Mrs. Sawyer in her speech, in the full setting and implications of what she said, engaged in a willful attack on the administration of justice in the particular trial in which she was then actively participating, and patently impugned, even if by clear implication rather than by blatant words, the integrity of the presiding judge, and thereby violated the obligations of one in her immediate situation, judged by conventional professional standards, so as to be reasonably deemed to have committed what the Hawaii Supreme Court termed "misconduct."

Problem 10. Advocacy Outside the Courtroom

One of the elements of the misconduct found by the Hawaii Supreme Court and the Court of Appeals was, without doubt, the attack on the integrity of the judge presiding at the trial in which she was engaged. Surely that does not mean she must have referred to Judge Wiig by name. Nor does it mean, as the opinion of Mr. Justice Brennan seems to assume, that any evidence which does not consist of a direct attack on the judge is irrelevant to the ultimate question: could the Hawaii Supreme Court have found petitioner guilty of misconduct as set forth in its opinion?

By carefully isolating various portions of the Matsuoka notes, concentrating on them as a self-contained, insulated document, the opinion of Mr. Justice Brennan labors to put a neutral, if indeed not an innocently attractive, patina on Mrs. Sawyer's remarks. But the speech must be interpreted in its entirety, not distorted as an exercise in disjointed parsing. It must be placed in its context of time and circumstances. Nor can we neglect the fact that what people say is what others reasonably hear and are meant to hear. When this is done what emerges is no abstract attack on the state of the law, no analysis of the dubieties of Smith Act trials with which even judges may agree or, at all events, which critics have an unquestioned right to make, no Dickensian strictures on the injustices of legal proceedings, but a plainly conveyed attack on the conduct of a particular trial, presided over by a particular judge, involving particular defendants in whose defense Mrs. Sawyer herself was professionally engaged. There is ample support for the reasonable conclusion that, in making the fairness of the conduct of this particular trial the target of her appeal to a crowd outside while the trial was proceeding inside the court-room, Mrs. Sawyer was including in her assault the judicial officer who both in fact and in common understanding bears ultimate responsibility for the fairness and evenhandedness of judicial proceedings — the presiding judge. In examining this record sight must never be lost of the limited scope of our reviewing power. We are only concerned with whether the findings have fair support in the record. If the findings are so supported we have the right to strike down the suspension only if it transgresses constitutional limits. We must indeed have in mind, as the opinion of Mr. Justice Brennan reminds us, the entire "context" of this speech. We must endeavor to understand the complete utterance in its setting, as it sounded and was meant to sound to its auditors in Honokaa, Hawaii, on December 14, 1952.

The Honokaa meeting was sponsored by a committee for the defense of Jack Hall, one of the principal defendants in the Smith Act trial then under way in Honolulu, in which Mrs. Sawyer was one of the group of lawyers for the defense. It was publicly announced and advertised that the topic of the meeting would be the Smith Act trial in Honolulu. The general public was invited and members of the press were present, as well they might be expected to be at a meeting where among the principal speakers were a defendant and a defense attorney in a highly controversial trial. It was controversial, not an obscure, run-of-the-mill trial; it had been receiving front-page publicity in the Hawaii press for weeks. The defendant Hall himself was one of the principal speakers and Mrs. Sawyer was on the platform. Her function was, as stated by Mr. Hall, "to explain the legal aspects of the prosecution." Certainly this setting precludes a naive conclusion that Mrs. Sawyer was delivering herself of an abstract dissertation on Smith Act trials, using illustrations from the Honolulu trial merely as "typical present examples" of the evils of such prosecutions. The enveloping environment of her talk, intensified by much other evidence, gives substantial support to the conclusion that Mrs. Sawyer was, in the main, discussing and attacking the Honolulu trial and that her more general condemnations were directed toward, and designed to have particular applicability to, that trial. . . .

When to this evidence is added the setting we have described, and the fact that to those who read the Hawaii papers "the" Smith Act trial, was the notorious, much-exploited trial of the "Hawaii Seven," how can one reasonably escape, on the basis of the record which determines our adjudication, the conclusion that Mrs. Sawyer was directly castigating the administration of the very trial in which she was then professionally engaged?[7] So viewed the specific statements which she made lose the aura of innocence the Court has cast about them and support the finding that Mrs. Sawyer was guilty of professional misconduct in attacking the administration of justice in the Honolulu trial and impugning the integrity of its presiding judge. . . .

This evidence establishes more than that Mrs. Sawyer was attacking the conduct of the Honolulu trial at large. It clearly reflects on the judge who was permitting or participating in these "shocking and horrible" things; at the lowest it allows the inference to be drawn, as the Hawaii Supreme Court did draw the inference, that she did so reflect. To suggest that the only reasonable inference we may draw from her speech is that petitioner was indicting the general

---

7. Petitioner's lawyer had no doubt regarding the meaning and purport of the speech.

"I will say to the Committee right now — I have read these speeches and I would agree with the conclusion implicit in Mr. Dodge's question; namely that this was a talk about what was going on in the Smith Act trial here in Honolulu. Now, let's not fool ourselves about that. We're lawyers here."

state of the law or merely reflecting on the prosecution, is to deny the obvious fact that when a lawyer harangues a lay audience, wholly unskilled in drawing subtle distinctions for exculpatory purposes, about the horrible and shocking things going on in a judicial proceeding, he inevitably reflects upon the total conduct of that trial and upon the integrity of all, not excluding the judge, responsible for the conduct of the trial. Certainly if we, as lawyers, were addressed by a doctor on the theme of the horrible and shocking things that go on at X hospital, and the speaker dwelt on specific examples of conduct at that particular hospital, we would not assume that merely the general sad state of medicine was being impugned rather than the doctors and the administrators at that hospital. . . .

More than that, the attack on the judge presiding at the trial does not rest merely on implication. It was direct and clear. Again the remarks about unfairness and the rules that were "made up" must be read not in isolation but in context. After outlining several examples of what she considered to be the outrageous evidence being admitted in this case, petitioner made her remark that there was "no such thing as a fair trial in a Smith Act case. All rules of evidence have to be scrapped or the government can't make a case." Matsuoka's notes reveal that she then proceeded to illustrate this remark by relating that in an earlier case of hers. . . . This portion of the speech dispels any illusions that the condemnatory remarks made by petitioner could not reasonably be thought to relate to the conduct of this trial. In the context of the entire speech it is inescapably a direct reflection on the fairness and integrity of this particular judge in this particular case. This was no abstract assault on the rigors of hearsay. Petitioner attacked the fairness of the trial and the scrapping of the rules of evidence. She then pointed to a ruling

Problem 10. Advocacy Outside the Courtroom

of Judge Wiig which she said was highly prejudicial and hardly left doubt that it was made in this particular trial. She then repeated her charge that the trial was unfair and the rules made up. To suggest that the only reasonable inference to be drawn from these remarks is that the conduct of the prosecution or the law of evidence in the abstract was impugned, is really asking too much from judges, even if we accept Mr. Justice Holmes' view that judges "are apt to be naif, simple-minded men." Holmes, Collected Legal Papers, p. 295....

Having arrived at this conclusion, our task is at an end, and the order suspending Mrs. Sawyer from the practice of law for one year should be affirmed. But throughout the opinion of Mr. Justice Brennan runs the strong intimation that if the findings are supportable, a suspension based on them would be unconstitutional. This must be the import of the opinion's discussion of a lawyer's right to criticize law. For if we find that the evidence supports the findings, no matter what we think of the wisdom of suspending an attorney on the basis of such findings, we can only reverse if the Constitution so commands....

The problem raised by this case — is the particular conduct in which this petitioner engaged constitutionally protected from the disciplinary proceedings of courts of law? — cannot be disposed of by general observations about freedom of speech. Of course, the free play of the human mind is an indispensable prerequisite of a free society. And freedom of thought is meaningless without freedom of expression. But the two great Justices to whom we mostly owe the shaping of the constitutional protection of freedom of speech, Mr. Justice Holmes and Mr. Justice Brandeis, did not erect freedom of speech into a dogma of absolute validity nor enforce it to doctrinaire limits. Time, place and circumstances determine the constitutional protection of utterance. The First Amendment and the Fourteenth Amendment, insofar as it protects freedom of speech, are no exception to the law of life enunciated by Ecclesiastes: "For everything there is a season, and a time for every purpose under heaven." And one of the instances specifically enumerated by the Preacher controls our situation: "[A] time to keep silence, and a time to speak." Eccles. 3:1, 7. Of course, a lawyer is a person and he too has a constitutional freedom of utterance and may exercise it to castigate courts and their administration of justice. But a lawyer actively participating in a trial, particularly an emotionally charged criminal prosecution, is not merely a person and not even merely a lawyer. If the prosecutor in this case had felt hampered by some of the rulings of the trial judge, and had assailed the judge for such rulings at a mass meeting, and a conviction had followed, and that prosecutor had been disciplined for such conduct according to the orderly procedure for such disciplinary action, is it thinkable that this Court would have found that such conduct by the prosecutor was a constitutionally protected exercise of his freedom of speech, or, indeed, would have allowed the conviction to stand? . . .

What we are concerned with is the specific conduct, as revealed by this record, of a particular lawyer, and not whether like findings applied to an abstract situation relating to an abstract lawyer would support a suspension. All the circumstances we have set forth must determine judgment. Here was a public meeting addressed by counsel for the defense, haranguing a crowd on the unfairness to the defendant of the proceedings in court, with the high probability indeed almost certainty under modern conditions that the goings-on of the meeting would come to the attention of the presiding judge and the jury. It took place in a case in

Problem 10. Advocacy Outside the Courtroom

which public interest and public tempers had been aroused. When the story of the meeting came to the attention of the judge, he felt obliged publicly to defend his conduct. It is hard to believe that this Court should hold that a member of the legal profession is constitutionally entitled to remove his case from the court in which he is an officer to the public and press, and express to them his grievances against the conduct of the trial and the judge. "Legal trials," said this Court, "are not like elections, to be won through the use of the meeting-hall, the radio, and the newspaper." *Bridges v. California,* 314 U.S. 252, 271, 62 S. Ct. 190, 197.

Even in the absence of the substantial likelihood that what was said at a public gathering would reach the judge or jury, conduct of the kind found here cannot be deemed to be protected by the Constitution. An attorney actively engaged in the conduct of a trial is not merely another citizen. He is an intimate and trusted and essential part of the machinery of justice, an "officer of the court" in the most compelling sense. He does not lack for a forum in which to make his charges of unfairness or failure to adhere to principles of law; he has ample chance to make such claims to the courts in which he litigates. As long as any tribunal bred in the fundamentals of our legal tradition, ultimately this Court, still exercises judicial power those claims will be heard and heeded.

Certainly courts are not, and cannot be, immune from criticism, and lawyers, of course, may indulge in criticism. Indeed, they are under a special responsibility to exercise fearlessness in doing so. But when a lawyer goes before a public gathering and fiercely charges that the trial in which he is a participant is unfair, that the judge lacks integrity, the circumstances under which he speaks not only sharpen what he says but he imparts to his attack inflaming and warping significance. He says that the very court-room into which he walks to plead his case is a travesty, that the procedures and reviews established to protect his client from such conduct are a sham. "We are a society governed by law, whose integrity it is the lawyer's special role to guard and champion." In re Howell, 10 N.J. 139, 142, 89 A.2d 652, 653 (concurring opinion). No matter how narrowly conceived this role may be, it has been betrayed by a lawyer who has engaged in the kind of conduct here found by the Hawaii court. Certainly this Court, the supreme tribunal charged with maintaining the rule of law, should be the last place in which these attacks on the fairness and integrity of a judge and the conduct of a trial should find constitutional sanction.

I would affirm the judgment.

[Justice CLARK also dissented.]

A.B.A. Formal Opinion 336
(June 3, 1974)

THE COMMITTEE has been asked from time to time whether the Code of Professional Responsibility is applicable to the conduct of a lawyer at a time when the lawyer is not engaged in the performance of his professional duties. The question has arisen since the "Watergate" episodes with some frequency in regard to D.R.1-102(A) (3) and (4), which read as follows: "(A) A lawyer shall not: . . . (3) Engage in illegal conduct involving moral turpitude. (4) Engage in conduct involving dishonesty, fraud, deceit, or misrepresentation."

The answer is that a lawyer must comply at all times with all applicable disciplinary rules of the Code of Pro-

Problem 10. Advocacy Outside the Courtroom

fessional Responsibility whether or not he is acting in his professional capacity.

Many, if not most, disciplinary rules by their nature relate only to conduct of a lawyer acting in his professional capacity. For example, D.R.7-106, which regulates the trial conduct of a lawyer, obviously is concerned with the conduct of a lawyer in his professional capacity of a trial lawyer. However, other disciplinary rules are equally clearly designed to be applicable to a lawyer without regard to whether he is acting individually or as a lawyer. Examples include D.R.8-102(A) and (B), proscribing false statements about judges and judicial candidates.

The provisions of D.R.1-102(A)(3) and (4) are not limited to a lawyer's conduct while he is acting in his professional capacity as a lawyer. They are applicable to all conduct of the nature specified in those provisions without regard to the capacity in which the lawyer may be acting.[1]

In regulating a lawyer's nonprofessional as well as professional conduct, the Code of Professional Responsibility charted no new course. It is recognized generally that lawyers are subject to discipline for improper conduct in connection with business activities,[2] individual or personal activities,[3] and activities as a judicial, governmental, or public official.[4] Furthermore, many states, by statute and indepen-

---

1. Accord, In re Kirtz, 494 S.W.2d 324 (Mo. 1973).

2. See In re Wilson, 391 S.W.2d 914 (Mo. 1965); In re Gould, 164 N.Y.S.2d 48 (1957); In re Kirtz, 494 S.W.2d 324 (Mo. 1973); Murphy v. Erie County Bar Association, 328 N.Y.S.2d 949 (1972).

3. See Fellner v. Bar Association of Baltimore, 131 A.2d 729 (Md. 1957); Committee on Legal Ethics v. Scherr, 143 S.E.2d 141 (W. Va. 1965); Kentucky State Bar Association v. Martin, 490 S.W.2d 759 (Ky. 1973), and Anno., 36 A.L.R.3d 735 (1968).

4. See In re Wilson, 216 N.E.2d 555 (Ind. 1966); In re Chernoff, 26 A. 2d 335 (Pa. 1942); Anno., 53 A.L.R.2d 305 (1957).

dent of the code, discipline lawyers for certain illegal conduct.[5] And the grossly improper conduct proscribed by D.R.1-102(A)(3) and (4) is the kind of conduct that is sufficient to evidence lack of the requisite good moral character required of all members of the bar.

As stated in E.C.1-2, the "public should be protected from those who are not qualified to be lawyers by reason of a deficiency in . . . moral standards." It would be utterly incongruous with the entire tenor of the code to find that its provisions regarding lawyers who engage in fraud, deceit, misrepresentation, or illegal conduct involving moral turpitude do not apply to them when they are acting as individuals or as public servants.

BACKGROUND READING

Compare the standard set forth in *Sawyer* and in Opinion 336 with the First Amendment test established by the Supreme Court for libel against public officials. See *New York Times Co. v. Sullivan,* 376 U.S. 54 (1964); and *Garrison v. Louisiana,* 379 U.S. 64 (1964). See also *Polk v. State Bar of Texas,* 374 F.Supp. 784 (N.D. Tex. 1974); *In re Buckley,* 10 Cal. 3d 237, 514 P.2d 1201, 110 Cal. Rptr. 121 (1973); *Justices of Appellate Div. v. Erdman,* 39 App. Div. 2d 223, 333 N.Y.S.2d 863 (1972); and *Chicago Council of Lawyers v. Bauer,* 522 F.2d 242 (7th Cir. 1975), rev'g 371 F.Supp. 689 (N.D. Ill. 1974), for divergent viewpoints on the right of lawyers to criticize judges.

---

5. See In re Adams, 331 N.Y.S.2d. 244 (1972); Note, Disbarment: Non-Professional Conduct Demonstrating Unfitness to Practice, 43 Cornell L.Q. 489 (1958).

PART III
Conflicts of Interest

PROBLEM 11

Representing Both Sides: When Is It Permissible?

Conflicting interests v. potentially conflicting interests: how informed is a layman's consent to representation of multiple clients? Can one be sure that litigation will not result?

Edwin Goodman and Victor Kresky formed the Good-Kres Corporation in 1925 and it grew to be a large manufacturer of women's dresses, with a net worth of one million dollars as of 1969 when Mr. Goodman died, leaving all of his stock to his widow, Clara Goodman, who never played a role in the business. Mr. Kresky has successfully carried on the business with the help of his son and daughter, both of whom are now in the business. The Goodmans had no children.

Ever since 1940 the corporation has been represented by Jeremy Goldsmith, who has also acted as personal attorney for Goodman and Kresky.

In February, 1976 Mr. Kresky and Mrs. Goodman appear in Mr. Goldsmith's office.

"We've decided that the business should buy out

Clara's interest," says Mr. Kresky, "and we'd like you to draw up the papers."

"Don't you think it would be better if you had your own lawyer?" says Mr. Goldsmith to Mrs. Goodman. "After all, I represent the company and this is an agreement between the company and you."

"Why do I need a lawyer?" asks Mrs. Goodman. "Ed had complete confidence in you, and so do I. A lawyer will only make trouble and charge high fees."

"Have you agreed on the terms?" asks Mr. Goldsmith.

"Yes," replies Mr. Kresky. "We'll buy half of Clara's stock now, paying twenty-five percent cash and the balance over ten years."

"What's the price?" asks Mr. Goldsmith.

"Book value as of last December 31," replies Mr. Kresky. "We'll pay eight percent interest on the unpaid balance."

"What about the rest of Clara's stock?"

"Clara and the company have agreed," replies Mr. Kresky, "that the company will have an option during the next ten years to acquire the remainder of her stock at whatever the book value is at the time we exercise the option. We'll have ten years to pay, same eight percent interest on any unpaid balance."

1. Is Mr. Goldsmith precluded from representing both the corporation and Mrs. Goodman?

2. If he feels he can represent both, what should he do to make certain that both parties knowingly consent?

3. Suppose it were a small business and the widow's stock was worth only $25,000? Would your answer to question one be different?

4. Would it be proper for Mr. Goldsmith to recommend another lawyer if requested?

Problem 11. Representing Both Sides: When Is It Permissible?

ASSIGNMENT

Canon 5; EC5-14, EC5-15, EC5-16, EC5-17, EC5-18, EC5-19; DR5-105(A), (B) and (C).
Canon 9; EC9-6.

BACKGROUND READING

The question of representing multiple parties arises often in the following contexts: (1) matrimonial matters, see Drinker, Problems of Professional Ethics in Matrimonial Litigation, 66 Harv. L. Rev. 443 (1953); *Halvorsen v. Halvorsen,* 3 Wash. App. 827, 479 P.2d 161 (1970); Drinker, Legal Ethics 122-128 (Columbia University Press, 1953); A.B.A. Informal Opinion 1125 (1969); Countryman, Finman, and Schneyer, The Lawyer in Modern Society 107-114 (Little, Brown and Company, 2d ed., 1976); (2) cases where the lawyer represents the insured and the insurance carrier, see A.B.A. Informal Opinion 1199 (1971); Countryman, Finman, and Schneyer, *supra,* 114-122; (3) representing codefendants in a criminal case, see *Glasser v. United States,* 315 U.S. 60 (1942); Note, Conflict of Interests in Criminal Proceedings, 23 Ark. L. Rev. 250 (1969). See generally American Bar Association, Opinions on Professional Ethics 22-39 (American Bar Foundation, 1967).

PROBLEM 12

Opposing a Former Client

Is it a matter of appearances, or the preservation of confidences?
Is it worth the risk?

Jerome King has been the family attorney for Mr. and Mrs. Harry Walker for ten years. During that time he has advised Mr. Walker on his business matters, has represented the estate of Mrs. Walker's father when he passed away, has drawn up wills for the Walkers and has represented them when they purchased their cooperative apartment in New York and their country home in Connecticut. He has also been consulted in the preparation of their tax returns. In recent years the Walkers have been having marital problems and Mr. King has been consulted by the Walkers (together and separately) in an effort to effect a reconciliation.

On January 15, 1975 Mr. Walker writes Mr. King a letter stating: "Things are going from bad to worse in my marriage. I have decided to obtain a new lawyer since it's probably not wise for you to continue representing both of us. I've heard about conflicts of interest, and my wife and I seem to conflict all the time."

Mr. King continues to advise Mrs. Walker on her per-

Problem 12. Opposing a Former Client

sonal business matters. Six months later Mrs. Walker asks Mr. King to institute a divorce action which will allege adultery as the sole grounds for divorce. At no time has Mr. Walker ever revealed to Mr. King any information concerning his relations with other women.

1. Was it proper for Mr. King to represent Mrs. Walker after January 15, 1975?

2. Would it be proper for Mr. King to represent Mrs. Walker in the divorce action?

ASSIGNMENT

Canon 9; EC9-1, EC9-2.
Canon 4; EC4-1, EC-4-2, EC4-4, EC4-5, EC4-6.
Canon 5; EC5-14, EC5-15.
Also read the following case: *T.C. Theatre Corp. v. Warner Bros. Pictures, Inc.*

T. C. Theatre Corp. v. Warner Bros. Pictures, Inc.
113 F.Supp. 265 (S.D.N.Y. 1953)

WEINFELD, D. J. This is a motion by the defendant Universal Pictures Company, Inc. and Universal Film Exchanges, Inc. (both of which are hereafter referred to as Universal) for an order (1) to disqualify Thomas Turner Cooke from acting as counsel for the plaintiff and from associating himself in any capacity with any attorney for the plantiff in the pending action as long as Universal is a party defendant; (2) to disqualify Alexander Kahan from acting as counsel for plantiff; and (3) to disqualify Gorfinkle & Adler, the attorneys of record for the plantiff, from continuing to represent the plantiff in this action.

Although Cooke is not the attorney of record for the plantiff, it is not disputed that thus far he has been actively associated with, and has played an important role in, the litigation.

The motions stem from the prior representation by Cooke of Universal in another matter.

In July 1946, Cooke was retained to represent Universal's interests in the well-known Paramount case after the Statutory Court had filed its opinion. The Court had directed the entry of a final decree, and its formulation and that of the proposed findings of fact and conclusions of law was a matter of considerable importance to all parties in the litigation, including, of course, the defendant Universal, with whom we are presently concerned. Cooke as counsel for Universal prepared its proposed findings and decree; appeared at hearings before the Statutory Court in support thereof and in opposition to those proposed by the government and some of the so-called "Big Five" defendants. Following the settlement of the findings of fact, conclusions of law and the entry of the decree, his further activities included general representation of Universal in connection with its appeal to the Supreme Court; obtaining a stay of some of the provisions of the decree; preparation of brief and reply brief and argument before the Supreme Court of Universal's appeal.

In May 1948, the Supreme Court rendered its opinion affirming in part and reversing in part the decree of the Statutory Court. Cooke then worked on a proposed petition for rehearing and on the order of mandate.

Cooke's representation of Universal ended, according to the latter, on July 7, 1948; according to him, on or about February 14, 1951. Subsequently, on October 17, 1951,

Problem 12. Opposing a Former Client 97

Cooke brought suit against Universal for a claimed balance due him on account of services rendered in the Paramount litigation. In that suit, which is still pending, he is represented by Mr. Kahan. The controversy as to dates is important here only to the extent that if we accept the date fixed by Cooke it narrows the gap between his former representation of Universal and his present representation of plaintiff against his former client Universal to less than a year. This gap is further narrowed when we consider that some of the complaints, admittedly prepared by Cooke, were in the process of preparation over an extended period of time.

The cases out of which this motion grew were commenced between January 23, 1952 and May 15, 1952. The motion presently relates to but one pending case. The complaint alleges that the defendants, including Universal, were engaged in a nation-wide conspiracy with each other and others unreasonably to restrain trade and that they combined with affiliated circuits, large unaffiliated circuits, and locally favored exhibitors to monopolize the motion picture exhibition industry in violation of §§1 and 2 of the Sherman Act, 15 U.S.C.A. §§1 and 2. It is alleged that (1) they conspired with each other and with affiliated exhibitors to maintain a system of minimum motion picture prices; (2) they acted in concert in establishing a uniform and fixed system of runs and clearances against independent competitors of the theatre-operating defendants; (3) they entered into master agreements, or blanket deals and formula deals with circuits of theatres, and other non-competitive agreements; and (4) they discriminated, in a number of ways, against independent exhibitors.

At this point it is noted that the conspiracy so charged is substantially the same nation-wide conspiracy which was found to exist on the part of the defendants in the Paramount case. All the eight distributor-defendants therein are named as distributor-defendants in this action. . . .

Universal seeks to disqualify Cooke from now acting as attorney against it upon two separate grounds: (1) that the causes of action asserted by the plantiff against Universal are based substantially on the identical charges made against it and the other distributor-defendants in the Paramount case, so that as present counsel for the plaintiff he will necessarily be called upon to prove against Universal, his former client, the very charges against which he had earlier defended it. Cooke's disqualification is urged irrespective of any showing that actual confidential information relating to the case had been received by him during the former representation; (2) that, in fact, matters of confidence were disclosed to Cooke while he acted as Universal's counsel in the Paramount litigation which are related to the issues at bar; and that his current representation of the plaintiff involves, or may involve, the disclosure or use of such confidences.

Cooke disputes that the Paramount litigation and the present triple damage suit involve the same matters. As to Universal's second ground for his disqualification, he contends that he received no confidential communications from Universal, that there was no necessity therefor; that his services as appeal counsel in the Paramount case were based upon the "cold record" and that prior to his entry into the case the government had fully exposed and made publicly available all the defendants' files and records, including, of course, Universal's. Finally, no attempt is made, he says, to relate any confidential communications allegedly received by him to any use which might be made of them in T.C.'s triple damage suit against Universal and others.

A lawyer's duty of absolute loyalty to his client's interests does not end with his retainer. He is enjoined for all

Problem 12. Opposing a Former Client

time, except as he may be released by law, from disclosing matters revealed to him by reason of the confidential relationship. Related to this principle is the rule that where any substantial relationship can be shown between the subject matter of a former representation and that of a subsequent adverse representation, the latter will be prohibited.

This salutory principle is summed up in Canon 6 of the Canons of Professional Ethics adopted by the American Bar Association,[4] which, in part, provides:

> The obligation to represent the client with undivided fidelity and not to divulge his secrets or confidences forbids also the subsequent acceptance of retainers or employment from others in matters adversely affecting any interest of the client with respect to which confidence has been reposed.

It is upon this Canon that movant places its principal reliance. I agree that if Cooke's present retainer by T.C. falls within this Canon, he is disqualified to represent it.

I am not in accord with Mr. Cooke that Universal is required to show that during the Paramount litigation it disclosed matters to him related to the instant case. Rather, I hold that the former client need show no more than that the matters embraced within the pending suit wherein his former attorney appears on behalf of his adversary are substantially related to the matters or cause of action wherein the attorney previously represented him, the former client. The Court will assume that during the course of the former representation confidences were disclosed to the attorney

---

4. The Canons of Ethics of the American Bar Association and the New York State Bar Association have been adopted by a rule of this court. General Rule 5(c).

bearing on the subject matter of the representation. It will not inquire into their nature and extent. Only in this manner can the lawyer's duty of absolute fidelity be enforced and the spirit of the rule relating to privileged communications be maintained.

To compel the client to show, in addition to establishing that the subject of the present adverse representation is related to the former, the actual confidential matters previously entrusted to the attorney and their possible value to the present client would tear aside the protective cloak drawn about the lawyer-client relationship. For the Court to probe further and sift the confidences in fact revealed would require the disclosure of the very matters intended to be protected by the rule. It would defeat an important purpose of the rule of secrecy — to encourage clients fully and freely to make known to their attorneys all facts pertinent to their cause. Considerations of public policy, no less than the client's private interest, require rigid enforcement of the rule against disclosure. No client should ever be concerned with the possible use against him in future litigation of what he may have revealed to his attorney. Matters disclosed by clients under the protective seal of the attorney-client relationship and intended in their defense should not be used as weapons of offense. The rule prevents a lawyer from placing himself in an anomalous position. Were he permitted to represent a client whose cause is related and adverse to that of his former client he would be called upon to decide what is confidential and what is not, and, perhaps, unintentionally to make use of confidential information received from the former client while espousing his cause. Lawyers should not put themselves in the position "where, even unconsciously, they might take, in the interests of a new client, an advan-

Problem 12. Opposing a Former Client

tage derived or traceable to, confidences reposed under the cloak of a prior, privileged relationship." In cases of this sort the Court must ask whether it can reasonably be said that in the course of the former representation the attorney might have acquired information related to the subject of his subsequent representation. If so, then the relationship between the two matters is sufficiently close to bring the later representation within the prohibition of Canon 6. In the instant case I think this can be said.

It is true that in the Paramount suit the government was the plantiff, whereas here an independent exhibitor is the plaintiff; that the exhibitor-defendants in the Paramount case did not include some of the exhibitor-defendants named here; that the Paramount case was concerned with a nation-wide conspiracy, whereas plantiff's charges here relate mainly to its local situation. In these respects it may be acknowledged that the two actions are not identical. But a comparison of the plantiff's complaint with the findings of fact, conclusions of law and decree in the Paramount case shows beyond peradventure that the plaintiff charges and relies upon the same conspiracy which the government established against the defendants in the Paramount case. The same distributor-defendants are named in both suits. The conspiracy charged in the two cases traverse substantially the same periods. Cooke in opposing a motion to dismiss the original complaint (drafted by him) categorically stated that the essential allegations charging a conspiracy by Universal and others against independent exhibitors, such as the present plaintiff, were pleaded in haec verba from the opinion and decree in the Paramount case. Thus, charges now made by Cooke on behalf of his present client against Universal parallel those against which he previously had defended

Universal. The only difference is that plaintiff here asserts that it was the victim of the conspiracy, whereas in the government suit specific individuals were not identified.

A government suit, while primarily in the public interest, if successful, also accrues to the immediate benefit of those injured by the wrongful conduct. . . . Thus, the decree obtained in the Paramount suit would prima facie establish that Universal and the other defendants, who are defendants here, were engaged in a nation-wide conspiracy which in enumerated ways affected the local independent exhibitor, within which group plaintiff belongs. The proof so offered, plus a showing that the conspiracy had an impact upon the plantiff and that it suffered damage as a result, would be sufficient to establish a prima facie case. . . .

The findings of fact and conclusions of law which are incorporated by reference in the decree, insofar as they are pertinent to the plaintiff's situation, may also be made use of to further the attack against Cooke's former client. Cooke replies, however, that these are matters of public record, available to all. Further, that his services were based upon the "cold record" on appeal and that the government's case prior to his entry into it had been drawn from Universal's files, all of which was, and is, exposed to public view. Even if we were to accept Cooke's contention that his services were solely those of an appellate counsel, it does not follow that he did not receive confidences based upon the attorney-client relationship. But, more important, this argument overlooks an important aspect of Cooke's representation of Universal following the original ruling by the Statutory Court. His services included the preparation, drafting, presentation and argument in support of the findings of fact, conclusions of law and decree proposed by Universal, as well as opposition to those offered by the government and some of the

Problem 12. Opposing a Former Client

other defendants. This was no mere mechanical job of paste pot and shears. It involved the acquisition of a thorough knowledge of Universal's entire business. To this end, whatever information, whatever documents, he sought from Universal were made available to him. During the preparation of the findings and decree he was in full command of Universal's legal forces; house and general counsel looked to him for leadership and he freely consulted with them as to various aspects of Universal's activities. It was Cooke's duty to his client to know Universal's individual trade practices, its relationship to other producers and distributors, to exhibitors, its methods of operation and procedures and all other matters relevant to the decree. I am satisfied that he fully discharged this duty.

In sum, enough appears to show that Mr. Cooke's present representation deals with matters as to which his former client reposed confidence in him. Hence, I hold that Mr. Cooke is disqualified from acting as counsel for the plantiff in this case in any capacity so long as Universal is a party defendant, and the motion is granted to this extent. This disposition makes it unnecessary to consider the second ground for the motion to disqualify, based on Canon 37. . . .

Finally, there is the application to disqualify Messrs. Kahan and Gorfinkle & Adler. Kahan, as already noted, is the attorney for Cooke in the suit to recover the balance of fees and has also been engaged as trial counsel for the plantiff in this case. Here I will assume that confidential information material to T.C.'s case was actually imparted to Cooke during the Paramount litigation. Universal contends that it must be presumed that Cooke has passed it on to those with whom he is associated in this suit. Universal admits that there is no direct evidence that this has been done, but asserts that because Kahan is Cooke's lawyer in the fee suit, it necessarily follows that Cooke in enumerating his services to him made full disclosure of all that Universal told him.

I have fully reviewed the deposition taken by Universal of Cooke in connection with that suit and nothing therein warrants such an inference and I am unwilling to draw it upon this record.

Cooke's right to recovery of additional fees, if any, does not depend upon the disclosure of confidential communications, but, rather, upon the nature, extent and importance of the services performed by him. He could enumerate the various conferences with his client without detailing the matters which might have been discussed. It seems to me that Kahan's representation of Cooke could be just as effective without such a disclosure. The Court is not required to indulge in any presumption that Cooke has divulged confidences reposed in him by his former clients simply because he is now engaged in a law suit with them. The presumption would be to the contrary.

There is even less basis for the claim against Messrs. Gorfinkle & Adler. Movant again presses upon the Court a "presumption" that they must have retained Cooke in order to make use of confidential information he received in the course of his former employment. It is not clear why it should presume the attorneys have acted unethically. On the contrary, I would presume that Messrs. Gorfinkle & Adler had no such motivation. Cooke was probably retained for the same reason that Universal retained him in the Paramount case — because of his special experience in antitrust matters.

The motion with respect to Messrs. Kahan and Gorfinkle & Adler is denied.

Problem 12. Opposing a Former Client

BACKGROUND READING

A.B.A. Informal Opinion 885 (1965) summarizes some of the authorities and other opinions relating to the issue of a lawyer taking a case against a former client. The opinion concludes: "The thrust of the foregoing authorities is, a lawyer should not accept litigation against a former client, under any circumstances if such would result in a conflict of interests or disclosure of confidences of the former client. In such a situation a court is justified in enjoining a lawyer from proceeding with the litigation against the former client. Moreover, the lawyer should avoid representation of a party in a suit against a former client, where there may be the appearance of a conflict of interest or a possible violation of a confidence, even though this may not be true in fact."

See Drinker, Problems of Professional Ethics in Matrimonial Litigation, 66 Harv. L. Rev. 443 (1953) and the discussion by the same author in Drinker, Legal Ethics 103-112 (1953).

PROBLEM 13

Disqualifying a Lawyer Because of What His Law Firm (Past or Present) Knew, Knows, or Is Assumed to Know

Is a partner's knowledge imputed to everyone else in the firm?
What about associates?
Does the size of the firm make a difference?
Does a member of the firm take this imputed knowledge into a new firm?
When is the chain broken?

Sylvia Lang is an associate in the San Francisco law firm of Batten and Lord. One of the major clients of the firm, Federated Electronics, is a manufacturer of pocket calculators and mini-computers. Ms. Lang's work for Federated Electronics has been confined entirely to tax matters. Federated has been involved for several years in a bitter patent infringement suit brought against it by International Electronic Machines, Inc. Named as codefendants are some customers of Federated. Under an indemnification agreement, Federated must defend all patent infringement suits, so Batten and Lord represents all defendants. International has

Problem 13. Disqualifying a Lawyer

been represented by another San Francisco firm, Herrod and Smyth.

One day Ms. Lang enters the office of George Blakeslee, the senior tax partner and says, "I'd like to talk to you about my future."

"Well, as you know," he interrupts, "we're pretty heavy on tax people."

"I know," she replies. "That's why I have accepted an offer to be a partner with Herrod and Smyth."

"Great!" says Mr. Blakeslee, quite relieved, since Ms. Lang was clearly one of the best tax lawyers around, but was not likely to become a partner because the firm did have a great many tax partners. (Sex discrimination had something to do with it, too, although Blakeslee was reluctant to admit it, even to himself.)

"I'm bothered about one thing," says Ms. Lang. "Herrod and Smyth represents International in that patent suit against Federated that's been keeping our patent and litigation departments alive during the recession."

"Have you done anything on the case?"

"Nothing at all. But I've given tax advice on a variety of matters, including the tax consequences of the acquisition and sale of patents. Some of those patents are involved in the International suit."

"But you've had nothing to do with infringement questions?"

"Nothing. And it is understood at Herrod and Smyth that I'll do no work at all for International until the patent suit is over, whenever that will be."

"Is this okay with our partners handling the patent case?"

"Yes, they have no objection."

"Good luck! Their gain is our loss."

1. Assuming Ms. Lang becomes a partner in Herrod and Smyth, should that firm be disqualified in the patent suit against International?

2. Would your answer be different if Ms. Lang had been a partner in Batten and Lord and left for a more lucrative partnership in Herrod and Smyth?

3. Is there anything that either, or both, law firms could have done to minimize the risk of litigation resulting from Ms. Lang's shift of firms?

ASSIGNMENT

Canon 4; EC4-4, EC4-5, EC4-6.
Canon 9; EC9-1, EC9-2.
Read *United States v. Standard Oil Co.*, 136 F.Supp. 345 (S.D.N.Y. 1955), reproduced after Problem 18 *infra*.
Read the following case: *Laskey Bros. v. Warner Bros. Pictures, Inc.*

Laskey Bros. v. Warner Bros. Pictures, Inc.
224 F.2d 824 (2d Cir. 1955)

CLARK, Ch. J. These appeals involve the qualification of the firm of Malkan & Ellner to serve as attorneys for plaintiffs in private anti-trust actions involving the motion picture industry. Disqualification was sought by the defendants on the basis of Malkan's prior partnership with one Isacson. In proceedings independent of those here under review, Isacson has been found to have obtained confidential information about the defendants in the course of his former employ-

Problem 13. Disqualifying a Lawyer

ment by the firm of Sargoy & Stein. The history of this litigation is set forth in detail in the opinion of the district court in this proceeding, so that we need not repeat it here. D.C.S.D.N.Y., 130 F.Supp. 514. Judge Dawson concluded that Malkan & Ellner should be disqualified in the Laskey case, which had originally come to the firm of Malkan & Isacson. The plaintiffs and the attorneys appeal from this determination. In the Austin case — the second of these two actions heard and decided together below — Judge Dawson decided that the new firm was not disqualified, since this client had come to it by channels completely apart from Malkan's former association with Isacson. Here the defendants appeal. . . .

[In the Laskey case the] plaintiff first came to the firm of Malkan & Isacson to initiate an anti-trust action in the Western District of Pennsylvania. Subsequently a new suit was begun for this plaintiff by Malkan & Ellner in the Southern District of New York, but it is not contended that these suits differ in any material respect. It seems clear that . . . the firm of Malkan & Isacson was barred from prosecuting this case . . . since all authorities agree that all members of a partnership are barred from participating in a case from which one partner is disqualified. *Consolidated Theatres v. Warner Bros. Circuit Management Corp.*, 2 Cir., 216 F.2d 920; Note, Disqualification of Attorneys for Representing Interests Adverse to Former Clients, 64 Yale L.J. 917, 920; Drinker, Legal Ethics 106 (1953). And once a partner is thus vicariously disqualified for a particular case, the subsequent dissolution of the partnership cannot cure his ineligibility to act as counsel in that case. The decision in Laskey is therefore affirmed.

This brings us to the more difficult question of legal ethics posed by the Austin case. This case came to the new firm of Malkan & Ellner through channels having nothing whatsoever to do with Malkan's prior association with Isacson. Judge Dawson decided that disqualification of the firm of Malkan & Isacson should not carry over to Malkan & Ellner in the absence of any showing that Malkan had received confidential information from Isacson.

Defendants contend that either receipt of confidential information should be conclusively presumed from the fact of partnership or alternatively Malkan should at least have the burden of rebutting such an inference. Within the framework of the original partnership the fact of access to confidential information through the person of the partner with such specialized knowledge is sufficient to bar the other partners, whether or not they actually profit from such access. Such a result, although an extension of the literal wording of Canons 6 and 37 of the Canons of Professional Ethics of the American Bar Association, is necessary to facilitate maximum disclosure of relevant facts on the part of clients. Once the partnership is dissolved, however, the inference from access to receipt of information, in a new case having no relationship to the old partnership, becomes logically less compelling and should therefore become rebuttable legally, lest the chain of disqualification become endless.

Thus an irrebuttable inference that confidential information had been received would result in Malkan's disqualification for partnership with Isacson, and Ellner's disqualification for partnership with Malkan. Since the degree of association to effect disqualification need not necessarily be that of a partner, young lawyers might seriously jeopardize their careers by temporary affiliation with large law firms. But even more important is the effect on litigants who may seriously feel they have claims worthy of judicial test-

Problem 13. Disqualifying a Lawyer

ing, but are prejudiced in securing proper representation. For the net effect of an overharsh rule of disqualification must be to hinder adequate protection of clients' interests in view of the difficulty in discovering technically trained attorneys in specialized areas who were not disqualified, due to their peripheral or temporally remote connections with attorneys for the other side. See Note, 64 Yale L.J. 917, 928. The necessity of judicial recognition of the contingent fee is an appropriate analogy.

In this case Malkan has successfully met the burden of rebutting the inference that he received confidential information from Isacson. Malkan testified in a hearing before Judge Dawson that he had received no such information, and Judge Dawson obviously believed him. The only indications to the contrary to which the defendants advert are that Malkan and Isacson signed complaints in several anti-trust actions involving the distribution of motion pictures, and that Malkan and Isacson together solicited clients for their firm. This is not enough to overcome the favorable effect of Malkan's testimony and demeanor as appraised by the trial judge. Malkan had long been engaged in private anti-trust actions in other fields before he met Isacson, and can be presumed to have had independent know-how on the drawing of an appropriate complaint in such an action. The alleged solicitation, on which there was no clear ruling in the Fisher proceedings, is irrelevant to the question of violation of confidences. It will not do to make the presumption of confidential information rebuttable and then to make the standard of proof for rebuttal unattainably high. This is particularly true where, as here, the attorney must prove a negative, which is always a difficult burden to meet.

We therefore conclude that the judgment in the Austin case must be affirmed.

RYAN, D. J. (dissenting). . . .

I disagree with my distinguished colleagues as to the Austin suit; as to it I would sustain the appeal, and enter an order of disqualification equally as broad in scope as in Laskey. . . .

To properly appraise the ethical obligations of Malkan and Ellner to the defendants their prior professional activities and associations must be ascertained and this is particularly so with respect to Malkan's association with David H. Isacson.

In November, 1946, Isacson entered the employ of the law firm of Sargoy & Stein. It was at the time a large office. He remained in their employ until March, 1951.

For several years prior to Isacson's employment the firm had represented a number of motion picture companies in prosecuting claims for rental of motion picture films arising from alleged underreporting of box office receipts by theatre licensees. Sargoy & Stein would cause theatre box office audits to be made by their staff and in almost 500 instances caused suit to be filed to collect on alleged underreportings. Isacson at first took part in these audits and later spent the major portion of his time taking depositions in examinations before trial. These depositions covered many phases of the relationship of the theatres with the motion picture companies. To assist him in taking these depositions Isacson had complete access to the firm's files which contained an abundance of data and information, not only gathered by this law firm but also disclosed to and confided in it by the motion picture companies concerning the manner in which the companies did business in the 16 mm. as well as the 35 mm. field.

The firm also assisted the general counsel of the motion picture companies in the preparation and defense of a number of private anti-trust suits filed against them. Much of the

Problem 13. Disqualifying a Lawyer

confidential data in the firm's files was collated and gathered in this work; it concerned the licensing of 16 mm. pictures for exhibition; the limitations, if any, on the distribution, and the terms of the licenses.

Isacson's professional status in the firm rose in importance within a short time. His name was placed on the firm letterhead by October, 1947. He soon left off routine work of the audits and took part in the ensuing litigation. Of the 464 under-reporting suits filed while he was with Sargoy & Stein, in at least 233 of them anti-trust defenses or counterclaims had been interposed. Isacson took some part in 170 of these suits and participated in taking depositions in 72, and at least in 31 interrogated witnesses concerning anti-trust claims. Isacson also participated in litigation involving 35 mm. pictures in which anti-trust violations were alleged.

Sargoy & Stein also investigated information which it had received from 16 mm. dealers, concerning the illegal duplicating of 16 mm. prints; among these dealers was Robert V. Fisher who occasionally visited the office of the firm and Carl J. Kunz.

There is no question but that Isacson, while in the employ of Sargoy & Stein, enjoyed the confidence and trust of the firm and of their clients in the motion picture industry. He had unrestricted access to the confidential data they had disclosed to the firm; and much of this would unquestionably be of great assistance to one prosecuting a claim of an anti-trust violation against those companies. An obligation of fidelity and loyalty was voluntarily assumed by his employers; Isacson was in the same way bound to the firm's clients; his obligation was no less than that of his employers, the partners of the firm; and that obligation remained with him after he left the firm in March, 1951 with respect to the confidences in which he had shared.

... For sixteen months or so he unsuccessfully sought

legal employment and tried to rejoin Sargoy & Stein. Finally, Isacson was introduced to Malkan by a cousin who had been a classmate of Malkan's in law school. After several months of discussion the law firm of Malkan & Isacson was formed in July, 1952. . . .

At the time of this association between Malkan and Isacson, Malkan had been consulted in connection with private anti-trust motion picture litigation but he had not been retained. While they were together the firm had a number of these cases. It is undisputed that in the major portion of the litigation in which the two-man firm of Malkan & Isacson appeared they represented plaintiffs in treble damage antitrust suits, and that prior to the formation of the firm Malkan had been quite active in litigation of this type, but not in the motion picture field. Isacson supplied the technical knowledge of the operations in this industry, which Malkan lacked; Malkan furnished the office, the practical experience in the prosecution of plaintiffs' anti-trust claims and, it seems from his statements, the financial support necessary to the firm. This was all well, except that Isacson also brought with him to this new venture in the motion picture field knowledge of all the anti-trust data which had been gathered by Sargoy & Stein from information imparted to them and their staff by their clients. . . .

At least sixty-five announcements were sent out; a half dozen or more went to exhibitors or attorneys for exhibitors; on some Isacson wrote personal notes. In one note to an attorney, who represents independent exhibitors, Isacson wrote that since his days with Sargoy & Stein he had "come to see the light and have undertaken to represent exhibitors (the salt of the earth, God bless them)." An announcement and copy of the altered article were sent to two motion picture exhibitors who were then parties to litigation against clients of Sargoy & Stein.

Problem 13. Disqualifying a Lawyer

It was against this background that the new combination of Malkan & Isacson appeared as attorneys for Fisher Studio Inc. and Robert V. Fisher, plaintiffs, in a private antitrust suit filed in the Eastern District of New York in September, 1952. This suit involves charges of restraints on 16 mm. film.

Robert V. Fisher had called at the office of Sargoy & Stein during 1946 and 1948. He had met Isacson in the Spring of 1948 there. In August, 1952, after Fisher read of the suit filed by the Government in the District Court for the Southern District of California against Twentieth-Century-Fox Film Corporation, et al., he discussed with Isacson the question of filing a complaint by Fisher Studio against the distributors of 16 mm. film and retained Isacson. Fisher apparently thought it a good idea to inform others in the industry of what he was doing and later Isacson addressed a meeting attended by 10 or 12 people out of 30 invited.

The defendants in the Fisher suit moved to disqualify Malkan and Isacson and the firm. Judge Abruzzo on November 19, 1952 referred the matter to Harold F. McNiece, Esq., as Special Master to hear and report. Mr. McNiece is a member of the Bar exceptionally well qualified and competent to perform such a task. Numerous hearings were held by him and he filed a comprehensive report on April 19, 1953. The report is part of the record before this Court. In it the facts recited above are found. The Master noted that —

> Mr. Isacson was present throughout the hearings. He ... was throughout a most unimpressive witness. . . . His memory was particularly poor on matters which were unfavorable to him, though ofttimes remarkably good on favorable ones. . . .

The Special Master found, when denying a motion to strike from the record evidence of solicitation —

> The evidence of solicitation shows that Mr. Isacson peddled confidential information and violated his duty toward his former clients and is therefore relevant on the confidential information issue.

After the filing of the Special Master's report, Judge Abruzzo by order filed April 13, 1954 disqualified Isacson and the firm of Malkan & Isacson from representing the plaintiffs in the Fisher suit....

Following Judge Abruzzo's order the firm of Malkan & Isacson was dissolved about July 1, 1954. About a month later the firm of Malkan & Ellner was formed....

It was after the firm of Malkan & Ellner was established that the Laskey and Austin suits were filed in the Southern District of New York on November 6, 1954. The defendants in both suits are substantially the same corporations — some 58 in number and all in the motion picture industry. Many of the defendants in these suits were clients of Sargoy & Stein, when Isacson was there employed and were also defendants in the Fisher suit. Both the Laskey and Austin suits are 35 mm. anti-trust actions against distributors. The claims alleged in both suits are in substance predicated upon the same restraints as alleged in the Fisher suit.

The Laskey matter came to Malkan & Isacson through Isacson; a suit was filed in 1953 in the Western District of Pennsylvania by Malkan & Isacson; the same issues are there presented as in the suit in the Southern District of New York; this prior suit in Pennsylvania is still pending. It was in the New York suit that the order of disqualification to which one of the appeals has been filed was made.

I agree with Judge Dawson's observation that —

> As Mr. Malkan, as well as Mr. Isacson, was disqualified from handling that case at a time when it first came to

Problem 13. Disqualifying a Lawyer 117

their office, this disqualification cannot be cured by the dissolution of the partnership. Once the attorney was disqualified from handling the case, he remains disqualified.

I am unable to follow the removal of this disqualification from Malkan and his new associate Ellner and the approval of the continuance of their employment in the Austin suit.

Isacson was disqualified because of his former engagement by a law firm representing the defendant corporations. While so employed he occupied a position of great moral trust and confidence. From his confidential position there attached to him an obligation which was voluntarily assumed by all who later joined with him in the practice of the law. It attached to Malkan if for no other reason than that he became a partner of Isacson and it attached to Ellner upon his association with Malkan.

Partners in a law firm do not dwell in cubicles; they all must observe and respect the confidence and trust a client has reposed in any one of them; they divide the fees and rewards of faithful service; they join in a common acceptance of responsibility to a client; they jointly and severally represent the clients; all are bound to each and every client of the firm by a relationship of trust and confidence, and are bound by such relationship which has at any time existed as to any former client of any one partner. It seems to me that to hold otherwise is to view the practice of the law as a business rather than as a profession. The principles to guide us in fixing the extent of professional obligations of the Bar are not to be looked for in the market place.

As to the Austin suit Judge Dawson found that it first came to Malkan after the partnership with Isacson had been dissolved and that Isacson had not had any connection with that case. He held that Malkan, Ellner and Malkan & Ellner were qualified to represent the plaintiff, and wrote —

> There has been no evidence presented that Mr. Malkan acquired such confidential information, and the burden would be upon the defendants to assert or offer proof that he had acquired such confidential information. This they have not done.

I do not agree that the burden is upon the defendants. It is far too great a task to place upon a former client seeking protection against disclosure of his confidences to require him to establish by proof that the confidence he placed in one partner has been disclosed to other partners. Assuming arguendo that such burden is upon the client, the record before us, while it contains no direct evidence of disclosure by Isacson to Malkan and subsequent disclosure by Malkan to Ellner, contains more than ample evidence to support the inference that such disclosure did in fact occur. Direct evidence would be well nigh impossible to obtain; the circumstances shown lead to one rational conclusion.

The defendants have the burden of establishing that a relationship of trust and confidence existed between them and the member of the Bar whom they seek to disqualify. This burden, they have concededly sustained as to Isacson by affirmative proof; Malkan and Ellner are bound by reason of the circumstances surrounding Malkan's association with Isacson and his subsequent association with Ellner. The defendants further need only show that these attorneys who owe them loyalty and fidelity have undertaken to represent adverse parties in matters in which the confidences given are involved. This, the defendants have done.

The ethics of the situation are tersely expressed in the

Problem 13. Disqualifying a Lawyer

third paragraph of Canon 6 of the Canons of Professional Ethics of The American Bar Association, which reads —

> The obligation to represent the client with undivided fidelity and not to divulge his secrets or confidences forbids also the subsequent acceptance of retainers or employment from others in matters adversely affecting any interest of the client with respect to which confidence has been reposed.

It is by application of this principle that Malkan, Ellner and the firm of Malkan & Ellner are disqualified in the Laskey suit. That disqualification attached to Malkan, not only by reason of association as a partner with Isacson in the practice of the law, but also by reason of the confidence which partners place in one another and the joint obligation to the former clients of any partner of the firm. Ethical obligations place both Malkan and Ellner individually in the same moral position as Isacson.

I would reverse in Austin and enter an order of disqualification as in Laskey. . . .

BACKGROUND READING

Note, Unchanging Rules in Changing Times: The Canons of Ethics and Intra-Firm Conflicts of Interest, 73 Yale L.J. 1058 (1964); *Emle Industries, Inc. v. Patentex, Inc.*, 478 F.2d 562 (2d Cir. 1973); *Silver Chrysler Plymouth, Inc. v. Chrysler Motors Corp.*, 370 F.Supp. 581 (E.D.N.Y. 1973).

A recent case which has some similarity to the instant problem is *Rotante v. Lawrence Hospital,* 46 App. Div. 2d 199, 361 N.Y.S. 2d 372 (1974). See also A.B.A. Formal Opinion 342 (1975), discussed *infra* p. 189.

PART IV
Special Problems of Government Lawyers

PROBLEM 14

Client Identification in a Government Context

Is the client the head of the agency, the government, the chief executive or the public? Is there any attorney-client privilege in government?

Frank Gleason is the city attorney for a city in central Texas. He is appointed by the mayor. The charter of the city states: "The city attorney shall be the attorney for the city, for all of its agencies and for all of its officers and employees in their official capacities. Neither the city nor its agencies or employees shall employ any other counsel."

A Texas State Commission has been appointed to look into prison systems throughout the state; and the warden of the city prison, Sol Lattimore, has been asked to testify before the commission. He consults with "his lawyer," City Attorney Gleason, in preparation for the testimony.

During the course of the interview, Warden Lattimore informs Mr. Gleason that one of the things he is concerned about is the report that some prisoners have been physically beaten for allegedly minor infractions of prison rules.

"What are the facts?" asks Mr. Gleason.

"Are you my lawyer?"

"Of course."

"It's all exaggerated," says the warden. "My men don't do anything unless it's absolutely necessary."

"Have you ever beaten a prisoner?" Mr. Gleason asks.

"Of course, we all do every now and then. It's the only way to keep some of those guys in line."

"Do you realize that your conduct is probably a violation of state and federal law?"

"Only if it can be proved," says the warden. "And remember, you're my lawyer."

"Does the commissioner of correction know about this?"

"I assume so."

"What about the mayor?"

"I have no idea."

1. What is the proper course of conduct for Mr. Gleason?

2. What advice should he give concerning Mr. Lattimore's testimony?

3. Suppose Mr. Lattimore testifies before the commission and is asked whether he discussed his testimony with anyone before appearing. If Mr. Lattimore answers truthfully, can Mr. Gleason be compelled to reveal the details of their conversation?

ASSIGNMENT

Canon 4; EC4-1, EC4-2, EC4-4; DR4-101.
Canon 5; EC5-17, EC5-18, EC5-19; DR5-105.
Canon 7; EC7-8.
Read the following news story:

Problem 14. Client Identification in a Government Context

Did Jaffurs Represent Liquor Control Board Clients or Public?
Philadelphia Evening and Sunday Bulletin, August 26, 1973, p. 14

"I'm serving a public organization, a public apparatus, and the public has a right to know how this public organization operates." — Alexander J. Jaffurs, Aug. 16, 1973

By Gerald McCullough

Harrisburg — The House Liquor Control Committee has completed nearly 2,000 pages of testimony this month without resolving the fundamental question raised by the firing of Alexander J. Jaffurs.

Did Jaffurs, a deputy attorney general assigned to the Liquor Control Board, represent the board, as Democratic committee counsel Elliott Goldstan has said? Or did Jaffurs have a higher duty as a government lawyer to represent the people?

Jaffurs lost his job because, in his words, "I felt I had a duty over and above the normal client-attorney relationship to keep the public informed as to the operation of a public organization."

FIRED BY PACKEL

He was dismissed by Attorney General Israel Packel because his public statements on alleged LCB improprieties by legislators and administration officials embarrassed the administration and alienated friendly legislators.

Democrats complained that Jaffurs was bound by the same attorney-client privilege that prohibits a private lawyer from revealing information given by a client.

When Jaffurs was accused by Goldstan of violating his client's confidence, he answered in language that could give a number of former White House lawyers, indicted in the Watergate scandal, pause for reflection.

'REPRESENTING THE PUBLIC'

"I was to perform legal services for the Liquor Control Board but I felt that ultimately I was representing the public," Jaffurs said.

"Assistant attorney generals in the past had always accommodated the board, even in most of their dealings. I felt my position was to be a watchdog and to call them as I saw them."

Goldstan, a Reading attorney, conceded the difficulty of challenging Jaffurs, a tall, 43-year-old former Penn football star, whom he described as a "straight arrow."

'DIFFICULT TO QUESTION'

"He sits there with his Savonarola-face, his gray hair and his wire-rim glasses and it's difficult to question his ethics," Goldstan said. (Savonarola, a 15th century Italian friar, was hanged for his reform preaching.)

Goldstan accused Jaffurs of violating Canon 4 of the American Bar Association's Code of Professional Responsibility which says that "A lawyer should preserve the confidences and secrets of a client."

"I think a client is a client and I think Jaffurs' client was the LCB," Goldstan said. "This guy screamed copper every time he disagreed with the board and that's a violation of ethics."

Problem 14. Client Identification in a Government Context

'DUAL RESPONSIBILITY'

Fred Bolton, executive director of the Pennsylvania Bar Association, said the state Ethics Committee had never ruled in a case involving a breach of confidence by an attorney for a state agency.

"It's a difficult question that has never been faced," Bolton said. "The lawyer here has a dual responsibility. He's advising a client on matters where the public has a right to know."

Pamela Wassman, a staff attorney at the American Bar Association's headquarters in Chicago, said the ABA Ethics Committee could not rule on the question until state courts had decided the exact relationship between a government attorney and his public "client."

Fred W. Speaker, former state Attorney General under Governor Shafer, said Pennsylvania courts "have never squarely faced the question."

"There is a special relationship between an attorney and a public agency but it is a relationship that's just not covered in the law," said Attorney General Packel. "It has not been determined by the courts."

Jaffurs said in an interview this week that he was forced to resolve the question during this two-year tenure as chief counsel to the LCB.

"The more I think about it the more I become convinced that nothing should be confidential when you're dealing with a public agency like the LCB," Jaffurs said. "The only exception I would make would be discussions of promotions where you're talking about private individuals."

"A lawyer is trained to think in terms of confidentiality and there is a natural tendency to cover things up when you get into government. That's what happened in Watergate."

"But I always felt the need to break this natural conspiracy of silence. I don't think there's anything unethical about that."

Read the following Opinion of the Federal Bar Association:

The Government Client and Confidentiality: Opinion 73-1
Professional Ethics Committee, Federal Bar Association
The Honorable Charles Fahy, Chairman

AT THE OUTSET of his Presidency of the Association Mr. Poirier submitted to the Committee under date of October 8, 1971, the following questions:

1. Under what circumstances may a federally employed lawyer disclose information concerning a Government official of any rank which would reveal corrupt, illegal, or grossly negligent conduct?

2. If disclosure may be properly made, to whom may it be made?

3. Who is the client of a Government attorney in the Executive or Legislative branches of Government?

A draft of proposed opinion was submitted to Mr. Poirier by the Committee, as then constituted, in June, 1972. It was circulated by him for their comments among a number of federally employed lawyers of high rank in Washington. Numerous comments were made. It was also discussed by the National Council of the Association at its meeting in September, 1972. At that meeting, at the suggestion of the Chairman of the Ethics Committee, the matter was referred

Problem 14. Client Identification in a Government Context

again to the Committee for reconsideration in light of the comments and discussion. The Committee now submits the result of its further consideration.

A few remarks as to terminology are in order. Thus, the "federally employed lawyer," for purposes of this opinion, is considered to be the lawyer employed by the federal government in a legal capacity. This opinion may at times refer to him as the government lawyer, or simply as the lawyer or attorney, without repetition that he is "federally employed." In defining the terms "corrupt, illegal or grossly negligent" conduct, as used in the opinion, and in judging whether particular conduct comes within those terms, special care is required. The "corrupt" conduct referred to in the request for an opinion was construed to be venal conduct in violation of law and duty, engaged in for personal gain or the gain of another, the gain ordinarily being of a pecuniary or other valuable nature which is measurable. Defining "illegal" conduct was not so easy for such conduct is often subject to reasonable differences of opinion as to its legality. The profession as well as the courts are constantly troubled and at odds about whether particular conduct is legal or not. For purposes of this opinion "illegal" conduct is divided into two general categories. One consists of the willful or knowing disregard of or breach of law, other than of a corrupt character, the latter type of illegal conduct having been separately defined. The second category of illegal conduct was considered to be that about which the lawyer may hold a firm position as to its illegality but which he nevertheless recognizes is in an area subject to reasonable differences of professional opinion as to its legality. Conduct which is "grossly negligent" would seem not to lend itself to greater clarification than those words themselves indicate.

One further general comment seems desirable. The federally employed lawyer in reaching a conclusion that the type of conduct referred to has occurred must be fully aware of the circumstances and exercise care commensurate with his own professional nature and responsibility, with a consciousness of the need always to avoid an unjust or mistaken derogatory characterization of the conduct of another.

Assuming the described conduct to have occurred, answers to the three questions can be more clearly developed by considering first the question posed as to who is the client of the federally employed lawyer in the Executive and Legislative branches of the government. Problems of disclosure involved in the other questions should be considered in light of the answer to the client question.

The client problem also divides according to the duties involved. There is the government lawyer who is designated to represent another in government service against whom proceedings are brought of a disciplinary, administrative or personnel character, including a court-martial. The answer to the client question in these situations seems clear. The person the lawyer is designated to represent is the client. The usual attorney-client relationship arises, with its privilege and professional responsibility to protect and defend the interest of the one represented.

The more usual situation of the federally employed lawyer, however, is that of the lawyer who is a principal legal officer of a department, agency or other legal entity of the Government, or a member of the legal staff of the department, agency, or entity.[1] This lawyer assumes a public trust, for the government, over-all and in each of its parts, is re-

---

1. In the course of this opinion when we use the term "agency" as a matter of convenience to include "Department" or other governmental entity.

Problem 14. Client Identification in a Government Context   131

sponsible to the people in our democracy with its representative form of government. Each part of the government has the obligation of carrying out, in the public interest, its assigned responsibility in a manner consistent with the Constitution, and the applicable laws and regulations. In contrast, the private practitioner represents the client's personal or private interest. In pointing out that the federally employed lawyer thus is engaged professionally in the furtherance of a particular governmental responsibility we do not suggest, however, that the public is the client as the client concept is usually understood. It is to say that the lawyer's employment requires him to observe in the performance of his professional responsibility the public interest sought to be served by the governmental organization of which he is a part.

Proceeding upon the foregoing background, the client of the federally employed lawyer, using the term in the sense of where lies his immediate professional obligation and responsibility, is the agency where he is employed, including those charged with its administration insofar as they are engaged in the conduct of the public business. The relationship is a confidential one, an attribute of the lawyer's profession which accompanies him in his government service. This confidential relationship is usually essential to the decision-making process to which the lawyer brings his professional talents. Moreover, it encourages resort to him for consultation and advice in the on-going operations of the agency.

The relationship above described gives rise to the question whether or to what degree the attorney-client privilege known to private practice attaches with respect to those to whom the government lawyer is professionally obligated in the conduct of the public business. No all-inclusive answer to the problem of the privilege is attempted herein, not only because no concrete factual situation has been posed, but also because the questions as submitted call for consideration of the privilege only as it bears upon the problem of disclosure: In that context the following is submitted.

The Committee does not believe there are any circumstances in which corrupt conduct may not be disclosed by the federally employed lawyer, apart from those situations to which we have referred in which the lawyer has been designated to defend an individual in a proceeding against him with respect to a personal problem.

In other instances of corruption the ethical aspect of the answer merges with the legal. Section 535 of Title 28 of the United States Code provides:

> (b) Any information, allegation, or complaint received in a department or agency of the executive branch of the Government relating to violations of Title 18 [the federal criminal code] involving Government officers and employees shall be expeditiously reported to the Attorney General by the head of the department or agency, unless —
>
> (1) the responsibility to perform an investigation with respect thereto is specifically assigned otherwise by another provision of law; or
>
> (2) as to any department or agency of the Government, the Attorney General directs otherwise with respect to a specified class of information, allegation, or complaint.
>
> (c) This section does not limit —
>
> (1) the authority of the military departments to investigate persons or offenses over which the armed forces have jurisdiction under the Uniform Code of Military Justice (chapter 47 of Title 10); or
>
> (2) the primary authority of the Postmaster General to investigate postal offenses.

Problem 14. Client Identification in a Government Context 133

In addition to this statute, there is House Concurrent Resolution No. 175 of July 11, 1958, 72 Stat. B12, entitled "Code of Ethics for Government Service." Its provisions have been made applicable to the entire Executive branch by Regulations of the Civil Service Commission, 5 C.F.R. §735.10.[2] The Resolution provides: "Any person in the Government service should: 9. Expose corruption wherever discovered." . . .[3]

Reading section 535 of Title 28 of the United States Code with the Joint Resolution and the Civil Service Commission Regulations, corrupt conduct and other illegal conduct of a criminal character, that is, the willful or knowing disregard of or breach of law, in either the Legislative or Executive branch may be disclosed by the federally employed lawyer, that is, reported to the "head of the department or agency" or other governmental entity, who shall report it to the Attorney General. If the head officer referred to is involved, the report in our opinion may be made directly to the Attorney General or other appropriate official of the Department of Justice.[4]

---

2. The legislative history of the Resolution (S. Rep. No. 1812, 85th Cong., 2d Sess. (1958)) states it is intended only as a guide and "creates no new law . . . and establishes no legal restraints on anyone."

3. Id.

4. The Committee adds at this point a strong recommendation that the federally employed lawyer, for himself personally and for his ability to assist others in his agency, acquaint himself with the full content of 5 C.F.R. §735.10. This section provides that each employee shall acquaint himself with each statute that relates to his ethical and other conduct as an employee of his agency and of the Government, and that the agency itself shall direct the attention of its employees, by specific reference in agency regulations issued under this Part 735, which is concerned with employee responsibilities and conduct, to each statute relating to the ethical and other conduct of employees of that agency, as well as to a listed number of provi-

With respect to the second category of illegal conduct, conduct about which there may be reasonable differences of opinion as to its legality, and grossly negligent conduct, the Committee considers the problem to be different. Ordinarily there is no need of disclosure of such conduct beyond the personnel of the agency where it arises. Differences of opinion as to the legality of action are often unavoidable in the process of arriving at a course of action to be recommended or adopted. The lawyer may not deem the decision reached or the action taken to be legally sound, but in the situations in which the question arises it may not be misconduct at all. Moreover, when we turn particularly to the grossly negligent category, one must consider that the particular conduct may be accidental by a person ordinarily careful. There should usually be an adequate remedy in the public interest calling for no disclosure beyond the immediate persons involved, including if need be other members of the agency. In all of these matters there may be regulations of the agency pointing to the course which should be followed. These should be observed unless for some very good reason the lawyer deems them inapplicable. In any event, the opportunity to correct these matters should first be within the agency itself.

Something more needs to be said. The confidential relationship of the lawyer with those entitled to consult with and be advised by him varies in degree according to the subject matter. It is one thing in the area of national security or the conduct of foreign affairs, for example, and quite another if there is involved, for example, a dispute over the

---

sions respecting employee conduct, including Chapter 11 of Title 18 U.S.C., which is concerned, inter alia with conflicts of interest.

Problem 14. Client Identification in a Government Context

validity of a particular order of the National Labor Relations Board. The diversity of situations is almost innumerable. It is to be borne in mind throughout that ours is an open society insofar as compatible with the orderly and effective conduct of government. This follows from the nature of the relationship of our Government with the people, and it has been given legislative recognition in recent years by the Freedom of Information Act, with its limited exemptions from the obligation of disclosure. Moreover, the government lawyer cannot be a refuge for the corrupt or looked upon as a secret repository for illegal or grossly negligent conduct of the business of the Government. There is a dividing line between conduct which falls in the area of strict confidentiality and that which falls within the area of appropriate public knowledge. This line cannot accurately be drawn except upon consideration of a particular factual situation, and even then not always easily or accurately drawn, certainly not to the satisfaction of all. Accordingly, the Committee feels obliged to limit its answer respecting disclosure to acceptance of the principle that disclosure beyond the confines of the agency or other law enforcing or disciplinary authorities of the Government is warranted only in the case when the lawyer, as a reasonable and prudent man, conscious of his professional obligation of care, confidentiality and responsibility, concludes that these authorities have without good cause failed in the performance of their own obligation to take remedial measures required in the public interest. In the absence of a concrete situation upon which to pass judgment as to the ethical course which should be followed we go no further than to adopt the above stated ethical principle. We think it appropriate for us to affirm the position that honesty and faithfulness is the prevailing rule in the Government service, and we warn against applying the principle we have stated to any situation without that care and sense of responsibility which is the hallmark of the legal profession at its best. Such care would call for resort by the lawyer himself to a trustworthy advisor as to the course to be followed. The ultimate decision, however, remains with him.

One final comment. The Committee has not considered it relevant to the present inquiries to embrace the subject of classified material or the Executive privilege.

This opinion has the unanimous approval of the Committee, composed as follows in alphabetical order: Circuit Judge Arlin M. Adams, Third Circuit; Superior Court Judge Sylvia Bacon, District of Columbia; Judge Earl Chudoff of the Court of Common Pleas, Philadelphia; Justin Dingfelder, Esquire, Office of the General Counsel, Federal Trade Commission; Senior Circuit Judge Charles Fahy, District of Columbia Circuit; Axel Kleiboemer, Esquire, Department of Justice, Washington, D.C.; Joseph G. O'Neill, Jr., Esquire, Assistant Legislative Counsel, Central Intelligence Agency; Honorable Harold E. Stassen, Philadelphia; Major Charles A. White, Jr., Judge Advocate General's School, U.S. Army, Charlottesville.

BACKGROUND READING

Cox, The Lawyer's Public Responsibilities, 4 Human Rights 1, 8-11 (1974); Lewis, Government Lawyers and Conscience, 59 A.B.A. Journal 1420 (1973); Dam, The Special Responsibility of Lawyers in the Executive Branch, 55 Chicago Bar Record 4 (1974). A recent case discussing the at-

Problem 14. Client Identification in a Government Context 137

torney-client privilege is *Hearn v. Rhay,* 44 U.S.L.W. 2207 (D.D.C. Sept. 26, 1975).

A.B.A. Informal Opinion 1282 (1973) discusses the conflicts inherent in a situation similar to that posed by the instant problem.

PROBLEM 15

Lawyer or Policymaker?

Does the government lawyer have a policymaking role?
Who resolves conflicts among a government lawyer's clients?
What consequences flow from a government lawyer's monopoly on legal affairs of government?

Frank Gleason, the city attorney in the previous problem, is also, by virtue of that office, the attorney for the city's board of education. The members of the board have asked to consult with Mr. Gleason concerning a situation which has arisen in the high school where the students, with the approval of the board, have set up a table in the main hall for the distribution of political literature. One of the publications is a pamphlet distributed by a "hate" group called the Pure American Party. It contains derogatory remarks about Jews, Blacks and Catholics. Irate parents have besieged the board with demands that the pamphlet be barred from the school. The matter has been placed on the calendar for next week's board meeting, and the Texas Civil Liberties Union

Problem 15. Lawyer or Policymaker?

has stated publicly that if the publication is removed, it will promptly bring a federal court action.

"Are you considering the removal of all publications of a political or controversial nature?" asks Mr. Gleason.

"No," replies the board chairman. "Only this one. The others haven't created any problems."

"Is the trouble coming from parents only, or are you also encountering disruption of the normal operation of the school as a result of the pamphlet?" inquires Mr. Gleason.

"No, I'm sure that some students feel uncomfortable, and one or two Jewish and Black kids have threatened to knock over the table, but it's nothing more serious than that. Most of the kids regard it as a far-out, screwball kind of thing."

Mr. Gleason assigns several lawyers to research the question and concludes that if the board bans the pamphlet he could not successfully defend its action, and he so advises the board.

"Is there a precedent dealing with this particular pamphlet?" asks the board chairman.

"No," replies Mr. Gleason, "but the law is fairly clear that a school board cannot selectively bar the distribution of material based solely on the content of the material. You might be able to stop the distribution of all political material, without discrimination, but the only way you could single out this one would be upon a showing of some disruptive effect in the school."

"Aren't we the judges of what's disruptive?"

"You told me there was no problem you couldn't handle. Isn't that still the case?"

There is no reply.

At the next meeting of the board of education, the board votes three to two to bar the publication. Right after the meeting Mr. Gleason calls the board chairman and says, "I told you it was illegal."

"You told us your view of the law, and we make policy. I guess a court will have to decide ultimately."

The next day Mr. Gleason receives a call from the clerk of a United States district court judge, advising Mr. Gleason that the Pure American Party, represented by an attorney from the Texas Civil Liberties Union, is moving for a preliminary injunction and declaratory judgment to prevent the board from implementing its decision. The plaintiffs are also seeking a temporary restraining order, and a hearing has been set by the judge for the following afternoon at two p.m.

Just then the phone rings again in Mr. Gleason's office. It is the mayor.

"Frank," says the mayor, "I hear that foolish school board is trying to burn a silly pamphlet. The civil liberties people are up in arms."

"I know," replies Gleason, "I advised them that they couldn't do it, and now we've been sued."

"Well," says the mayor, "I really don't think that we should be trying to prevent people from exercising their constitutional rights no matter how much we disagree with them. Remember, I was elected on a platform saying that we had to stop dragging our heels and provide constitutional rights for all. I'd sure look hypocritical if we took a different position just because of that crackpot Pure American group."

"I've got a lawsuit on my hands, though."

"That's true, but remember, you're the lawyer for the whole city, as well as the board of education."

1. Should Mr. Gleason defend the board of education in this matter? Assume that the charter provision under which Mr. Gleason functions is the same as in Problem 14.

Problem 15. Lawyer or Policymaker?

2. Suppose Mr. Gleason had furnished the board of education with a written opinion setting forth his reasoning as to the unconstitutionality of the board's proposed action, and that this opinion had been made public at the board's meeting by one of the dissenting members. Should this affect Mr. Gleason's decision on his handling of the case?

3. Suppose Mr. Gleason takes the case and the court grants the application for the restraining order and also grants a preliminary injunction, deciding the case almost exactly along the lines predicted by Mr. Gleason in his opinion. The board then directs Mr. Gleason to appeal to the court of appeals. Does he have the right to refuse to take the appeal?

4. Would your answers to these questions differ if Mr. Gleason were the full-time counsel of the board of education, assuming, of course, that the board had the legal right to be represented by its own staff counsel?

5. Would your answers differ if the board acted without consulting Mr. Gleason?

ASSIGNMENT

Canon 5; EC5-15, EC5-18, EC5-21, EC5-22.
Canon 7; EC7-4, EC7-5, EC7-7, EC7-8, EC7-9, EC7-14.
Also the following case: *Kay v. Board of Higher Education.*

BACKGROUND READING

Weinstein, Some Ethical and Political Problems of a Government Attorney, 18 Maine L. Rev. 155 (1966); Countryman, Finman, and Schneyer, The Lawyer in Modern Society 46-51 (Little, Brown & Company, 2d ed., 1976).

In considering whether a lawyer should defend a position he had previously advised was illegal, if the previous advice is on public record (see question two above), consider the relevance of these opinions which state that a lawyer should not accept employment to attack the validity of his prior work. See Drinker, Legal Ethics 113-114 (1953); and, e.g., A.B.A. Formal Opinions 177 (1938) and 64 (1932).

Matter of Kay v. Board of Higher Education, N.Y. City
260 App. Div. 9, 20 N.Y.S.2d 898 (1940)

PER CURIAM. The present status of the corporation counsel with respect to his duties and powers has remained substantially unchanged since the office was first established by statute. Subdivision a of section 394 of the New York City Charter provides that ". . . the corporation counsel shall be attorney and counsel for the city and every agency thereof and shall have charge and conduct of *all* the law business of the city and its agencies and in which the city is interested." (Italics ours.)

His authority to conduct all law business of the city and its agencies is exclusive. While exceptions are found, they are not here applicable.

By section 395 of the Charter it is provided that ". . . no officer or agency, . . . shall have or employ any attorney or counsel, except where a judgment or order in an action or proceeding may affect him or them individually or may be followed by a motion to commit for contempt of court, in which case he or they may employ and be represented by attorney or counsel at his own or their own expense."

In our opinion the majority of the board of higher educa-

Problem 15. Lawyer or Policymaker? 143

tion, neither individually nor as a body, come within the purview of the exception contained in this latter section.

In the first place, they do not now assert that they intend to be contumacious and disobey the order. Nor are they placed in a position of jeopardy such as the comptroller found himself in *Buck v. City of New York* (214 App. Div. 629). In that case, after rejecting a claim against the city, the comptroller was met with a situation where, in an action brought on the claim, the corporation counsel first defaulted and thereafter entered into a stipulation which the comptroller opposed because he thought it waived all defenses. In such situation, the comptroller, if he refused to pay the claim, might have been met with an order of the court directing him to pay, for violation of which he could be punished for contempt. If he did pay pursuant to the order, he would be violating his oath of office.

A different situation here prevails. There is no duty resting upon the board to engage the services of Russell. The order restraining them from so doing, therefore, may properly be obeyed by the board.

The other exceptions to the rule, that the corporation counsel is the sole judge as to the conduct of litigation and other law matters, are those in which fraud, collusion or corruption are charged with respect to his doing or not doing an act. Even in such case, the aggrieved officer or agency is not granted the right of appeal, but relegated to actions or proceedings to set aside an order or judgment so obtained. (*Sharp v. Mayor, etc., of N. Y.*, 31 Barb. 578.) It is not here contended but that the corporation counsel who represents the city as a whole (*Lowber v. Mayor, etc., of N.Y.*, 5 Abb. Pr. 325; *Ramson v. Mayor, etc., of N.Y.*, 24 Barb. 226) acted in the exercise of his best judgment.

Another situation where other counsel may be retained

is where the official attorney is called upon to represent conflicting interests or is otherwise disqualified. (*Judson v. City of Niagara Falls,* 140 App. Div. 62; affd., 204 N.Y. 630; *Matter of Fleischmann v. Graves,* 235 *id.* 84, 91.) Here, there are no conflicting interests.

Under the circumstances, the decision of the corporation counsel with respect to the advisability of appealing from the order setting aside the appointment of Russell is binding. (*People ex rel. Sherrill v. Guggenheimer,* 47 App. Div. 9; *People ex rel. Forty-first and Park Avenue Corp. v. Walsh,* 199 *id.* 925.)

It follows, therefore, that the appeal by the board of higher education from the order setting aside its appointment of Russell should be dismissed as not being properly before the court; that the order denying the motion of the board to substitute private attorneys be affirmed and that the order denying the motion of certain members of the board to intervene and for other relief, likewise be affirmed.

In disposing of these appeals we deem it unnecessary, at this time, to pass upon the other questions presented by the briefs which have been submitted to the court and express no opinion with respect thereto.

The appeal from the order entered on the 17th day of April, 1940, should be dismissed, without costs. The orders entered on the 1st day of May 1940, should be affirmed, without costs.

PROBLEM 16

The Prosecutor's Decision to Prosecute

Response to political pressures; selective enforcement as an ethical question — should the prosecutor go after the crime, or the person?

William Rogers is district attorney of Dade County, Florida, where the cities of Miami and Miami Beach are located. Although prostitution is a crime in Florida, Rogers, who has been D.A. for three years, has brought only three cases. This is not because there are no prostitutes in Dade County, but rather because there is very little overt streetwalking and few public complaints, and Rogers finds it personally distasteful to prosecute for what he regards as a "victimless crime" involving the sexual practices of consenting adults.

In recent weeks, however, about a dozen prostitutes have been observed soliciting in the neighborhood of some of Miami Beach's most elegant hotels. The managers have complained to the police, and there have been editorials in the local newspapers saying that the law enforcement officials should do something about it.

Police Commissioner Larry Walsh phones D.A. Rogers and says, "Look, we're getting these complaints about the girls in front of some of the posh hotels on the Beach. But I don't think it's right just to go after those girls. What instructions should I give my men about other prostitutes in downtown Miami? Are you going to prosecute all prostitutes, or just the ones that people are complaining about?"

"Look, Larry. We have to be selective, and the girls in Miami aren't bothering anyone. The problem is in Miami Beach, and that's what we should focus on. Oh, one more thing."

"What's that?"

"The FBI has alerted us that Lou Castaldo is down here trying to set up a gambling operation."

"The Mafia boss?"

"That's right. He's staying at the Americana Hotel. I'd like to let him know that he's unwelcome here. Keep tabs on him and pick him up for whatever you can, even if it's patronizing a prostitute."

"But we've never arrested anyone for that before."

"It's a crime, isn't it? You arrest and I'll prosecute. I want him out of town."

1. Is it proper for the district attorney to confine his enforcement of the prostitution law only to Miami Beach and to ignore similar violations in other cities under his jurisdiction?

2. Is it proper for the district attorney to decline to prosecute the so-called "Johns," who would be guilty of the crime of patronizing prostitutes?

3. Is it proper for the district attorney to try to convict a particular individual of *any* crime, quite apart from the seriousness of the crime or the extent to which there is equitable enforcement of the criminal laws?

Problem 16. The Prosecutor's Decision to Prosecute

ASSIGNMENT

EC7-13.

Consider the standards of prosecutorial discretion as articulated in Section 3.9 of the A.B.A. Standards Relating to the Prosecution Function and the Defense Function:

> 3.9 Discretion in the charging decision.
>
> (a) It is unprofessional conduct for a prosecutor to institute or cause to be instituted criminal charges when he knows that the charges are not supported by probable cause.
>
> (b) The prosecutor is not obliged to present all charges which the evidence might support. The prosecutor may in some circumstances and for good cause consistent with the public interest decline to prosecute, notwithstanding that evidence may exist which would support a conviction. Illustrative of the factors which the prosecutor may properly consider in exercising his discretion are:
>
> (i) the prosecutor's reasonable doubt that the accused is in fact guilty;
> (ii) the extent of the harm caused by the offense;
> (iii) the disproportion of the authorized punishment in relation to the particular offense or the offender;
> (iv) possible improper motives of a complainant;
> (v) reluctance of the victim to testify;
> (vi) cooperation of the accused in the apprehension or conviction of others;

(vii) availability and likelihood of prosecution by another jurisdiction.

(c) In making the decision to prosecute, the prosecutor should give no weight to the personal or political advantages or disadvantages which might be involved or to a desire to enhance his record of convictions.

(d) In cases which involve a serious threat to the community, the prosecutor should not be deterred from prosecution by the fact that in his jurisdiction juries have tended to acquit persons accused of the particular kind of criminal act in question.

(e) The prosecutor should not bring or seek charges greater in number or degree than he can reasonably support with evidence at trial.

BACKGROUND READING

Uviller, The Virtuous Prosecutor in Quest of an Ethical Standard: Guidance from the ABA, 71 Mich. L. Rev. 1145 (1973); Freedman, Lawyers' Ethics in an Adversary System 79-98 (Bobbs-Merrill, 1975); Breitel, Controls in Criminal Law Enforcement, 27 U. Chi. L. Rev. 427 (1960); Rabin, Agency Criminal Referrals in the Federal System, 24 Stan. L. Rev. 1036 (1972).

PROBLEM 17

The Standard of Prosecution

How convinced of guilt must the prosecutor be?

Charles Witherspoon is an elementary school English teacher in Chicago, Illinois. At six p.m. in mid-October, when it was still light out, Mr. Witherspoon emerged from the subway station nearest his home and was attacked by a group of teenagers who knocked him to the ground, kicked him, and stole his wallet containing $200 and a watch worth $500. He suffered a mild concussion and two broken ribs. Two weeks later, while shopping on a Saturday in a neighborhood store, Mr. Witherspoon recognized a youth who he believed was one of the gang that attacked him. He followed the boy until he saw a police officer who, at Mr. Witherspoon's urging, arrested the boy.

Mr. Witherspoon has spoken to Assistant District Attorney John Freeman and is now prepared to testify positively that the young man he has identified was one of those who mugged him.

"This young man is black," says Mr. Freeman to Mr. Witherspoon. "Do you know many black kids?"

"No," answers Mr. Witherspoon. "The school where I

teach is predominantly white, but I'm sure he was one of the gang."

"You were attacked from behind, weren't you?"

"Yes, but I could see them briefly and clearly as they kicked me."

The young man's only alibi is that he was walking with his girl friend at the time of the attack. He has a clean record.

There is a considerable doubt in Mr. Freeman's mind about whether the man Mr. Witherspoon has identified is actually one of the men who attacked him. Mr. Witherspoon is positive of his identification, however, and Mr. Freeman thinks there is a good chance of obtaining a conviction.

1. Should Mr. Freeman prosecute?
2. Would it be permissible to decline to prosecute?
3. Would it be proper, instead of proceeding to the grand jury for an indictment for robbery and grand theft, for Mr. Freeman to offer to accept a plea of assault?

ASSIGNMENT

EC7-13; DR7-103(A). Section 3.9 of the ABA Standards (see Problem 16 *supra*).

BACKGROUND READING

Dean Monroe Freedman and Professor Richard Uviller have carried on a lively debate concerning the issues raised by this problem. In addition to the material cited at the end of Problem 16, *supra*, see Freedman, Legal Ethics: Prosecutorial Discretion, 172 N.Y.L. Journal, Sept. 25, 1974, at 1;

Problem 17. The Standard of Prosecution

Uviller, Prosecutorial Discretion: Another View of Ethics, 172 N.Y.L. Journal, Oct. 17, 1974, at 4; Freedman, Legal Ethics: Criminal Trial Ethics Revisited, 172 N.Y.L. Journal, Nov. 27, 1974, at 1.

PROBLEM 18

The Former Government Lawyer

When can the former government lawyer litigate against the government?
On the same side?
Are private rules concerning side-switching and appearance of impropriety applicable for lawyers leaving government for private practice?

Marilyn Freed was an attorney with the Civil Rights Division of the United States Department of Justice from January 1971 to August 1974. During 1973 and 1974 she worked on a school desegregation suit which the department brought against the City of Dayton, Ohio. While working on the case, she urged her superiors to ask the federal court to issue an order which would have required busing children across school district lines dividing Dayton and the suburbs, in order to achieve racial integration. This position was rejected since the Justice Department was asserting, in other cases, that the Fourteenth Amendment did not permit such relief unless it could be shown that the suburban district was also guilty of intentional segregation.

Problem 18. The Former Government Lawyer

In April, 1974, the Justice Department obtained an order requiring redrawing of attendance lines within Dayton and a limited amount of busing within the city. Civil rights groups which had intervened in the case had urged the interdistrict remedy which Ms. Freed had been advocating within the Justice Department, but were unsuccessful. Ms. Freed had worked actively on the case for the United States, loyally arguing the Justice Department's position despite her strong feeling that it did not go far enough.

In July, 1974, the United States Supreme Court, in *Milliken v. Bradley*, 418 U.S. 717 (1974), adopted the position of the Justice Department on interdistrict busing. In August, 1974, Ms. Freed left the department and came to Cleveland, Ohio to work in a large private law firm.

Dayton remained in the news, however, because of continuing unrest over school segregation. In September, 1975, Ms. Freed was approached by the Ohio office of the NAACP Legal Defense and Education Fund, Inc., one of the groups which had intervened in the original Justice Department desegregation suit. The chief counsel to the Defense Fund in Ohio, Jeffrey Greene, asked Ms. Freed to work on a new case which the Fund was planning to bring in Dayton to obtain relief that would require interdistrict busing between Dayton and the predominantly white suburbs.

"Isn't that the same issue you lost before?" Ms. Freed asked.

"No, we're aware of *Milliken v. Bradley*. We think we can show that the suburbs and the State Department of Education have been practicing, since the original decree, a policy which promotes segregation. This could justify interdistrict relief even within *Milliken v. Bradley*."

"Has my old office been involved?" asked Ms. Freed.

"No," replied Mr. Greene. "The Justice Department is

staying out of this one. I think they believe we don't have much of a case."

"Do you?"

"We think so. And with your help, I think we can win."

Ms. Freed returned to her office and checked the Federal Conflict of Interest Act, 18 U.S.C. §207, which makes it unlawful for a person who was an employee of the executive branch of the United States Government to act as an attorney for any one other than the United States in connection with any "particular matter . . . in which the United States is a party or has a direct and substantial interest and in which he participated personally and substantially as an officer or employee, through decision, approval, disapproval, recommendation, the rendering of advice, investigation, or otherwise, while so employed. . . ."

Another provision of the act forbids such an employee, for a period of one year after the termination of his employment, from appearing for anyone other than the United States in a matter in which the United States ". . . is a party or directly and substantially interested, and which was under his official responsibility as an officer or employee of the Government at any time within a period of one year prior to the termination of such responsibility. . . ."

The federal statute prescribes criminal sanctions for violations of its provisions.

1. Should Ms. Freed work on the new Dayton case?

2. Assume that during Ms. Freed's service with the Civil Rights Division, a group of lawyers in the next office was investigating the possibility of bringing a desegregation suit against Columbus, Ohio, involving the same legal issues as the Dayton case. Ms. Freed did no work on that investigation which had been terminated when the head of the Civil Rights Division concluded that there was little likelihood of

Problem 18. The Former Government Lawyer

a successful result. Could Ms. Freed bring a desegregation suit against Columbus, Ohio on behalf of the NAACP Legal Defense and Education Fund, Inc. in September, 1975?

3. Suppose that, in question two, the Justice Department informed the Defense Fund in September, 1975, that the department was planning to intervene on the side of the City of Columbus because it was satisfied that the suit was designed to overturn the Justice Department's position on interdistrict busing which it had established in *Milliken v. Bradley*. Should Ms. Freed participate in the Columbus case?

ASSIGNMENT

Canon 4; EC4-1, EC4-2, EC4-4, EC4-5, EC4-6; DR4-101(A) and (B)
Canon 9; EC9-3; DR9-101(B).
Also read the following cases: *United States v. Standard Oil Co.* and *General Motors Corp. v. City of New York*.

United States v. Standard Oil Co.
136 F.Supp. 345 (S.D.N.Y. 1955)

IRVING R. KAUFMAN, D. J. In a civil suit by the United States Government to recover refunds from Standard Oil Company (New Jersey) and its subsidiary, Esso Export Corporation, for alleged overcharges in ECA financed transactions, defendant Esso Export moved for an order decreeing that the law firm of Sullivan & Cromwell, its counsel, may properly represent Esso Export in this action, and the government cross-moved for an order disqualifying Sullivan & Cromwell from acting as attorneys for defendant in this suit. The basis for the motion and cross-motion was a request made by the Department of Justice on June 2, 1955 that Sullivan & Cromwell withdraw as attorneys because one of their partners, Mr. Garfield Horn, who is actively working on the case, was a government counsel for a Paris office of the Economic Cooperation Administration (ECA) during the period in question. The government contends that Mr. Horn and his firm are barred from participation in this suit by Canons 6, 36 and 37 of the Canons of Legal Ethics adopted as Rules of this Court. Succinctly stated, these Canons forbid an attorney to accept employment in matters adversely affecting any interest of a former client with respect to which confidence has been reposed. They forbid his revealing or using such confidences to the disadvantage of the former client even though there are other available sources of this information. Further, they forbid a former government attorney to accept employment "in connection with any matter which he has investigated or passed upon while in such office or employ." Canon 36. In order to intelligently decide whether Mr. Horn and his firm have in fact violated these Canons, a thorough understanding of the factual and legal questions posed by the main controversy is necessary.

THE MAIN ACTION

In the main action, the United States seeks recovery of $35,862,288.08 claiming that Esso Export charged excessive prices in sales of Arabian crude oil to private importers in European countries participating in the Marshall Plan. Under this plan, authorized by the Economic Cooperation Act of 1948, 22 U.S.C.A. §1501, et seq., the ECA allocated funds in United States currency to various European nations

Problem 18. The Former Government Lawyer

participating in the program through the issuance of "procurement authorizations" setting forth the conditions for procurement of commodities. Firms in participating countries which desired crude oil, for example, after obtaining the approval of their respective governments, contracted to purchase such crude oil from various suppliers (including Esso Export). Such purchasers made payment to their local governments in local currencies and the money so paid was placed in "counterpart fund" accounts for use locally in connection with foreign aid programs. . . .

With regard to the specific transactions which are the subject matter of this suit, the United States claims that the prices charged by Esso Export for Arabian crude oil were higher than the maximum prices permitted by the Act and by the ECA Regulations which were promulgated [purportedly] pursuant to the Act. . . .

It is against this background of the case that we must examine the government service and private employment record of Mr. Garfield Horn, the partner in Sullivan & Cromwell whose former employment by ECA is the cause of these motions.[4]

MR. HORN'S EMPLOYMENT RECORD

Mr. Horn joined the staff of Sullivan & Cromwell as a salaried associate upon his graduation from Harvard Law School in 1946. A major part of his work for the firm was in the area of foreign legal and economic problems, an area of work for which he had specially prepared during his un-

---

4. It is conceded by Sullivan & Cromwell that if Mr. Horn is disqualified, the entire firm is disqualified. The reasons for this will be discussed *infra* in relation to the theory of imputed knowledge within a partnership. Even without this theory, if he is disqualified so is his work product which would be difficult to distinguish from that of the rest of the firm.

dergraduate training. In April 1949, Mr. Horn completely terminated his relationship with Sullivan & Cromwell, and on May 31, 1949, he entered the employ of ECA. At the time he left the employ of Sullivan & Cromwell there was no understanding with respect to his being re-employed by the firm; rather he was clearly told that any application for re-employment would have to be considered anew on the basis of the situation at the time such application was made. Mr. Horn served with the ECA until October 11, 1951, and in November 1951, he again entered the employ of Sullivan & Cromwell, pursuant to arrangements made during the summer of 1951, and he became a partner of the firm on January 1, 1953. Since his return to the firm, he has continued to concentrate on problems with foreign aspects. In the spring of 1952, Sullivan & Cromwell was retained to represent Esso Export in this case; the retainer came personally to Arthur H. Dean, senior partner of the firm, who is also quite familiar with aspects of the Marshall Plan and related problems. Since Mr. Horn had often worked under Mr. Dean in such matters before, Mr. Dean chose Mr. Horn to act as his assistant in this case. Mr. Horn assured Mr. Dean at that time that while in ECA he had never worked on the subject of the present controversy, that he had never investigated or passed upon it, and that in all respects the matter was completely new to him, and he had never heard of it while he was with ECA.

The government has been aware of Mr. Horn's active participation in the case since the fall of 1952, but not until June 2, 1955 did it make a request for Mr. Horn's and his firm's withdrawal. The government contends that it was not until Mr. Horn displayed "peculiar knowledge" of the inner workings of ECA during a conference in March of 1955 that it considered whether there might be any impropriety in his

Problem 18. The Former Government Lawyer

serving as attorney for defendant and that an investigation then of Mr. Horn's government service record convinced it that a request for withdrawal was necessary.

During the entire two and a half years Mr. Horn served with the ECA he was in the General Counsel's Office of the Office of the Special Representative in Paris (OSR/Paris). The only periods during which he was in Washington were ten days of personnel processing and indoctrination at the time of his initial assignment to Paris, approximately two days personnel processing at the termination of his duties, and two trips to Washington on OSR/Paris business. . . .

RESPECTIVE INTERPRETATIONS OF MR. HORN'S GOVERNMENT SERVICE RECORD

Mr. Horn's period of service with ECA from May 1949 to October 1951 falls entirely within the period of time during which the contested transactions occurred, i.e., April 1948 to August 1952. His position in the OSR/Paris hierarchy was an important one. Nevertheless, defendant contends that due to a division in functions between ECA/Washington and OSR/Paris, Mr. Horn's office in OSR/Paris knew nothing of the subject matter of these transactions, and none of his work for OSR/Paris was related to the subject of this case.

Defendant contends that OSR/Paris was concerned with implementing the operating phases of the ECA program, that its function in chief was to work closely with the various European countries and the ECA Missions in them on problems such as eliminating trade restrictions between the participating countries, clearing European payments and working out foreign currency problems, the allocation of scarce materials, and problems of manpower supply. It claims that the General Counsel's Office furnished legal advice on such problems, its chief job being the determination of whether various activities could be undertaken under the terms of the Act or financed with counterpart funds. Defendant further asserts that the only petroleum problems considered by OSR/Paris were those that dealt with the compiling of data estimating the oil requirements of the various countries, and recommending where and how much additional refinery capacity should be built in Europe. It is defendant's contention that ECA/Washington had exclusive responsibility for the drafting, promulgation and enforcement of the ECA policies relating to procurement and prices set forth in ECA Regulation 1, the Regulation which implemented the Marshall Plan procurement program. Defendant further says that this sharp division in functions between ECA/Washington and OSR/Paris also applied to the two separate General Counsel's Offices; that while the General Counsel's Office in Washington played an active part in the drafting, promulgation and enforcement of the procurement and price provisions of Regulation 1, the General Counsel's Office in Paris played no role in these matters, and that as to the very controversy on which the lawsuit is based, the General Counsel in Washington was continuously involved in the controversy while the Paris office played no part in it. The defendant urges, therefore, that Mr. Horn never received any confidences of the government with regard to the subject matter of this case; that he cannot be considered as having represented the government in matters relating to this case; that he never investigated or passed upon the matters involved in this controversy; and that he is, therefore, free to act as attorney for defendant, Esso Export.

    The government's reply to defendant's contentions is largely based on the key legal position Mr. Horn held during the time of the transactions in question. It urges that his

Problem 18. The Former Government Lawyer 161

duties in Paris included proposing legislation necessary to implement the operating phases of the program, solving legal problems arising under the Act, interpreting legislative provisions under the Act and drafting new legislative provisions. The government contends, therefore, that while Mr. Horn was employed by the government, he should have pointed out any invalidity in Regulation 1 which defendant now asserts. It is the government's position that whether or not Mr. Horn ever actually considered the validity of Regulation 1, he is disqualified because he should have done so.[9] Further, it claims that he actually did pass on Regulation 1 and pricing problems under it, more specifically, petroleum pricing problems.

It is urged further by the government that Mr. Horn had access to confidential data relating to the present controversy, and that in connection with the broad estoppel defense urged by defendant, many of the matters which must necessarily have come to Mr. Horn's attention while he was counsel and General Counsel in Paris, and because of his official position, are closely related to and interwoven with the question of the government's knowledge of the purported overcharges. It points out that many of his duties related to the counterpart funds mentioned in defendant's answer as having been expended for the benefit of the United States thus nullifying the government's claim of damages, and asserts that this fact also disqualifies him. The

---

9. The language of Canon 36 bars a former government attorney from accepting employment in connection with any matter "which he has investigated or passed upon while in such office or employ." The government contends that this includes matters which "he should have passed upon." This is a novel contention and the government cites no case to support it. The possible application of such a theory and its limitations, if applied, will be considered in discussing the appearance of evil, *infra*.

government summarizes its position by asserting that Mr. Horn is disqualified from acting in this case by Canons 6 and 37 because he had access to and obtained confidential information from the plaintiff and because he owed a duty of fidelity to plaintiff; and that he is further disqualified by Canon 36 because he passed upon or should have passed upon matters relating to the present controversy....

THE CANONS OF ETHICS INVOLVED

The pertinent provisions of these Canons follow:

Canon 6. Adverse Influences and Conflicting Interests
[See C.P.R. Canon 4 and 5]

"... The obligation to represent the client with undivided fidelity and not to divulge his secrets or confidences forbids also the subsequent acceptance of retainers or employment from others in matters adversely affecting any interest of the client with respect to which confidence has been reposed."

Canon 37. Confidences of a Client

"It is the duty of a lawyer to preserve his client's confidences. This duty outlasts the lawyer's employment, and extends as well to his employees; and neither of them should accept employment which involves or may involve the disclosure or use of these confidences, either for the private advantage of the lawyer or his employees or to the disadvantage of the client, without his knowledge and consent, and even though there are other available sources of such information. A lawyer should not continue employment when he discovers that this obligation prevents the performance of his full duty to his former or to his new client...."

Problem 18. The Former Government Lawyer

Canon 36. Retirement from Judicial Position or Public Employment
[See C.P.R. Canon 9]

". . . A lawyer, having once held public office or having been in the public employ, should not after his retirement accept employment in connection with any matter which he has investigated or passed upon while in such office or employ."

INFERENCES ARISING UNDER THE CANONS

Decisions interpreting these Canons have created three inferences operating against the attorney in question which the government contends are operative here. These must be examined to determine if they are applicable in the present case.

I. Inference of Access to Confidential Information

Insofar as these canons relate to the question of preservation of a former client's confidences, they disqualify an attorney who has received confidences which might possibly be relevant to the controversy at hand as they seek to avoid unconscious as well as conscious betrayal.[10]

---

10. "It would be unjust to the bar as a whole and to the litigants appearing before our courts to place advocates in a position where, even unconsciously, they might take, in the interests of a new client, an advantage derived or traceable to confidences reposed under the cloak of a prior, privileged, relationship." Watson v. Watson, Sup. Ct. 1939, 171 Misc. 175, 11 N.Y.S.2d 537, 540. See Consolidated Theatres, Inc., v. Warner Bros. Circuit Management Corp., 2 Cir., 1954, 216 F.2d 920, 925; Brown v. Miller, 1923, 52 App. D.C. 330, 286 F. 994; T. C. Theatre Corp. v. Warner Bros. Pictures, Inc., D.C.S.D.N.Y. 1953, 113 F.Supp. 265, 269; American Bar Association, Committee on Professional Ethics and Grievances, Opinions #83 and 177 (hereafter cited as A.B.A. Opinion # __); Association of the Bar of

As to who must carry the burden of showing that relevant confidences were reposed, an inference favorable to complainant has been reaffirmed recently in this Circuit. In *T. C. Theatre Corp. v. Warner Bros. Pictures, Inc.*, D.C.S.D. N.Y. 1953, 113 F.Supp. 265, 268, Judge Weinfeld said:

> A lawyer's duty of absolute loyalty to his client's interests does not end with his retainer. He is enjoined for all time, except as he may be released by law, from disclosing matters revealed to him by reason of the confidential relationship. Related to this principle is the rule that where any substantial relationship can be shown between the subject matter of a former representation and that of a subsequent adverse representation, the latter will be prohibited.

The court disagreed with the contention of the attorney whose conduct was questioned in the *T. C. Theatre* case. The attorney urged that the former client was required to show that it had disclosed to the attorney confidential matters related to the instant case. The court stated:

> [T]he former client need show no more than that the matters embraced within the pending suit wherein his former attorney appears on behalf of his adversary are *substantially related* to the matters or cause of action wherein the attorney previously represented him, the former client. *The Court will assume that during the course of the former representation confidences were*

---

the City of New York, Committee on Professional Ethics, Opinions #2 and B-39 (hereafter cited as City Opinion # __).

Where it is clear that betrayal of confidences can be avoided, however, it is permissible for an attorney to take a case adverse to the interests of a former client. See City Opinions #87, 119, 383, 508, B-26, B-32, B-172.

Problem 18. The Former Government Lawyer

disclosed to the attorney bearing on the subject matter of the representation. (Italics supplied.) at page 268.

. . .

The rule is clear, therefore, that complainant's burden extends only to showing the existence of a substantial relationship between the subject matter of the lawsuit and the matters in which the attorney represented his former client. This substantial relationship creates an inference that confidential information was reposed. Further, complainant need only show *access* to such *substantially related* material and the inference that defendant received these confidences will follow.[11]

[T]o guarantee that these confidences remain inviolate, the courts will assume that when a client entrusts an attorney with the handling of a particular matter, the client will reveal to that counsel all the information at his disposal, including confidential matter. It is upon this assumption that the courts will bar an attorney from taking a position adverse to a former client in regard to any matters substantially related to those in which the attorney represented that client. This assumption, however, is reasonable only so

---

11. The reason for the access extension to this rule is that there might be a situation where the client does not consult orally with the particular attorney (e.g., if the attorney is a junior attorney assigned to the case); nevertheless, records, files and other materials substantially related to the controversy at hand are made available to that attorney by the client. The attorney thus has access to the various documents, and the assumption is that these were made available to him only because of the confidential nature of the attorney-client relationship.

The question of whether this inference follows from access alone where there is no proof of use by the attorney of the materials in question will be discussed *infra* under the headnotes dealing with government attorneys.

long as there is a substantial relationship between those former matters and the lawsuit in which the confidence question is raised.

Unfortunately, the cases furnish no applicable guide as to what creates a "substantial" relationship. . . .

But, clearly, the word "substantial" must be given some restrictive content.

In the present case, Mr. Horn was formerly employed in a Paris office of the very agency which is making a claim against his client. His job was concerned with legal questions arising during the implementation in Europe of the operating phases of the ECA program, the program under which the contested transactions occurred. However, ECA was a vast agency with a network of offices throughout Europe and in Washington, D. C. It administered a billion dollar foreign aid program which dealt with almost every sort of problem that could arise in financing a project aimed at helping Europe recover from the devastations of World War II. It is easy to visualize a situation where an official in one office of that agency would be unaware of some of the functions of other branches of the agency. Indeed, this is the very contention that defendant makes here. It claims that the job of implementing the operating phases of the program in no way involved consideration of any pricing, procurement or refund problems of the type involved in the present controversy. Defendant supports its assertion that Mr. Horn's former duties had nothing to do with any matters relating to the present controversy by the affidavits of 13 men who held key positions in ECA in Paris and in Washington during the period in question. Typical of their recollections is the affidavit of Isaac N. P. Stokes, who served as Acting General Counsel, General Counsel and Acting Special Representative in OSR/Paris from February 1949 through September 1952, at

Problem 18. The Former Government Lawyer 167

which time he became General Counsel in Washington, a position in which he served until March 1953. In his affidavit of September 26, 1955, he states:

> In connection with the preparation of this affidavit, I have carefully searched my recollection as to all aspects of this case of which I had any knowledge and as to the functions, responsibilities, and activities of GC/Paris. I am unable to recall any instance in which there was referred to or considered by GC/Paris any question relating to the promulgation, interpretation, operation, or validity of any of the pricing or refund provisions of ECA Regulation 1, either in connection with Arabian crude oil or any other commodity; any question involving the consideration of whether prices charged in ECA-financed sales of Arabian crude oil complied or failed to comply with the provisions of ECA Regulation 1; any question concerning prices charged for Arabian crude oil whether in ECA-financed sales or non-ECA-financed sales; any question involving comparisons between prices of Arabian crude oil shipped to European destinations and prices of Arabian crude oil shipped to Western Hemisphere or other destinations; or any question concerning refunds to be obtained in respect of ECA-financed shipments of Arabian crude oil. Nor can I recall any other instance in which GC/Paris would have had any occasion to acquire any information regarding any of the above-mentioned questions, or any instance when or any reason why any member of the staff of GC/Paris would have had any occasion, on his own initiative, to inquire into the subject matter of this case.
>
> Any reference of any such questions to GC/Paris or to any other part of OSR/Paris would have been inconsistent with the recognized division of responsibilities and functions as between Washington and Paris.

I find that these affidavits establish that there was no such substantial relationship between Mr. Horn's former work and his present position as would disqualify him in this suit. Any other ruling would delete all meaning from the word "substantial." These affidavits deprive of any significance the fact that Horn had access to the file rooms of OSR/Paris by their assertion that the functions of that office were such that it would not maintain relevant files. . . .

II. Inferences Arising From the Appearance of Evil

Interpretations of the Canons of Ethics have held that it is the duty of an attorney to avoid not only the actuality but the appearance of evil. In discussing Canon 36, H. S. Drinker in his Legal Ethics, p. 130, points out that one of the reasons for the rule forbidding the former public attorney to act in relation to any matter he passed upon while in government service is to prevent the appearance of evil — i.e. to prevent even the appearance that the government servant may take a certain stand in the hope of later being privately employed to uphold or upset what he had done.[24] This rule finds application here in the government's contention that Mr. Horn should be disqualified if he passed upon or should have

---

24. This appearance of evil rationale would also seem to explain the rule applied to privately employed attorneys that the attorney may not attack the validity of his own work. It has been held that where an attorney draws a document for a client, or advises a client to take a certain legal position, he is forever barred from asserting that that position was unsound or that document invalid. See Thatcher v. United States, 6 Cir., 1914, 212 F. 801; Federal Trust Co. v. Damron, 1933, 124 Neb. 655, 247 N.W. 589; A.B.A. Opinions #33, 64, 71, 177; City Opinion #32; County Opinion #156. See also Drinker, op. cit. pp. 113-114. Outside these restrictions, however, an attorney is free to change his legal viewpoint generally; the ethical question is posed only when the lawyer attempts to change his viewpoint with respect to the merits of a specific matter with which he has previously dealt.

Problem 18. The Former Government Lawyer 169

passed upon the validity of the pricing regulations in question in this controversy. Of course, if Mr. Horn did actually pass on the validity of these regulations, he is barred from participating in this case by the language of Canon 36. However, if he did not actually consider the question of whether these regulations were valid, I find that there is no appearance of evil arising from his now questioning their validity unless it is proven that he was specifically ordered to consider that question while in government employ. If he was so ordered, he cannot now be heard to urge that he shirked his duty in the past and is, therefore, free to raise the question presently. This exception to the necessity of proving actual investigation of the matter in question will be applied, however, only when the attorney's duty to pass upon that particular matter, was very clear. The factual questions raised by this rule as applied to this case will be discussed after consideration of one more inference arising under these Canons.

III. Inference of Imputed Knowledge Within a Partnership

It has been repeatedly held by courts and ethics committees which have considered these canons, that the knowledge of one member of a law firm will be imputed by inference to all members of that firm. In *Laskey Bros. of West Virginia v. Warner Bros. Pictures, Inc.*, 2 Cir., 1955, 224 F.2d 824, 826-827, the Court said:

> [A]ll authorities agree that all members of a partnership are barred from participating in a case from which one partner is disqualified....
>
> Within the framework of the original partnership the fact of access to confidential information through the person of the partner with such specialized knowl-

edge is sufficient to bar the other partners, whether or not they actually profit from such access. Such a result, although an extension of the literal wording of Canons 6 and 37 of the Canons of Professional Ethics of the American Bar Association, is necessary to facilitate maximum disclosure of relevant facts on the part of clients.

This chain of imputed knowledge has been held to extend, not only to the partners in a law firm, but to salaried law clerks in a firm. Applied to the instant case, treating the entire OSR/Paris office as a partnership, the government argues that if anyone in the OSR/Paris office would have been barred from taking part in this controversy, then Horn is barred. It then urges that there was such a close association between the Counsel's Office in Washington and the Counsel's Office in Paris, that the chain of disqualification must necessarily extend from one office to another, and the Washington Counsel's Office was clearly involved in the present controversy from its inception.

The major premise on which the partnership disqualification theory is based, however, is that there was in the partnership office confidential information pertinent to the pending law suit to which all the partners had access. In this case, that basic premise is challenged by affidavits denying this alleged closeness between Washington and Paris, and the government has attempted to meet that challenge by producing documents from its files. If none of the documents the government has introduced rebut the import of those affidavits, the basic premise of knowledge within the office fails, the inference fails also, and the government is again left with the burden of proving actual knowledge.

Applying this doctrine of imputed knowledge within a

Problem 18. The Former Government Lawyer

partnership to the present case, however, presents a difficulty not found when dealing with private law firms. As stated, the doctrine's basic premise is that there is a free flow of information within a *partnership office* so that the knowledge of one member is the knowledge of all. When dealing with a government attorney, the question remains, within what *office* is that free flow of information assumed to exist. In this case, for example, is the office the overall ECA agency itself, OSR/Paris, or the General Counsel's Office of OSR/Paris.

This question arises in analogous form with relation to the inference set forth in the *T. C. Theatre* case that if an attorney had access to materials of the former client which are substantially related to the present controversy, it will be presumed that he came into contact with confidential information relating to the controversy, and he will be disqualified. Who is the client which the former government attorney represented and to whose files will access be presumed? Through what divisions and sub-divisions of a large government office will an attorney, who actually can go to any file, be presumed to have gone to such files regardless of his personal job assignments? At this point, when dealing with the government attorney, the client he represented and the partnership of which he was a member become merged. This is so because the basic problem is not merely to identify the former client here, which is in a larger sense the United States Government *in toto,* but rather to identify the interests with respect to which the attorney represented the client, for it is only as to these interests that he is disqualified. In identifying these interests one is confronted by the question of whether this attorney is to be considered as having represented the government in matters pending within his immediate office, or within a broader agency to which that office is attached, or solely in matters which he himself handled. In other words, the full circle has been swung and a decision must be made as to whether the theory of imputed knowledge as applied to members of a law partnership applies to attorneys working for the government; if it does, what office marks the boundary of imputation?

Guidance on this point can be taken from the language of Canon 36 which was enacted in 1928, twenty years after the American Bar Association originally adopted the first 32 Canons, and which deals specifically with lawyers retiring from public positions. This Canon forbids a former government attorney to accept employment "in connection with any matter which he has *investigated or passed upon* while in such office or employ." (Italics supplied.) The main purpose of this Canon was to clarify the duties in Canon 6 as related to government attorneys — chiefly, it avoids the "client" language of Canon 6 which presents serious difficulties in this sphere. Although it cannot be considered as completely superseding Canon 6 in dealing with a lawyer's duty to a former client, Canon 36 undoubtedly serves as a guide to the chief purpose of the ethical principle involved and the words "investigated" or "passed upon" imply a test of actual personal knowledge or action. However, it is also undoubtedly the purpose of the Canons generally to avoid the appearance that an attorney has taken a position contradictory to his former client's interests although, in fact, he may not have done so. This second purpose makes it impossible to hold that Canon 36 permits of none of the previously discussed inferences where a former government attorney is involved. The language of that Canon, however, must be held to require that a practical test be employed in determining when an appearance of evil exists: i.e. in each instance the fact finder must determine whether it was likely that the

Problem 18. The Former Government Lawyer

particular government attorney would have attained knowledge of or taken a stand on the subject matter of the particular controversy. If there is no practical likelihood, there is no appearance of evil.

Where an attorney is head of his office or a subdivision of it, as was Mr. Horn during part of his tenure, there is, of course, imputed to him knowledge of the proceedings taken by his juniors. This is a vertical theory of imputed knowledge well founded in rules of ultimate responsibility. However, for such an official there is still the problem of horizontal imputation of the knowledge of another division head of coordinate rank within the same larger agency. Again, there may sometimes be a rebuttable presumption of imputed knowledge, but this is the kind of question which must be decided on an *ad hoc* basis depending on the particular factual relationship between the two divisions or the two personalities involved and the likelihood that knowledge passed freely between them. In the instant case, the decision as to imputed knowledge, if any, must await closer examination of these facts....

Support for applying this practical, factual test in cases involving the disqualification of former government attorneys can be found in recognition of the serious problems which would otherwise arise — problems particularly acute where the employment was with the United States Government as opposed to some smaller public body. The government itself does not expect to bar a former government servant from participating in any case against the government involving in any way the agency in which he was employed. The size and diversity of function of many government agencies prohibit any such broad conclusion. The fact that the government is a client difficult to identify, and that the "firm" of which the government attorney is a part is difficult to limit in scope, were factors in the establishment of the more specific "investigated" or "passed upon" language of Canon 36. Although the confidence and adverse interests rules of Canons 6 and 37 still bind the former government attorney with a duty of fidelity, that duty must be given a practical scope. This is important for the benefit of the government which must constantly recruit attorneys from private practice. If service with the government will tend to sterilize an attorney in too large an area of law for too long a time, or will prevent him from engaging in practice of the very specialty for which the government sought his service — and if that sterilization will spread to the firm with which he becomes associated — the sacrifices of entering government service will be too great for most men to make. As for those men willing to make these sacrifices, not only will they and their firms suffer a restricted practice thereafter, but clients will find it difficult to obtain counsel, particularly in those specialties and suits dealing with the government.[34]...

34. A converse problem arises when an attorney who has represented several corporate clients enters government service as the head of a department or as a lower ranking official, and that department wished to undertake an investigation of or lawsuit against his former clients. If he is head of the department, knowledge of his subordinates' activities is imputed to him as is responsibility for their actions. A former department chief is barred from undertaking to represent in private practice any interests adverse to the government in any matters which were pending in his department during his tenure; why should not the present chief be barred while in government service from undertaking any activities adverse to interests of his former client. And if he is barred, why not his subordinates since he is held responsible for their actions. The answer which has been reached is that the hands of the government cannot be tied because of the former associations of one of its officials; therefore, that top person disqualifies himself from handling that particular matter, and the conflict of interest

Problem 18. The Former Government Lawyer

In *Laskey Bros. of West Virginia v. Warner Bros. Pictures, Inc.*, 2 Cir., 1955, 224 F.2d 824, in a disqualification proceeding, the Second Circuit was confronted with a former partner in a private law firm, who would have been barred from taking the case in question if he had remained a member of that firm because of the theory of imputed knowledge. The Court held that although the presumption of imputed knowledge is irrebuttable while a partnership exists, after its dissolution or after an attorney leaves the firm, a former partner barred only by imputed knowledge may rebut the inference that he received confidential information from the attorney with actual knowledge.[36] It held further that the testimony of the former partner was itself sufficient rebuttal. Discussing the practical problems which would be raised by any stricter application of the partnership-imputed knowledge rule, the Court said:

> Since the degree of association to effect disqualification need not necessarily be that of a partner, young lawyers might seriously jeopardize their careers by temporary affiliation with large law firms. But even more important is the effect on litigants who may seriously feel

question is considered resolved. Similarly, the particular lower ranking attorney disqualifies himself and another attorney handles the matter. No such opportunity is given to one partner in a law firm to disqualify himself and qualify the firm. The only explanation for the difference in result is that the practical exigencies are more compelling in the former situation than the latter. This is another illustration of the fact that ethical problems cannot be viewed in a vacuum; practical, everyday facts of life must be considered.

36. In the District Court opinion in Laskey, and in the T. C. Theatre case, the burden of proving that the knowledgeable attorney had conveyed that information to his former partner was placed upon the complainant. For other treatment of this problem see A.B.A. Opinion #167 and City Opinion #793.

they have claims worthy of judicial testing, but are prejudiced in securing proper representation. For the net effect of an overharsh rule of disqualification must be to hinder adequate protection of clients' interests in view of the difficulty in discovering technically trained attorneys in specialized areas who were not disqualified, due to their peripheral or temporally remote connections with attorneys for the other side. See Note, 64 Yale L.J. 917, 928. The necessity of judicial recognition of the contingent fee is an appropriate analogy.

Aside from these practical problems, it is doubtful if the Canons of Ethics are intended to disqualify an attorney who did not actually come into contact with materials substantially related to the controversy at hand when he was acting as attorney for a former client now adverse to his position. I agree, that where there is a close question as to whether particular confidences of the former client will be pertinent to the instant case, an attorney should be disqualified to avoid the appearance if not the actuality of evil. But, where an attorney has worked for a vast agency of the United States government, as in the instant case, it is hardly reasonable to hold that an appearance of evil can be found in his undertaking a case against the government where there is not some closer factual relationship between his former job and the case at hand other than that the same vast agency is involved. . . .

The government, complainant herein, had the burden of coming forward with evidence to dispel the effect of these affidavits. Specifically, to show grounds for disqualifying Mr. Horn in the present controversy, the government had the burden of either showing that he actually received relevant confidences or passed on the subject of the controversy, or

Problem 18. The Former Government Lawyer

that, although such personal active participation cannot be proved, his former duties were so substantially related to the present controversy that an appearance of evil arises from his taking part in this suit.

To support its contention that Mr. Horn's duties did bring him into contact with the subject matter of the present controversy in such a way as to disqualify him from proceeding as attorney for defendant in this action, the government has submitted some 25 assorted documents from its files, and two explanatory affidavits by Judge Stanley N. Barnes, Assistant Attorney General in charge of the Anti-trust Division, United States Department of Justice. Unlike the affidavits submitted by defendant, Judge Barnes' affidavits are based, not upon personal knowledge of ECA and OSR operations during the time in question, but upon interpretations which he has given the submitted documents without such personal knowledge.

CONCLUSION

After careful study of these documents, . . . it is my considered opinion that the government has failed to present grounds for ordering the disqualification of Mr. Horn and his firm as defense attorneys in this case, and that the division in functions between OSR/Paris and ECA/Washington has been clearly established.

Specifically, the government has failed to prove:

(1) that Mr. Horn had access to documents substantially related to the subject matter of the instant case;

(2) that he ever had access to and/or actually saw or worked on any relevant confidential materials;

(3) that he ever investigated or passed upon the subject matter of the instant case;

(4) that he ever rendered any legal advice or opinion in relation to the regulations which are the subject matter of the instant case; and

(5) that despite these conclusions, Mr. Horn's present position creates an appearance of evil requiring disqualification.

These conclusions have been reached after a thorough document-by-document analysis of the papers upon which the government bases its motion. . . .

When dealing with ethical principles, it is apparent that we cannot paint with broad strokes. The lines are fine and must be so marked. Guide-posts can be established when virgin ground is being explored, and the conclusion in a particular case can be reached only after painstaking analysis of the facts and precise application of precedent. After full consideration of all applicable principles, I hold that the motion of the government to disqualify Mr. Horn and his firm as defense attorneys is denied, and the motion of Sullivan & Cromwell for an order decreeing them to be qualified as attorneys herein is granted. So ordered.

General Motors Corp. v. City of New York
501 F.2d 639 (2d Cir. 1974)

KAUFMAN, Ch. J. Suits involving large damage claims inevitably spark intensive pretrial skirmishing, as the litigants bombard each other and the district court with a variety of motions. In this case, brought by the City of New York [City], which alone has a $12,000,000 claim, as a class action alleging that General Motors Corporation [GM] has violated the antitrust laws principally by monopolizing or attempt-

Problem 18. The Former Government Lawyer 179

ing to monopolize the nationwide market for city buses, we face appeals by GM from interlocutory orders deciding two bitterly contested pretrial, although unrelated, motions. The first is the City's successful motion to permit the suit to proceed as a class action; the second, GM's unsuccessful motion to have the City's privately-retained counsel, George D. Reycraft, disqualified for breach of the ethical precepts embodied in Canon 9 of the Code of Professional Responsibility. . . . With respect to the motion to disqualify counsel, however, we conclude, without intending to suggest any actual impropriety on the part of Reycraft, that his disqualification is required to "avoid even the appearance of professional impropriety." Accordingly, the court's order denying disqualification of Reycraft is reversed.

The facts necessary to an understanding of our disposition of these appeals have been gleaned, in the main, from the complaint and from the affidavits filed by the parties in support of and in opposition to the respective motions at issue. They are, thankfully, rather straightforward and, in all material respects, undisputed.

On October 4, 1972, the City filed a complaint alleging that GM had violated Section 2 of the Sherman Act by attempting to monopolize and monopolizing "trade and commerce in the manufacture and sale of city buses." The complaint contained, as a second cause of action, the allegation that GM had breached Section 7 of the Clayton Act by acquiring, in 1925, a controlling interest in Yellow Truck & Coach Manufacturing Co. [Yellow Coach] — an acquisition which purportedly "threatens substantially to lessen competition and to tend to create a monopoly in the manufacture and sale of buses within the United States. . . ." The action, furthermore, was commenced on behalf of a class consisting of "all non-federal governmental units and instrumentalities in the

United States which have purchased or have contributed to the purchase of city buses or city bus parts. . . ." The relief sought was, *inter alia,* for appropriate divestiture, treble damages, costs and attorneys' fees.

According to Reycraft's affidavit, filed in opposition to the disqualification motion, he was asked by the Office of the Corporation Counsel, sometime in July 1972, to assist in the preparation of the complaint. When approached by the Corporation Counsel, then J. Lee Rankin, Reycraft responded by informing Rankin of his prior and substantial involvement in an action brought by the United States against GM, under Section 2 of the Sherman Act, based on GM's alleged monopolization of a nationwide market for the manufacture and sale of city and intercity buses. *United States v. General Motors* (No. 15816, E.D. Mich. 1956) [1956 *Bus* case].

In his affidavit, Reycraft described his participation in the 1956 *Bus* case, and his work for the Antitrust Division of the Department of Justice, in these words:

> I was employed as an attorney for the Antitrust Division of the Department of Justice from the end of December, 1952 through the end of December, 1962. From sometime during the middle of 1954 through the end of 1962 I was employed in the Washington Office of the Antitrust Division. My initial assignment in the Washington Office of the Antitrust Division in 1954 was as a trial attorney in the General Litigation Section.
>
> One of my first assignments as a member of the General Litigation Section was to work on an investigation of alleged monopolization by General Motors of the city and intercity bus business. The chief counsel in that matter from at least 1954 until the case was settled by Consent Decree in 1965 was Walter D. Murphy. At

Problem 18. The Former Government Lawyer

no time was I in active charge of the case. *That investigation culminated in the complaint filed on July 6, 1956 which I signed and in the preparation of which I participated substantially.*

In 1958, I became Chief of the Special Trial Section of the Antitrust Division and no longer had any direct or indirect involvement with the 1956 *Bus* case. Subsequently in 1961 I became Chief of Section Operations of the Antitrust Division and had technical responsibility for all matters within the Washington Office of the Antitrust Division, including the 1956 *Bus* case. I have no recollection of any active participation on my part in the 1956 *Bus* case from 1958 through the time I departed from the Antitrust Division in December of 1962. The case was in the charge of Walter D. Murphy from its inception and he continued in charge until the Consent Decree was entered on December 31, 1965. (emphasis added)

In light of his substantial involvement as an employee of the Department of Justice in a matter which, at the very least, was similar to the dispute for which his retention was sought, Reycraft initially consulted his partners in the firm of Cadwalader, Wickersham & Taft and, subsequently, requested the advice of the Antitrust Division on the applicability of the Federal conflict of interest statute.[7] That statute, we note, is penal in nature and its prohibitory rules, only two in number, must therefore be specifically defined and strictly construed. With that in mind, the Justice Department had little difficulty in concluding that the statute placed no bar on Reycraft's employment by the City. Its response to Reycraft states, in pertinent part:

7. 18 U.S.C. §207.

It is clear that section 207(b) [which applies for only one year after separation from government employ] has no bearing on your case. As for section 207(a) [which applies only where the United States is a party or has a direct and substantial interest in the matter], although it appears that you participated personally and substantially in the case brought by the United States against General Motors, the Antitrust Division advises us that the United States will not be a party to or have a direct and substantial interest in the private antitrust suit by the City of New York against General Motors. Therefore, section 207(a) has no application.

Accordingly, with Cadwalader's approval and the absence of any barrier posed by federal law, Reycraft agreed to represent the City on a contingent fee basis, a not infrequent arrangement in actions where recovery is at the same time uncertain but potentially great. . . .

Turning to the disqualification motion, the district court recognized that DR9-101(B) requires Reycraft's disqualification, in order to avoid "even the appearance of impropriety," if his participation in this action would constitute "private employment in a matter in which he had substantial responsibility while he was a public employee." Since it was virtually conceded that Reycraft had "substantial responsibility" over the 1956 *Bus* case, the only questions which remained were whether his engagement to represent the City was "private employment," and whether the City's antitrust action was, for purposes of DR9-101(B), the same "matter" as the 1956 *Bus* case. Judge Carter answered both questions in the negative. . . .

We turn now to GM's unsuccessful motion to disqualify the City's privately-retained counsel, George Reycraft. It is necessary that we begin our discussion by

Problem 18. The Former Government Lawyer 183

focusing again on the language of Canon 9 of the Code of Professional Responsibility:

> A lawyer should avoid even the appearance of professional impropriety.

Providing a measure of specificity to this general caveat, DR9-101(B) commands:

> A lawyer shall not accept private employment in a matter in which he had substantial responsibility while he was a public employee.

The purpose behind this plain interdiction is not difficult to discern. Indeed, the City recognizes its salutary goal, as stated by the ABA Comm. on Professional Ethics, Opinions, No. 37 (1931) to be:

> [to avoid] the manifest possibility that . . . [a former Government lawyer's] action as a public legal official might be influenced (or open to the charge that it had been influenced) by the hope of later being employed privately to *uphold or upset* what he had done.

Id. at 124 (emphasis added). Viewed in this light, the question before us is whether Reycraft's decision to represent the City on a contingent fee basis in an antitrust suit strikingly similar, though perhaps not identical in every respect, to an antitrust action brought over his signature by the Department of Justice would raise an "appearance of impropriety," as private employment "to uphold . . . what he had done" as a Government lawyer. Unlike the court below, we are constrained to answer in the affirmative.

Before we commence our analysis, we would do well to recall the following description of our task:

> We approach our task as a reviewing court in this case conscious of our responsibility to preserve a balance, delicate though it may be, between an individual's right to his own freely chosen counsel [we do not presume the City to have a lesser right] and the need to maintain the highest ethical standards of professional responsibility. This balance is essential if the public's trust in the integrity of the Bar is to be preserved.

Emle Industries, Inc. v. Patentex, Inc., 478 F.2d 562, 564-65 (2d Cir. 1973).

Indeed, the "public's trust" is the raison d'être for Canon 9's "appearance-of-evil" doctrine. Now explicitly incorporated in the profession's ethical Code, this doctrine is directed at maintaining, in the public mind, a high regard for the legal profession. The standard it sets — i.e. what creates an appearance of evil — is largely a question of current ethical-legal mores. See Kaufman, The Former Government Attorney and the Canons of Professional Ethics, 70 Harv. L. Rev. 657, 660 (1957).

Nor can we overlook that the Code of Professional Responsibility is not designed for Holmes' proverbial "bad man" who wants to know just how many corners he may cut, how close to the line he may play, without running into trouble with the law. Holmes, The Path of the Law, in Collected Legal Papers 170 (1920). Rather, it is drawn for the "good man," as a beacon to assist him in navigating an ethical course through the sometimes murky waters of professional conduct. Accordingly, without in the least even intimating that Reycraft himself was improperly influenced while in Government service, or that he is guilty of any

Problem 18. The Former Government Lawyer

actual impropriety in agreeing to represent the City here, we must act with scrupulous care to avoid any *appearance* of impropriety lest it taint both the public and private segments of the legal profession.

It is undisputed that Reycraft had "substantial responsibility" in initiating the Government's Sherman §2 claim against GM for monopolizing or attempting to monopolize the nationwide market for city and intercity buses. Thus, we are left to determine whether the City's antitrust suit is the same "matter" as the Government's action and whether Reycraft's contingent fee arrangement with the City constitutes "private employment."

Directing our attention to the simpler question first, we are convinced beyond doubt that Reycraft's and, indeed, his firm's opportunity to earn a substantial fee for Reycraft's services is plainly "private employment" under DR9-101(B). The district judge apparently grounded his contrary decision on the rationale that Reycraft "has not changed sides" — i.e. "there is nothing antithetical in the postures of the two governments in the actions in question. . . ." But, as we have already noted, Opinion No. 37 of the ABA Commission on Professional Ethics unequivocally applies the ethical precepts of Canon 9 and DR9-101(B) irrespective of the side chosen in private practice. And see *Allied Realty of St. Paul v. Exchange Nat. Bank of Chicago,* 283 F.Supp. 464, 466 (D.Minn. 1968). We believe, moreover, that this is as it should be for there lurks great potential for lucrative returns in following into private practice the course already charted with the aid of governmental resources. And, with such a large contingent fee at stake, we could hardly accept "pro bono publico" as a proper characterization of Reycraft's work, simply because the keeper of the purse is the City of New York or other governmental entities in the class.

It is manifest also, from an examination of the respective complaints (see the appendix to this opinion [not reproduced here]), that the City's antitrust action is sufficiently similar to the 1956 *Bus* case to be the same "matter" under DR9-101(B). Indeed, virtually *every* overt act of attempted monopolization alleged in the City's complaint is lifted *in haec verba* from the Justice Department complaint. We cite, merely by way of illustration, paragraphs appearing in both complaints alleging the withdrawal of more than 20 companies from bus manufacturing, the coincidence of directors on the boards of GM and another bus manufacturer, the Flexible Company, and GM's acquisition of a controlling stock interest in Yellow Coach in 1925.

To be sure, as the City urges, the four-year statute of limitations, embodied in 15 U.S.C. §15b, requires the City to focus on market conditions since 1968, some ten years after Reycraft ceased his involvement in the *Bus* case. But, an equally essential element in proving a violation of Section 2 of the Sherman Act is either an intent to monopolize or an abuse of monopoly power. See *United States v. Grinnell Corp.*, 384 U.S. 563, 570-71 (1966); *Coniglio v. Highwood Services, Inc.*, slip op. at 2911, 2924 (2d Cir. Apr. 17, 1974); *United States v. Aluminum Co. of America,* 148 F.2d 416, 429-30 (2d Cir. 1945). Moreover, to decide the question whether GM is a passive recipient of monopoly power, a history of its operations will be imperative. See e.g. *United States v. Aluminum Co. of America, supra* (included an exhaustive study of Alcoa's operations from 1902 to the date of the lawsuit). Accordingly, at the very forefront of the City's case will be proof of alleged predatory practices amassed by the United States, with the substantial participation of Reycraft, when the Justice Department built its case against GM in 1956.

Problem 18. The Former Government Lawyer

The addition of the Clayton Act claim based solely on the same 1925 Yellow Coach acquisition which was part of the Sherman Act violation alleged by both the United States and the City, hardly alters the nuclear identity of these two suits. Both, after all, allege monopolization or attempted monopolization of the *same* product line — city buses — and, in the *same* geographic market — the United States. The subtleties of differential proof will not obviate the "appearance of impropriety" to an unsophisticated public. We opined in *Emle:*

> Nowhere is Shakespeare's observation that "there is nothing either good or bad but thinking makes it so," more apt than in the realm of ethical considerations.

Emle Industries, Inc. v. Patentex, Inc., supra, 478 F.2d at 571.

The City maintains, in the end, that if we reverse the court below and disqualify Reycraft, we will chill the ardor for Government service by rendering worthless the experience gained in Government employ. Indeed, the author of this opinion is hardly unaware of this claim, for he has cautioned:

> If the government service will tend to sterilize an attorney in too large an area of law for too long a time, or will prevent him from engaging in the practice of a technical specialty which he has devoted years in acquiring, and if that sterilization will spread to the firm with which he becomes associated, the sacrifice of entering government service will be too great for most men to make.

Kaufman, *supra,* 70 Harv. L. Rev. at 668. But, in that commentary, and the case upon which it was based (*United*

States v. Standard Oil Co. (N.J.), 136 F.Supp. 345 (S.D.N.Y. 1955) — *Esso Export Case*), the accommodation between maintaining high ethical standards for former Government employees, on the one hand, and encouraging entry into Government service, on the other, was struck under far different circumstances. Unlike the instant case, in which Reycraft's "substantial responsibility" in the *Bus* case is undisputed, the writer of this opinion concluded in *Esso Export* that the lawyer:

> never investigated or passed upon the subject matter of the pending case . . . never rendered or had any specific duty to render any legal advice in relation to the regulations involved in the litigation.

Kaufman, *supra*, 70 Harv. L. Rev. at 664. More to the point, therefore, is another admonition voiced in that article:

> If there was a likelihood that information *pertaining* to the pending matter reached the attorney, although he did not "investigate" or "pass upon" it, . . . there would undoubtedly be an appearance of evil if he were not disqualified.

Id. at 665 (emphasis added)

Esso Export unquestionably presented a case for the cautious application of the "appearance-of-evil doctrine," because the former Government lawyer's connection with the matter at issue was the tenuous one of mere employment in the same Government agency. If, for example, Reycraft had not worked on the 1956 *Bus* case, but was simply a member of the Antitrust Division at that time, a case not unlike *Esso Export* would be before us. To the contrary, however, Reycraft not only participated in the *Bus* case, but

Problem 18. The Former Government Lawyer 189

he signed the complaint in that action and admittedly had "substantial responsibility" in its investigatory and preparatory stages. Where the overlap of issues is so plain, and the involvement while in Government employ so direct, the resulting appearance of impropriety must be avoided through disqualification.

Accordingly, we . . . reverse the court's order denying disqualification of Reycraft.

BACKGROUND READING

A recent A.B.A. Opinion has interpreted DR9-101(B) and has considered such questions as: What constitutes "substantial responsibility"? What is "private employment"? What is "a matter"? How far does the disqualification of DR9-101(B) extend with regard to affiliated attorneys? Some of these issues are also discussed as they relate to the lawyer entering the government from private practice. A.B.A. Formal Opinion 342 (1975), 62 A.B.A. Journal 517 (1976).

PROBLEM 19

Structuring the Facts

The fine line between advising as to the law and suggesting perjury or false evidence.

John Wiggins is a lawyer specializing in tax matters. One day his seventy-year-old client, Henry Halloway, walks into Mr. Wiggins' office and says, "John, I haven't been feeling quite right lately. I guess I can't live forever. I'd like to transfer ownership in that Miracle Mile Shopping Center to my son. I know that if I hold on to it until I die, it will be included in my estate and we'll be hit with a large estate tax."

"You know, Henry," says Mr. Wiggins, "that a so-called 'gift in contemplation' of death is also included in your estate."

"I'm aware of that," replies Halloway. "That's why I'm here."

Scenario One

"My advice to you is that you investigate new business opportunities in Florida, consult with an architect about the construction of a new wing on your factory, and even talk to real estate brokers about buying a new cooperative apartment."

Problem 19. Structuring the Facts

"Why on earth should I do those things. I have no intention of following through on any of those things."

"Maybe not" advises Mr. Wiggins, "but they would sure indicate that you are contemplating living a long time."

Scenario Two

"Well, Henry, I'll have to look up the law on gifts in contemplation of death. Let's meet tomorrow."

The next day Mr. Wiggins advises his client as follows: "The key question is your state of mind at the time of the gift. This will, of course, be a question of fact, and you can be certain that if you die within three years after making the gift, the Internal Revenue Service will claim that it was in contemplation of death. Now, one's state of mind is a subjective concept, but the IRS, and the courts, often look to the actions of the decedent to help determine whether, at the time of the gift, the donor was contemplating death or life. For example, where the donor could show that he had been investigating new business opportunities, or that he had been consulting with an architect for the construction of a new wing on his factory, or that he had been talking to real estate brokers about the purchase of a new cooperative apartment — these have been strong evidentiary considerations in support of the claim that living, rather than dying, was very much in the donor's mind."

"That's very helpful, John," says Mr. Halloway. "I feel better already."

1. Is the first scenario unethical?
2. Ethically, does it differ from the second?

ASSIGNMENT

Canon 7; EC7-6; DR7-102(A)(6) and (7).

BACKGROUND READING

Freedman, Lawyers' Ethics in an Adversary System 59-77 (Bobbs-Merrill, 1975); Noonan, The Purposes of Advocacy and the Limits of Confidentiality, 64 Mich. L. Rev. 1485 (1966); Sellin, Professional Responsibility of the Tax Practitioner, 31 N.Y.U. Inst. on Fed. Taxation 9-11 (1973).

PROBLEM 20

Responsibilities of Advisors to Non-clients

Is there a special responsibility owed by lawyers when they render opinions which will be relied on by third parties?
Is there a responsibility to inform law enforcement officials about a client's illegal conduct when others are being harmed?
Does the lawyer have a responsibility to investigate facts in order to protect persons other than the client?

The firm of Stringer and Fones handles securities and general corporate matters for Interstate Industries, a publicly held conglomerate corporation whose stock is widely traded on major stock exchanges. Among its other business operations, Interstate has a wholly owned subsidiary, American Castings Corp., which is engaged in the manufacture and sale of brass plumbing fixtures.

The federal securities laws require a form (10K) to be submitted each year to the SEC indicating any material changes in the registrant's business, including information regarding "the sources and availability of raw materials essential to the business." A young associate in the law firm usually prepares the form, although it is filed by the corporation.

Just prior to the filing of the form, a vice president of Interstate informs the associate that a plant in Italy which supplies brass forgings for hundreds of the products of American Castings Corp., the manufacturing subsidiary, is having serious labor difficulties. In the light of the generally chaotic labor conditions in Italy, there is serious doubt about the factory's continued availability as a source of supply. The associate promptly notifies Dorothy Stringer, a senior partner in the firm, who immediately phones Ralph Whitney, the president of Interstate.

"What about the situation in Italy?" Ms. Stringer asks Mr. Whitney.

"Nothing serious," he replies. "It will get settled."

"Do you think it's a 'material' change in condition?"

"Absolutely not. I'm the best judge of that and I tell you there is nothing to be concerned about. And besides, we're negotiating the sale of that manufacturing subsidiary and this would make the buyer nervous for no reason at all."

If Ms. Stringer had investigated the matter by calling the plant manager in Italy, she would have learned that a partial strike had already begun, that the union was led by a politically radical clique that didn't really care whether the plant remained in business or not, and that many of the workers had already started looking for new jobs.

Form 10K is completed by the law firm and filed by the corporation without the disclosure of the labor situation in Italy. The report contains generally favorable financial information and Interstate's stock rises moderately in price, resisting a general market downswing.

Several weeks later, at an Interstate staff party in New

Problem 20. Responsibilities of Advisors to Non-clients

York, Ms. Stringer meets Frank DiCesare, manager of the Italian plant who reveals the details of the seriousness of the labor situation. He tells her that the work stoppage is now about seventy-five percent effective and that they think the situation will get worse.

The next day Ms. Stringer confronts Mr. Whitney with these facts.

"Did you know about the seriousness of the labor situation in Italy?" she asks.

"Well, I knew that there was no picnic over there."

"Did you know it when I first asked you about it?"

"Look, I told you I thought that it wasn't a 'material' change in condition, and I still stick by that. The plant is still in production, the strike will get settled, and it's important that we don't rock the boat on the sale of American Castings."

As negotiations for the sale of the subsidiary reach the final stage, the prospective buyer asks for an opinion from Interstate's counsel, Stringer and Fones, that all data required to be filed with the SEC, with regard to the subsidiary, have been filed. Copies of such data are also requested. Stringer and Fones provide such an opinion and attach a copy of the above-mentioned form.

The sale of American Castings is consummated. A few weeks later the plant in Italy shuts down completely, shutting off the supply of the forged component parts. This causes an almost complete termination of the manufacturing operations of Interstate's former subsidiary, a decline in its income and a severe drop on the market price of the securites of the purchaser, which are also publicly held.

1. Should Ms. Stringer have investigated the Italian labor situation further before preparing Interstate's 10K form for filing?

Part IV. Special Problems of Government Lawyers

2. Should she have done so before preparing the opinion requested by the purchaser of American Castings Corp.?

3. When, if at all, should the law firm have disclosed the facts to the Interstate Board of Directors, the SEC or the purchaser of American Castings?

4. When, if at all, should the firm have resigned from further representation of Interstate?

ASSIGNMENT

Canon 4; EC4-1, EC4-2, EC4-3, EC4-4, EC4-5; DR4-101(A), (B) and (C).
Canon 6; EC6-4, EC6-5; DR6-101(A).
　　　DR7-102(B).
Also read the material which follows:
1. A.B.A. Formal Opinion 341 (1975).
2. *SEC v. Spectrum, Ltd.*
3. Excerpts from the SEC's complaint in the National Student Marketing proceeding. The complaint states allegations only and should not be viewed as a statement of proven facts. Particularly noteworthy, for purposes of this problem, are the allegations against the law firm of White and Case as set forth in paragraph 48 of the complaint. The complaint has generated much discussion. See background reading at the end of assignment.
4. Statement of Policy Adopted by American Bar Association Regarding Responsibilities and Liabilities of Lawyers in Advising with Respect to the Compliance by Clients with Laws Administered by the Securities and Exchange Commission. Adopted August 12, 1975.

Problem 20. Responsibilities of Advisors to Non-clients

A.B.A. Formal Opinion 341
(September 30, 1975)

This opinion is made in response to several inquiries regarding the effect of the February, 1974, amendment to Disciplinary Rule 7-102(B), which presently reads: "(B) A lawyer who receives information clearly establishing that (1) His client has, in the course of the representation, perpetrated a fraud upon a person or tribunal shall promptly call upon his client to rectify the same, and if his client refuses or is unable to do so, he shall reveal the fraud to the affected person or tribunal, *except when the information is protected as a privileged communication.*" [Italicized language added by amendment February, 1974.][1]

---

1. Compare Rule 11, Code of Trial Conduct of the American College of Trial Lawyers (1971): "(d) Subject to whatever qualifications may exist from the confidential privilege that exists between a lawyer and his client, the lawyer should expose without fear before the proper tribunals perjury, subornation of perjury and any professional misconduct."

See Casenote, 50 Tex. L. Rev. 1265 (1972), for a view critical of D.R.7-102(B)(1) prior to its amendment.

Some commentators are concerned that the 1974 amendment might encourage lawyers to refuse to reveal communications that are not within the attorney-client privilege; however, the rule exempts from disclosure only confidences and secrets. Other commentators seem concerned that even with the amendment there is too heavy a burden upon a lawyer to reveal a client's misconduct; see, e.g., Lipman, The SEC's Reluctant Police Force: A New Role for Lawyers, 49 N.Y.U.L. Rev. 437 (1974); Monroe Freedman, Legal Ethics, N.Y.L.J., July 24, 1974; Freedman, Letter to Editor, 59 A.B.A.J. 114 (1973) (reporting the rejection of the original version of D.R.7-102(B)(1) when the C.P.R. was adopted in the District of Columbia).

Part IV. Special Problems of Government Lawyers

The derivation of D.R.7-102(B)(1) is informative. The prior American Bar Association Canons of Professional Ethics contained three mandatory revelation rules: Canon 1 (complaint against judge), Canon 29 (exposing dishonest conduct of lawyers and exposing perjury), and Canon 41 (informing injured person of fraud or deception by client). In the Code of Professional Responsibility, D.R.1-103 contains a duty to reveal knowledge of misconduct by judge or lawyer.[2] But the preliminary draft of the Code of Professional Responsibility (January, 1969) did not contain a disciplinary rule requiring a lawyer to reveal misconduct of a client.

Perhaps the omission was due to the committee's consideration of the high fiduciary duty owed by lawyer to client and consideration of the firm support found in the law of evidence for the attorney-client privilege. The preliminary draft contained a disciplinary rule virtually identical to present D.R.4-101(C), forbidding a lawyer, with certain exceptions, from knowingly revealing a confidence or secret of his client.[3] Some lawyers objected, however, to the preliminary draft because it did not carry into the Code of Professional Responsibility the substance of prior Canon 41. The result was the addition to the Code of Professional Responsibility, at that time, of D.R.7-102(B).

When D.R.7-102(B) was added to the Code of Professional Responsibility prior to its adoption in August, 1969, the full significance of D.R.4-101(C) apparently was not appreciated, even though the preliminary draft contained a virtually identical provision stating that "[a] lawyer may

---

2. D.R.7-108(G), revealing misconduct regarding juror, and D.R.7-102(B)(2), revealing fraud on tribunal by one other than client, are other revelation rules contained in the Code of Professional Responsibility.

3. D.R.5-101(A), (B), (C), and (E), Preliminary Draft, C.P.R., are identical, except for minor textual changes, with D.R.4-101(A), (B), (C), and (D).

Problem 20. Responsibilities of Advisors to Non-clients

reveal . . . [c]onfidences or secrets when permitted [under] Disciplinary Rules or required by law or court order."[4] That provision of D.R.4-101(C), while quite proper in the preliminary draft, had the unacceptable result when combined with new D.R.7-102(B)(1) of requiring a lawyer in certain instances to reveal privileged communications which he also was duty bound not to reveal according to the law of evidence. The amendment of February, 1974, was necessary in order to relieve lawyers of exposure to such diametrically opposed professional duties.

A similar impasse arising under the prior Canons of Professional Ethics was considered by this committee in Formal Opinion 287 (1953). Then Canon 37 required a lawyer to "preserve his client's confidences," although Canon 29 required a lawyer to reveal perjury to the prosecuting authorities and Canon 41 required a lawyer to inform against his client in certain circumstances in regard to "fraud or deception." The situation in Opinion 287 was that of a client who had committed perjury (which we assume constituted intrinsic fraud upon the tribunal) during the trial of his divorce action. Three months later the client sought advice from the same lawyer who had represented him in the divorce action. The advice was sought in regard to a dispute with his former wife over support money; in connection with this consultation the client told the lawyer that he had given false material testimony in the divorce action in which he had been represented by the same lawyer. Tracing the background of the evidentiary law concerning the attorney-client privilege, this committee held that the duty of the lawyer to preserve his client's confidences prevailed over the duty under Canon

---

4. In the preliminary draft, "by" rather than "under" was used. The rule appeared as 4-101(C)(2) in the preliminary draft.

41 to reveal fraud or deception, and over the duty under Canon 29 to bring knowledge of perjury to the attention of others. In Opinion 287 it was said that the lawyer, "despite Canons 29 and 41, should not disclose the facts to the court or to the authorities."[5]

One effect of the 1974 amendment to D.R.7-102(B)(1) is to reinstate the essence of Opinion 287 which had prevailed from 1953 until 1969. It was as unthinkable then as now that a lawyer should be subject to disciplinary action for failing to reveal information which by law is not to be revealed without the consent of the client, and the lawyer is not now in that untenable position. The lawyer no longer can be confronted with the necessity of either breaching his client's privilege at law or breaching a disciplinary rule.[6]

While the derivation of D.R.7-102(B)(1) indicates the necessity for the 1974 amendment, the scope of the 1974 amendment can be indicated only by considering the coverage of the basic requirement of D.R.7-102(B)(1) and by examining the interrelation of D.R.7-102(B)(1) and D.R.4-101. The conflicting duties to reveal fraud and to preserve confidences have existed side-by-side for some time.

However, it is clear that there has long been an accommodation in favor of preserving confidences either through practice or interpretation. Through the bar's interpretation in practice of its responsibility to preserve confidences and secrets of clients, and through its interpretations like Formal

---

5. See also New Jersey Ethics Opinion 163 (1969), 92 N.J.L.J. 825, citing A.B.A. Opinion 287 with approval.

6. A lawyer who breaches his fiduciary duty to client by revealing confidences protected by the attorney-client privilege may be liable to client in tort. He also may be guilty of a crime in some jurisdictions. See Weinberg, Confidential and Other Communications 16 (1967).

Problem 20. Responsibilities of Advisors to Non-clients

Opinion 287, significant exceptions to any general duty to reveal fraud have been long accepted. Apparently, the exceptions were so broad or the policy underlying the duty to reveal so weak that the earlier drafts of the Code of Professional Responsibility omitted altogether the concept embodied in Canon 41. Nonetheless, D.R.7-102(B) is a part of the Code of Professional Responsibility and must be given some meaning. Some of the exceptions to a general duty to reveal have been built into the disciplinary rule itself (for example, that the information must "clearly establish" fraud; that it must be received "in the course of representation" and (since 1974) that it must not be information "protected as a privileged communication").

Formal Opinion 287, which dealt with a lawyer's duty to reveal a perjury committed earlier by his client, represents merely one of the exceptions to old Canon 41 (it also pertained to old Canon 29, dealing with revealing perjury to the affected tribunal). We do not think that Formal Opinion 287 was intended to be an *exclusive* exception to old Canon 41. Accordingly, limiting the 1974 amendment to matters of attorney-client privilege covered in Formal Opinion 287 will not necessarily bring D.R.7-102 into line with past interpretations of a lawyer's duty when a client's confidences and secrets are involved.

The tradition (which is backed by substantial policy considerations) that permits a lawyer to assure a client that information (whether a confidence or a secret) given to him will not be revealed to third parties is so important that it should take precedence, in all the most serious cases, over the duty imposed by D.R.7-102(B). The many annotations to D.R.4-101 reflect this policy. Of course, there will be situations where a lawyer may reveal the secrets and confidences of his client. Some of these are recognized in D.R.4-101(C).

The balancing of the lawyer's duty to preserve confidences and to reveal frauds is best made by interpreting the phrase "privileged communication" in the 1974 amendment to D.R.7-102(B) as referring to those confidences and secrets that are required to be preserved by D.R.4-101.

Such an interpretation does not wipe out D.R.7-102(B), because D.R.7-102(B) applies to information received from any source, and it is not limited to information gained in the professional relationship as is D.R.4-101. Under the suggested interpretation, the duty imposed by D.R.7-102(B) would remain in force if the information clearly establishing a fraud on a person or tribunal and committed by a client in the course of representation were obtained by the lawyer from a third party (but not in connection with his professional relationship with the client), because it would not be a confidence or secret of a client entitled to confidentiality. D.R.4-102(C) sets out several circumstances under which revelation of a secret or confidence is permissible, and thus in cases where these exceptions apply, D.R.7-102(B) may make the optional disclosure of information under D.R.4-101 a mandatory one. For example, when disclosure is required by a law, the "privileged communication" exception of D.R.7-102(B) is not applicable and disclosure may be required.

An interpretation of the 1974 amendment which would limit its scope to the attorney-client privilege as it exists in each jurisdiction and under the Federal Rules of Evidence is undesirable because the lawyer's ethical duty would depend upon the rules of evidence in a particular jurisdiction. There may be significant problems in knowing which jurisdiction's evidentiary rule would be applied in a given case, and

Problem 20. Responsibilities of Advisors to Non-clients

the scope of that privilege may vary widely among jurisdictions.[7] Furthermore, limiting the 1974 amendment to the scope of the attorney-client privilege raises problems as to the difference between waiver of privilege by a client and a consent to the lawyer's disclosure of a confidence.

It is not reasonable to put a lawyer at peril of discipline if, after determining that he has information that "clearly" establishes fraud (a difficult task in itself), he must also determine the relevant rule of attorney-client privilege in order to determine whether he must reveal the client's confidences and secrets. Also, we believe that it is inconsistent with the lawyer's confidential relationship with his client to impose at the same time a duty to evaluate the client's confidences to determine whether the level of evidence of "fraud" has been reached that would require disclosure of such confidences. The lawyer's problem is not lessened, in this respect, by interpreting fraud in D.R.7-102(B), as we do, as being used in the sense of active fraud, with a requirement of *scienter* or intent to deceive.

The interpretation here adopted by the committee, which would preserve confidential information received in connection with the professional relationship, minimizes the problems. The committee believes that this interpretation does not go too far in relieving a lawyer of any responsibility to others because it does not alter the standing sanctions against the lawyer's involvement in a fraud nor alter the lawyer's duty under D.R.7-102(B) when his information is obtained outside the confidential relationship.

---

7. Compare Rule 5-3 of the Federal Rules of Evidence with the Texas rule discussed in Opinion 378 of the State Bar of Texas (1975).

SEC v. Spectrum, Ltd.
489 F.2d 535 (2d Cir. 1973)

KAUFMAN, Ch. J. The securities laws provide a myriad of safeguards designed to protect the interests of the investing public. Effective implementation of these safeguards, however, depends in large measure on the members of the bar who serve in an advisory capacity to those engaged in securities transactions. The standard of diligence demanded of the legal profession to meet this responsibility is a matter on which we are required to comment in the resolution of this appeal.

On April 2, 1971, the Securities and Exchange Commission [SEC] filed a complaint charging twelve defendants, including the appellee, Stuart Schiffman, with participation in a partially successful scheme to distribute over one million unregistered shares of the common stock of Spectrum, Ltd. in violation of the registration provisions of the Securities Act of 1933 [the 1933 Act] (15 U.S.C. §77e) and the antifraud provisions of that Act (15 U.S.C. §77q(a)) and of the Securities Exchange Act of 1934 [the 1934 Act] (15 U.S.C. §78j(b)). Although the Commission has obtained permanent injunctions against at least ten of the defendants, it was unsuccessful in its effort to gain preliminary injunctive relief against Schiffman, an attorney who allegedly prepared an opinion letter on the basis of which some of the unregistered securities were sold. Judge Tenney, after reviewing the affidavits, cross-affidavits, exhibits, and depositions filed by the SEC and by Schiffman, denied the SEC's request

Problem 20. Responsibilities of Advisors to Non-clients

for an evidentiary hearing, on the grounds that there were no material facts in dispute, and concluded that Schiffman's conduct, although perhaps negligent, did not rise to a violation of the securities laws. Upon a careful examination of the record, we find the existence of a highly material factual conflict. Accordingly, we reverse and remand to Judge Tenney for an evidentiary hearing in which the disputed issues can be resolved.

I.

A detailed account of the intricacies of the multi-party stock manipulation venture which prompted this action, the principal features of which were unchallenged below, is set forth in the extensive supporting affidavit filed by the SEC. . . .

In September, 1969, Louis Marder, representing the Westward Investment Corporation, and Bernard Goldenberg and Joseph Dye, representing Spectrum, Ltd., agreed to a merger of Westward into Spectrum. The purpose of this merger was to provide a vehicle for the distribution of unregistered Spectrum securities which could later be sold to an unwitting public.

Section 5(c) of the 1933 Act states that "it shall be unlawful for any person, directly or indirectly . . . to sell . . . any security unless a registration statement has been filed as to such security." 15 U.S.C. §77(e). To avoid this registration requirement, a plan was devised, principally by Marder and Goldenberg, which relied on a two-step procedure for securing exemption from Section 5. First, a large block of unregistered Spectrum common stock would be issued to the shareholders of Westward in the merger of Westward into Spectrum. This stock would be exempt from the registration mandate of Section 5 pursuant to Commission Rule 133,[5] which provided that the exchange of shares between a surviving corporation and the shareholders of a disappearing corporation in the course of a merger would not be considered a "sale" within the purview of Section 5. Second, under Section 4(1) of the 1933 Act, the recipients of this unregistered Spectrum stock would be able to dispose of these securities, again without the filing of a registration statement as a predicate to the transaction, as long as the seller was not deemed to be "an issuer, underwriter or dealer" under the Act.

For Marder, who controlled Westward, successful implementation of this plan presented one obvious stumbling block — Rule 133 classified a controlling shareholder of the "constituent corporation" (Westward) as an "underwriter" and, therefore, a person not qualified for exemption under Section 4(1). Accordingly, prior to the merger Marder commenced distributing some of his Westward shares to various friends, many of whom, as the court below found, were in fact unaware of their status as Westward shareholders. Following the merger, Marder intended to effect the sale of the Spectrum stock received by his acquaintances in transactions which, because of the stock's nominal ownership by noncontrolling former Westward shareholders, would appear to satisfy the criteria for a Section 4(1) exemption.

The stage was set for the successful charade upon consummation of the Spectrum-Westward merger on November 10, 1969. Of the 4,596,465 shares of Spectrum stock issued in the exchange, approximately one million shares went to

---

5. 17 CFR §230.133 (1973). Rule 133 was rescinded effective January 1, 1973. 37 Fed. Reg. 23636 (1972). It has been replaced by Rule 145, 17 C.F.R. §230.145 (1973), which no longer provides a registration exemption for securities issued in the course of a merger.

Problem 20. Responsibilities of Advisors to Non-clients

Marder's corps of nominees. By obtaining the necessary stock powers from these individuals, Marder was in a position to begin the illicit sale of unregistered Spectrum securities.

On the day of the merger, November 10, Spectrum's general counsel, Morton Berger, wrote an opinion letter to Spectrum's transfer agent in which he instructed the agent on the proper classification of the Spectrum shares then being issued. Berger's letter, based upon representations by Goldenberg and Marder, included his opinion that the merger complied with the requirements of Rule 133 and that certain recipients of the newly-issued Spectrum stock should receive shares labelled "restricted" — i.e. not for public sale — because these former Westward shareholders, whom Berger listed, were considered to be "underwriters" pursuant to Rule 133(c). Berger concluded his letter by opining that the remaining former Westward shareholders, whose names Berger did not recite, could be issued Spectrum securities without a restrictive legend.

On November 25, 1969, Berger wrote a second letter, this time to the president of Spectrum, in which he listed those persons who had received unrestricted shares of Spectrum stock pursuant to the merger. This letter, however, was not in the form of an opinion letter.

Retracing our steps, on November 13 and November 28, 1969, Marder delivered for sale a total of 125,000 shares of unrestricted Spectrum stock, nominally owned by William and John Doyen, to Michael Gardner, a principal at the registered broker-dealer firm of Gardner Securities. Gardner balked at the sale of these unregistered securities, despite their unrestricted nature, insisting upon an opinion letter which stated that these shares were considered exempt from the registration requirements of Section 5. Although Marder possessed the Berger letters of November 10 and November 25, Gardner viewed them as insufficient, apparently because the November 10 letter failed to specify the individuals entitled to exemption, while the November 25 letter did not purport to be an opinion letter.

Although Gardner called Berger about preparing the requisite opinion letter, Berger refused to issue such a letter on behalf of any shareholder. Because of this refusal, Gardner communicated with Schiffman stating that he wished to discuss a securities matter the details of which Gardner failed to provide on the telephone. Schiffman responded by meeting Gardner at his office.

It is at this juncture — Schiffman's debut so to speak — that the crucial factual controversy arises. According to Schiffman's affidavit submitted in opposition to the motion for a preliminary injunction, he visited Gardner's office twice in late November. On the first occasion, he and Gardner spoke in general terms about Gardner's securities business and Gardner introduced him to James Morse, one of Gardner's clients. At the second meeting, several days later, Morse was again present at Gardner's office. On this occasion, Morse mentioned that a friend of his, a Mr. Doyen, was in need of some help and asked Schiffman if he would speak to Doyen. After Schiffman agreed, Morse telephoned Doyen. Morse handed the instrument to Schiffman and Doyen proceeded to explain to Schiffman that he owned some unregistered stock in Spectrum, Ltd. for which he wanted an opinion letter that would indicate that the securities could be sold without registration. Schiffman allegedly responded that since he had no knowledge of the underlying transactions, he would be hesitant to write such a letter. But, Schiffman claims that his reluctance was overcome when Morse showed him the two Berger letters.

Problem 20. Responsibilities of Advisors to Non-clients

Schiffman then proceeded to advise Doyen that he would prepare an opinion letter which would "verify" Berger's opinion.

Schiffman's version of these meetings at Gardner's office is sharply in conflict with Gardner's recollection of the events, as described in his affidavit submitted by the SEC. Gardner recalls only one meeting with Schiffman at which not only Morse was present but Louis Marder as well. Gardner's affidavit then notes, quite specifically, that

> I [Gardner] introduced Schiffman to Marder and Morse for the purpose of Schiffman representing Marder and Morse. Marder and Morse asked Schiffman, in my presence, to prepare an opinion letter for securities of Spectrum that were going to be sold *by Marder and Morse.* [emphasis added]

The affidavit concludes with the statement:

> I do not recall at any time . . . Morse telephoning one William Doyen, giving the telephone to Schiffman, and Schiffman speaking to Doyen about an opinion letter to be prepared by Schiffman concerning either Doyen's stock, or any other stock.

In any event, Gardner was evidently satisfied that Schiffman would write the opinion letter because, sometime before its preparation, he proceeded to sell 50,000 shares of Spectrum stock jointly owned by the Doyens. As for Schiffman, he claims to have arranged a conference with Berger so that he could learn more about the Spectrum stock for which he had agreed to write an opinion letter.

What transpired at this meeting between Schiffman and Berger is also the subject of conflicting documentary versions. Both men agree that Berger gave Schiffman the two letters dated November 10 and November 25. Berger, however, in his affidavit submitted in the preliminary injunction proceeding, added that he warned Schiffman that he "suspected that this stock [the unregistered Spectrum securities] was going to be traded by a control person and therefore the stock should not be freely traded." This account did not appear in Berger's two prior depositions, also part of the record below. Schiffman, on the other hand, in his reply affidavit, denied that Berger uttered any warning whatsoever.

It is uncontroverted that following this meeting Schiffman prepared an opinion letter which closely paralleled the Berger opinion letter of November 10 with one key addition — it contained the names of those shareholders, mentioned only as a group by Berger, who could sell their Spectrum stock in a transaction exempt from the registration requirement of Section 5. Although Schiffman's letter, dated December 4, was addressed to Doyen, Schiffman delivered it to Gardner's office because Schiffman had never received Doyen's address. Subsequently, on December 8, Schiffman sent a second letter to Doyen, again through Gardner's office, in which Schiffman stated that his opinion letter of December 4 was not to be used for the sale of unregistered Spectrum stock. No such caveat, however, was incorporated in the December 4 letter.

The use to which Schiffman's opinion letter of December 4 was put is a matter of some uncertainty. The SEC has alleged that in January, 1970, Marder showed the Schiffman letter to "Canadian citizen #1" in order to assure this anonymous Canadian that the Spectrum shares that he had agreed to purchase from Marder could be traded without registration. The SEC charges that "Canadian citizen #1"

Problem 20. Responsibilities of Advisors to Non-clients   211

subsequently sold 15,000 shares of this unregistered Spectrum stock in the Canadian market. Although these allegations were never contested by Schiffman, they also remain unsupported by any independent evidence.

Eighteen months after this documentary joust commenced, Judge Tenney, on October 10, 1972, denied the SEC's request for a preliminary injunction to enjoin Schiffman from further violations of §§5(a), 5(c) and 17(a) of the 1933 Act and §10(b) of the 1934 Act. He concluded that there was no evidence, apart from the bare allegations by the SEC, that any unregistered Spectrum stock had been sold on the basis of Schiffman's opinion letter. Recognizing that Schiffman might still have violated the securities laws as an aider and abettor, the district court, after pronouncing a standard of liability which required actual knowledge of the illegal scheme, found a dearth of credible evidence in the papers before him to sustain a finding of such knowledge on Schiffman's part. Judge Tenney finally noted that even if Schiffman were considered negligent in preparing his opinion letter, there had been no showing that, unless enjoined, he would be likely to run afoul of the law in the future.

II.

We should note, at the outset, that had the denial of temporary injunctive relief been based solely on the failure to demonstrate a propensity for future violations, we would hesitate before disturbing such conclusion. . . . Judge Tenney, however, went well beyond this rationale, finding no evidence whatsoever of any violation, nor even sufficient factual uncertainty to justify an evidentiary hearing. It is especially as to this latter holding, the declination to hold an evidentiary hearing, that we find error for we believe that the district judge failed to properly heed our admonition that "a judge should not resolve a factual dispute on affidavits or depositions, for then he is merely showing a preference for 'one piece of paper to another.' . . ." . . .

On Schiffman's part, he has steadfastly maintained that he was ignorant of the Marder plan. Yet, these protestations of innocence are met squarely on two fronts — by the affidavits of Gardner and Berger. Although we do not disagree with the district court that the Berger affidavit would seem to be incredible on its face in light of Berger's failure to make any mention of his alleged warning to Schiffman in the course of two prior depositions, we cannot overlook the dispute between Gardner and Schiffman over the events and participants at the crucial meeting at Gardner's office in late November, 1969. If Gardner's statement that Marder personally asked Schiffman for an opinion letter so that Marder could sell unregistered Spectrum stock is true — and only a hearing could determine this — then Schiffman's claim of unawareness of the Scheme would appear thin. To be sure, Gardner's veracity may be questioned, but no more nor less than Schiffman's in view of Schiffman's stake in the outcome of this lawsuit. Accordingly, since oral testimony is a medium far superior for evaluating credibility than the cold written word, we consider an evidentiary hearing essential to the proper disposition of this case. . . .

III.

Since our decision necessitates further proceedings in the lower court, we would be remiss if we failed to comment on the appropriate rule of law to be applied by the district judge. Judge Tenney properly recognized that if Schiffman's opinion letter were in fact used to sell unregistered Spectrum stock in violation of Section 5, although his status as an "underwriter" might be uncertain, he could be liable, never-

Problem 20. Responsibilities of Advisors to Non-clients 213

theless, as an aider and abettor to Marder's illicit venture. . . . In assessing liability as an aider and abettor, however, the district judge formulated a requisite standard of culpability — actual knowledge of the improper scheme plus an intent to further that scheme — which we find to be a sharp and unjustified departure from the negligence standard which we have repeatedly held to be sufficient in the context of enforcement proceedings seeking equitable or prophylactic relief. . . .

We do not believe, moreover, that imposition of a negligence standard with respect to the conduct of a secondary participant is overly strict, at least in the context of this case. The legal profession plays a unique and pivotal role in the effective implementation of the securities laws. Questions of compliance with the intricate provisions of these statutes are ever present and the smooth functioning of the securities markets will be seriously disturbed if the public cannot rely on the expertise proffered by an attorney when he renders an opinion on such matters. Schiffman, himself, realized that his opinion letter of December 4 could be used in due course to sell unregistered securities and sought to prevent that use by his subsequent letter to Doyen of December 8. This belated effort was ineffectual, however, since the limitation expressed in the second letter could hardly affect the potency of the December 4 opinion letter which remained unrestricted on its face.

We do not find persuasive the argument by one recent commentator that since "the alleged aider and abettor will merely be engaging in customary business activities, such as loaning money, managing a corporation, preparing financial statements, distributing press releases, completing brokerage transactions, or giving legal advice, [a requirement that he] investigate the ultimate activities of the party whom he is assisting [may impose] a burden . . . upon business activities that is too great." Ruder, Multiple Defendants in Securities Law Fraud Cases: Aiding and Abetting, Conspiracy, In Pari Delicto, Indemnification and Contribution, 120 U. Pa. L. Rev. 597, 632-633 (1972). In the distribution of unregistered securities, the preparation of an opinion letter is too essential and the reliance of the public too high to permit due diligence to be cast aside in the name of convenience. The public trust demands more of its legal advisers than "customary" activities which prove to be careless. And, to be sure, where expediency precludes thorough investigation, an attorney can prevent the illicit use of his opinion letter by prohibiting its utilization in the sale of unregistered securities by a statement to that effect clearly appearing on the face of the letter.

Nor does Professor Ruder's analogy to the strict scienter requirement for *criminal* liability of an aider and abettor seem appropriate to gauge the quality of conduct sufficient to warrant injunctive relief in a civil action. *Cf. United States v. Peoni,* 100 F.2d 401, 402 (2d Cir. 1938). The disparate consequences cannot be glossed over when striking the balance between private rights and the public interest.

We could not conclude without emphasizing that the standard of culpability we find appropriate for the author of an opinion letter in an action for injunctive relief only should not be construed to apply to more peripheral participants in an illicit scheme or, for that matter, to criminal prosecutions or private suits for damages. Those questions are not before us.

Nor do we suggest that the degree of scienter may not be highly relevant to a determination of whether the defendant has the propensity to commit future violations, a requisite to injunctive relief. In this regard, the SEC has indicated

Problem 20. Responsibilities of Advisors to Non-clients

on this appeal that, subsequent to the argument of the instant case in the district court, Schiffman has been enjoined for violations of the securities laws on two separate occasions and has pleaded guilty to a third such violation. On remand of this case, we can see no reason for precluding the SEC from introducing this evidence on the propensity issue.

For the reasons stated, the order of the district court is reversed and the case remanded for further proceedings....

SEC v. National Student Marketing Corp.
Civil Action No. 225-72 (Feb. 3, 1972, D.D.C.)

COMPLAINT

The Defendants

Defendant NSMC, which has approximately 2,400 stockholders, is a corporation . . . which now maintains its principal place of business at 175 West Jackson Boulevard, Chicago, Illinois. . . . The fraudulent scheme which is the subject of this complaint commenced in 1968 and resulted in the issuance of approximately 11,200,000 shares of unregistered securities of NSMC between the fall of 1968 and June 1970 in 83 separate transactions. During this period of time the price of NSMC's stock ranged from a low of $6.00 per share, the initial public offering price in April 1968, to a high of $144.00 per share on December 15, 1969 (reported as $72.00 per share after the first 2 for 1 split in December 1968 but before the second split in December 1969). On Feb. 1, 1972, NSMC's stock was quoted at 2¼ bid, 2½ asked....

Defendant PMM is a national firm of certified public accountants with a local office at 1025 Connecticut Avenue,

N. W., Washington, D.C. Defendant PMM has been defendant NSMC's independent auditors for the fiscal years ended August 31, 1968 and 1969, and December 31, 1969 and 1970 and issued opinions as to the fairness of the financial position of defendant NSMC as of the four above noted dates and on the results of operations for the periods then ended. . . .

Defendant White & Case is a law firm with offices at 14 Wall Street, New York, New York, and has been a law firm representing defendant NSMC since approximately August 1968.

Defendant Epley, who resides at 30 Summit Avenue, Bronxville, New York, has been a partner of the law firm of White & Case since July 1, 1969. . . .

48. On October 31, 1969, at the closing of the merger between defendant NSMC and Interstate defendants NSMC [National Student Marketing Corporation], Randell, Davies, Joy, White & Case, Epley, Brown, Allison, Bach, Tate, Lord, Bissell & Brook, Meyer and Schauer received a comfort letter ("comfort letter") from PMM [the accounting firm of Peat, Marwick, Mitchell and Co.]. The comfort letter, a condition of the merger was required to state that PMM had no reason to believe that unaudited interim financial statements of NSMC as of May 31, 1969 and for the nine months then ended were not prepared in accordance with generally accepted accounting principles and practices or required any material adjustments in order that the results of operations of NSMC be fairly presented. In addition the comfort letter was to state that NSMC had not suffered any material adverse change in its financial position or results of operations from May 31, 1969 until five business days prior to the effective date of the merger. Unaudited financial statements of NSMC for the nine-month period ended May 31, 1969 were contained in the proxy soliciting material which was mailed

Problem 20. Responsibilities of Advisors to Non-clients 217

to the shareholders of NSMC and Interstate in seeking their approval of, among other things, the merger between NSMC and Interstate. These financial statements reflected net earnings of NSMC of approximately $700,000. At the time, Interstate had approximately 1200 shareholders. As a result of the merger, the shareholders of Interstate sold their shares in Interstate and received in exchange approximately 1,650,000 shares of NSMC.

(a) Said comfort letter did not, however, satisfy the stated condition in the merger agreement. The comfort letter presented at the closing (which had been dictated over the telephone and was unsigned) stated in part:

> [O]ur examination in connection with the year ended August 31, 1969 which is still in process, disclosed the following significant adjustments which in our opinion should be reflected retroactive to May 31, 1969:
>
> 1. In adjusting the amortization of deferred costs at May 31, 1969, to eliminate therefrom all costs for programs substantially completed or which commenced 12 months or more prior, an adjustment of $500,000 was required. Upon analysis of the retroactive effect of this adjustment, it appears that the entire amount could be determined applicable to the period prior to May 31, 1969.
>
> 2. In August 1969, management wrote off receivables in amounts of $300,000. It appears that the uncollectibility of these receivables could have been determined at May 31, 1969 and such charge off should have been reflected as of that date.
>
> 3. Acquisition costs in the amount of $84,000 for proposed acquisitions which the company decided not to pursue were transferred from additional paid-in capital to general and administrative expenses. In our opin-

ion these should have been so transferred as of May 31, 1969.

In furtherance of a fraudulent scheme among defendants NSMC, Randell, Davies, Joy, White & Case, Epley, Brown, Allison, Bach, Tate, Lord, Bissell & Brook, Meyer and Schauer, the merger was closed on October 31, 1969 without the contents of the comfort letter being disclosed to public investors and the shareholders of NSMC or Interstate, even though said defendants knew shareholder approval of the merger had been obtained on the basis of materially false and misleading financial statements of NSMC for the period ended May 31, 1969.

(b) On October 31, 1969, at the closing meeting but before the merger between NSMC and Interstate was actually consummated, PMM informed defendants White & Case, Epley and Davies that PMM wished to add another paragraph to the comfort letter which paragraph would state that if the necessary adjustments had been made to NSMC's unaudited consolidated statement of earnings for the period ended May 31, 1969, then NSMC would have shown a net loss for that period and that the consolidated operations of the company as it existed at May 31, 1969 would show a break-even as to net earnings for the year ended August 31, 1969. Defendants White & Case, Epley and Davies failed to inform the other persons present at the closing of this additional paragraph.

(c) On October 31, 1969, about an hour after the closing meeting had been concluded, defendant PMM informed defendants White & Case and Epley that PMM wished to add still another paragraph to the comfort letter which paragraph would state:

Problem 20. Responsibilities of Advisors to Non-clients 219

> In view of the above mentioned facts, we believe the companies should consider submitting corrected interim unaudited financial information to the shareholders prior to proceeding with the closing.

Later that day, a final version of the comfort letter was delivered by PMM to defendants White & Case and Epley. It was materially unchanged from that set forth in subparagraphs (a), (b) and (c) above, except that the amount of receivables written off by mangement of NSMC and referred to in subparagraph 3 of the letter had been reduced from $300,000 to $200,000. Defendants White & Case and Epley made no effort to communicate the contents of the final version of the comfort letter to the representatives of Interstate who had been present at the closing.

(d) As part of the fraudulent scheme, defendant White & Case, contemporaneous with receipt of the comfort letter, issued an opinion at the direction of the defendant Epley stating that all steps taken to consummate the merger had been validly taken and that NSMC had incurred no violation of any federal or state statute or regulation to the knowledge of counsel. Issuance of such an opinion was a condition to the merger, as had been represented to the shareholders of NSMC and Interstate in the proxy statements.

(e) As part of the fraudulent scheme defendant Lord, Bissell & Brook, contemporaneous with receipt of the comfort letter, issued an opinion at the direction of defendants Meyer and Schauer stating that all steps taken to consummate the merger had been validly taken and that Interstate had incurred no violation of any federal or state statute or regulation to the knowledge of counsel. Issuance of such an opinion was a condition to the merger, as had been represented to the shareholders of NSMC and Interstate in the proxy statements.

(f) On or about November 3, 1969, PMM mailed the final version of the comfort letter, as described above in subparagraphs (a), (b), and (c), to each of the directors of defendant NSMC and Interstate, including but not limited to defendants Randell, Davies, Joy, Walther, Brown, Bach, Allison, Meyer and Tate. As part of their fraudulent scheme of conduct, defendants NSMC, Randell, Walther, Joy and Davies failed and refused to issue a release or disseminate to the press, to shareholders of defendant NSMC or to file with the plaintiff Commission any report, press release or statement which indicated that NSMC's consolidated statement of income for the nine months ended May 31, 1969, materially overstated net income or to restate said financial statement. As part of their fraudulent scheme of conduct, defendants Brown, Meyer, Allison, Bach and Tate failed and refused to inform the Interstate shareholders, numbering approximately 1,200, of the comfort letter.

(g) As part of the fraudulent scheme, defendants NSMC, Randell, Davies, Walther, Joy and Kurek failed to revise or amend information contained within defendant NSMC's registration statement on Form S-14 referred to in paragraph 34 above, failed to revise or amend defendant NSMC's proxy statement referred to in paragraph 33 above and failed to revise defendant's NSMC's publicly announced financial figures contained in the Third Quarter Report to Shareholders and the press release referred to in paragraph 32 above.

(h) As part of the fraudulent scheme, defendant PMM, who assisted in the preparation of and reviewed the NSMC financial statements as of May 31, 1969 and who issued the comfort letter for the nine months then ended, failed in accor-

Problem 20. Responsibilities of Advisors to Non-clients   221

dance with their professional obligation to insist that the NSMC financial statements be revised in accordance with the comfort letter, and, failing that, to withdraw from the engagement and to come forward and notify plaintiff Commission or the NSMC and Interstate shareholders as to the materially misleading nature of the nine month financial statements.

(i) As part of the fraudulent scheme White & Case, Epley, Lord, Bissell & Brook, Meyer and Schauer failed to refuse to issue their opinions referred to in subparagraphs (d) and (e) above and failed to insist that the financial statements be revised and shareholders be resolicited, and failing that, to cease representing their respective clients and, under the circumstances, notify the plaintiff Commission concerning the misleading nature of the nine month financial statements.

(j) Defendant NSMC filed with the Commission its monthly reports on Form 8-K for the months of October and November 1969. The reports which contained representations as to the fairness, truthfulness and accuracy of NSMC's financial statements as of May 31, 1969, were signed by Davies and transmitted to the Commission by defendant White & Case. As part of the fraudulent scheme defendants White & Case, Epley and Davies continued to conceal the existence of the comfort letter or the contents thereof.

(k) By the acts and practices described in subparagraphs (a) through (j) above, defendants NSMC, Randell, Davies, Joy, Kurek, Walther, PMM, White & Case, Epley, Brown, Allison, Bach, Tate, Lord, Bissell & Brook, Meyer and Schauer singly and in concert, directly and indirectly violated and aided and abetted violations of Section 17(a) of the Securities Act and Section 10(b) of the Exchange Act and Rule 10b-5 thereunder.

(1) By the acts and practices described in paragraphs (a) through (j) above, defendants NSMC, Randell, Davies, Kurek, Walther, White & Case and Epley singly and in concert directly and indirectly violated and aided and abetted violations of Section 13(a) of the Exchange Act and Rules 13a-1 and 13a-13 thereunder.

(m) By the acts and practices described in paragraphs (a) through (i) above, defendants NSMC, Randell, Davies, Joy, Kurek, Walther, PMM, Natelli, White & Case and Epley singly and in concert directly and indirectly violated and aided and abetted violations of Section 14(a) of the Exchange Act and Rules 14a-3 and 14a-9 thereunder.

**Statement of Policy Adopted
by American Bar Association
Regarding Responsibilities and Liabilities
of Lawyers in Advising with Respect to
the Compliance by Clients with Laws
Administered by the
Securities and Exchange Commission**
American Bar Association —
Report to the House of Delegates —
Section of Corporation, Banking
and Business Law Recommendation

The Section of Corporation, Banking and Business Law recommends adoption of the following resolution:

BE IT RESOLVED, that this Association adopts the following Statement of Policy regarding responsibilities and liabilities of lawyers in advising with respect to the compliance by clients with laws administered by the Securities and Exchange Commission ("SEC"):

Problem 20. Responsibilities of Advisors to Non-clients

1. The confidentiality of lawyer-client consultations and advice and the fiduciary loyalty of the lawyer to the client, as prescribed in the American Bar Association's Code of Professional Responsibility ("CPR"), are vital to the basic function of the lawyer as legal counselor because they enable and encourage clients to consult legal counsel freely, with assurance that counsel will respect the confidentiality of the client's communications and will advise independently and in the client's best interest without conflicting loyalties or obligations.

2. This vital confidentiality of consultation and advice would be destroyed or seriously impaired if it is accepted as a general principle that lawyers must inform the SEC or others regarding confidential information received by lawyers from their clients even though such action would not be permitted or required by the CPR. Any such compelled disclosure would seriously and adversely affect the lawyers' function as counselor, and may seriously and adversely affect the ability of lawyers as advocates to represent and defend their clients' interests.

3. In light of the foregoing considerations, it must be recognized that a lawyer cannot, consistently with his essential role as legal adviser, be regarded as a source of information concerning possible wrong-doing by clients. Accordingly, any principle of law which, except as permitted or required by the CPR, permits or obliges a lawyer to disclose to the SEC otherwise confidential information, should be established only by statute after full and careful consideration of the public interests involved, and should be resisted unless clearly mandated by law.

4. Lawyers have an obligation under the CPR to advise clients, to the best of their ability, concerning the need for or advisability of public disclosure of a broad range of events

and circumstances, including the obligation of the client to make appropriate disclosures as required by various laws and regulations administered by the SEC. In appropriate circumstances, a lawyer may be permitted or required by the Disciplinary Rules under the CPR to resign his engagement if his advice concerning disclosures is disregarded by the client and, if the conduct of a client clearly establishes his prospective commission of a crime or the past or prospective perpetration of a fraud in the course of the lawyer's representation, even to make the disclosures himself. However, the lawyer has neither the obligation nor the right to make disclosure when any reasonable doubt exists concerning the client's obligation of disclosure, i.e., the client's failure to meet his obligation is not clearly established, except to the extent that the lawyer should consider appropriate action, as required or permitted by the CPR, in cases where the lawyer's opinion is expected to be relied on by third parties and the opinion is discovered to be not correct, whether because it is based on erroneous information or otherwise.

    5. Fulfillment by attorneys of their obligations to clients under the CPR best serves the public interest of assisting and furthering clients' compliance with legal requirements. Efforts by the government to impose responsibility upon lawyers to assure the quality of their clients' compliance with the law or to compel lawyers to give advice resolving all doubts in favor of regulatory restrictions would evoke serious and far-reaching disruption in the role of the lawyer as counselor, which would be detrimental to the public, clients and the legal profession. In fulfillment of their responsibility to clients under the CPR, lawyers must be free to advise clients as to the full range of their legitimately available courses of action and the relative attendant risks involved. Furthermore, it is often desirable for the lawyer to

Problem 20. Responsibilities of Advisors to Non-clients

point out those factors which may suggest a decision that is morally just as well as legally permissible. However, the decision as to the course to be taken should be made by the client. The client's actions should not be improperly narrowed through the insistence of an attorney who may, perhaps unconsciously, eliminate available choices from consideration because of his concern over possible personal risks if the position is taken which, though supportable, is subject to uncertainty or contrary to a known, but perhaps erroneous, position of the SEC or a questionable lower court decision. Public policy, we strongly believe, is best served by lawyers acting in conformance with their obligations to their clients and others as prescribed under the CPR. Accordingly, liability should not be imposed upon lawyers whose conduct is in conformance with the CPR.

REPORT

I. Introduction

Lawyers are often called upon for legal advice when the answer is not clear. The statute or regulation in question may be ambiguous; judicial opinions may be in conflict or not directly in point; counsel may be of the opinion that an existing precedent is wrong and should be reversed on appeal; or the issue, in the absence of a precedent directly in point, may involve a high degree of subjective judgment, particularly when considering various central concepts deliberately imprecise in laws administered by the Securities and Exchange Commission ("SEC"). Illustrative are concepts such as "materiality," "control," "adequate disclosure," "average prudent investor," "public distribution," "care of a prudent man," "manipulative or deceptive device or contrivance," and "untrue statement of a material fact or to omit to state a material fact necessary in order to make the statements made, in light of the circumstances in which they were made, not misleading." Furthermore, there are often questions of fact presented, sometimes involving technical problems in diversified and complicated industries, regarding which clients or others are better qualified to determine than lawyers.

Various proceedings by the SEC, speeches by members and staff of the Commission, and certain statements in recent judicial opinions have caused many lawyers serious concern as to their responsibility to their clients and to the public when advising in the areas of SEC laws. Their advice is, of course, reviewed by the SEC with the benefit of "hindsight" when something has gone wrong. Must the lawyer in such matters resolve all uncertainties in favor of the law having application, e.g., if there is any question whether something may be "material" it should be treated as "material," and if the client fails to follow such advice must the lawyer report such failure to the SEC?

II. Public Policy

It is a basic principle that the lawyer's role is essentially that of counselor to his client. The effectiveness of this role is highly dependent upon the long-accepted confidentiality of the attorney-client relationship. For this reason a role for the lawyer as investigator or informant would be a seriously inconsistent one, and the Bar should critically scrutinize any proposal, however limited, that the lawyer can be so regarded.

Whenever a proposal is made that a lawyer go beyond his fundamental role of advising his client and assume a function that could require him publicly to contradict his client or disclose possible deficiencies, on the basis of infor-

Problem 20. Responsibilities of Advisors to Non-clients

mation gained in the course of his professional engagement, there is cause for concern on the part of the public as well as the Bar, since the attorney-client relationship is of fundamental importance to our legal system.

The lawyer's ability to serve his client and the public by assisting and furthering the client's compliance with legal requirements rests largely on the effectiveness of his relationship with his client. This relationship is undermined to the extent that client communications with lawyers are made with the risk that the lawyer will, if not satisfied with the client's response to his advice or if concerned over his own potential personal liabilities, report possible deficiencies to third parties. Accordingly, it has long been recognized by the Code of Professional Responsibility ("CPR") and its predecessor Canons of Ethics that only in the clearest cases of illegal or fraudulent activities by a client in the course of the lawyer's representation should the lawyer be called upon or permitted to take such action. (The text of relevant provisions of the CPR is attached).

We do not believe that the policy of disclosure as embodied in the SEC laws warrants an exception to the basic confidentiality of the attorney-client relationship. Such exceptions have to date been carefully reserved by the CPR for far more critical and limited situations. The statutes administered by the SEC give it no power to require disclosure by lawyers concerning their clients beyond what is provided in the CPR.

For the foregoing reasons we strongly urge that the American Bar Association adopt a general statement of policy concerning lawyers' responsibilities and liabilities regarding a client's failure to comply with a law administered by the SEC which will reflect the basic principles we, as lawyers, believe are essential to the preservation of the concept of the attorney-client relationship as part of our legal system.[1]

The statement should recognize that the lawyer has a duty to advise his client candidly and responsibly as to the client's legal obligations, including the obligation to make appropriate disclosures as required by various laws and regulations administered by the SEC, and that a lawyer must take appropriate action, as required by the CPR (as adopted in his particular State), when faced with conduct of a client which clearly establishes his prospective commission of a crime, or the past or prospective perpetration of a fraud, in the course of the lawyer's representation. Similarly, the lawyer should consider appropriate action, as required or permitted by the CPR, in cases where the lawyer's opinion is expected to be relied on by third parties and the opinion is discovered to be not correct, whether because it is based on erroneous information or otherwise. The statement should also acknowledge that a lawyer need not confine his advice to purely legal considerations, but in appropriate cases should bring to the attention of the client considerations of fairness and avoidance of infliction of needless harm.

We firmly believe that such an approach will be in the long-term public interest and will provide for greater assurance of compliance with our laws, including those relating to disclosure, than would an approach requiring lawyers to disclose possible SEC violations by clients.

The Recommendation preceding this Report has been adopted by the Council of the Section of Corporation, Banking and Business Law.

---

1. No implication is intended that such policy should apply only to those advising with respect to SEC laws.

Problem 20. Responsibilities of Advisors to Non-clients

BACKGROUND READING

SEC v. Spectrum, Ltd. must now be read in the light of the Supreme Court's recent opinion in *Ernst & Ernst v. Hochfelder,* 44 U.S.L.W. 4451 (U.S. March 30, 1976). There the Court held that an accounting firm would not be liable under SEC Rule 10b-5, in the absence of an intent to deceive, manipulate or defraud.

See A.B.A. Formal Opinion 335 (1974) for a discussion of the role of lawyers in the preparation of opinions in the area of securities regulation. The National Student Marketing complaint has generated a great deal of comment. See, for example, Garrett, New Directions in Professional Responsibility, 29 Bus. Law. 7 (Special Issue — Revolution in Securities Regulation, 1974); Goldberg, Policing Responsibilities of the Securities Bar: The Attorney-Client Relationship and the Code of Professional Responsibility — Considerations for Expertizing Securities Attorneys, 19 N.Y.L.F. 221 (1973); Lipman, The SEC's Reluctant Police Force: A New Role for Lawyers, 49 N.Y.U.L. Rev. 437 (1974); Lowenfels, Expanding Public Responsibilities of Securities Lawyers: An Analysis of the New Trend in Standard of Care and Priorities of Duties, 74 Colum. L. Rev. 412 (1974); Shipman, The Need for SEC Rules to Govern the Duties and Civil Liabilities of Attorneys Under the Federal Securities Statutes, 34 Ohio St. L.J. 231 (1973); Sonde, Professional Responsibility — A New Religion, or the Old Gospel?, 24 Emory L.J. 827 (1975).

PART V
Testing Your Ethics: Five Self-Administered Quizzes

The twenty preceding problems were designed to raise important and difficult questions concerning a lawyer's varying professional roles. For most of these questions the Code of Professional Responsibility provides an essential starting point for discussion, although not necessarily the answers. Students should not lose sight of the fact, however, that many, if not most, ethical questions do have specific answers in the Code of Professional Responsibility, or in opinions of the American Bar Association, or state and local bar associations. The following quizzes may be taken either during, or outside of, class time, and are intended to cover some of these more specific areas of professional responsibility. The answers follow each quiz.

A similar version of these quizzes was prepared for, and distributed by, the New York State Bar Association.

Quiz No. 1 — General Questions

1. May a lawyer contribute to the campaign of a judicial candidate before whom he may appear in the future as an advocate?
2. May an attorney charge a client interest on delinquent accounts?
3. May a lawyer send a notice every five years to clients for whom he has drawn wills, suggesting that they come in and review their wills for any necessary updating?
4. May a city councilman serve as a lawyer for a corporation which competes for city contracts?
5. May a personal injury lawyer make a personal loan to a client to help him over some "rough spots" on the understanding that the attorney will be reimbursed out of the settlement or judgement eventually obtained from pending litigation?
6. May a lawyer represent both husband and wife in a "friendly" separation or an uncontested divorce if he has explained any possible conflicts of interest to the parties and both have knowingly consented to the arrangement?
7. May the name of a former member of a law firm who has been elected a full-time district attorney be continued in the firm name? May the name of a partner who serves as a part-time D.A. but practices regularly with the firm be continued in the firm name?
8. As a legal aid attorney, Mr. Goodfellow represented Ms. Abercrombie in her dealings with the Welfare Department regarding supplementary stipends. He subsequently learned that Ms. Abercrombie inherited a sizable amount of money from her uncle. Must he automatically report that fact

Quiz No. 1—General

to the Welfare Department? Assume Ms. Abercrombie now wants him to represent her again at a welfare hearing. It is clear to Mr. Goodfellow that Ms. Abercrombie has failed to report her inheritance on her welfare applications, as the law requires her to do. Does this fact change the answer to the first question?

Quiz No. 1
Answers

1. Yes, providing the following conditions are observed: the contribution is not unreasonably large; it is made to a committee rather than to the candidate himself; and neither the contributor nor the committee informs the candidate of the contribution. See N.Y.S.B.A. Opinion 186. In this case, as in all others involving ethical issues, any doubts about the propriety of the donation should be resolved against it, as "a lawyer should avoid even the appearance of impropriety." See Canon 9.

2. No.

See N.Y.S.B.A. Opinion 193. This does not include, however, any interest awarded by the court if the debt is reduced to judgement.

3. Yes.

Such renewal notices may in fact be required if there has been a material change in fact or law since the will was drawn. At any rate, such a renewal notice system does not violate the prohibition of solicitation contained in DR2-104(A), since the person notified is a client.

4. No.

Even if no actual conflict of interest were to be involved in such a situation, a lawyer should avoid actions which even suggest impropriety. See DR5-101, DR8-101, Canon 9 and N.Y.S.B.A. Opinion 209. This conduct may also be proscribed by local conflict of interest laws.

5. No.

Generally, a lawyer should not acquire a propriety interest in his client's litigation. A contingent fee arrangement is a permissible, though not always desirable, exception to this rule. While a lawyer may advance to a client the costs of litigation, other monetary assistance should not be provided. See EC5-7, EC5-8 and DR5-103(A), (B).

6. No.

Although the Code does not prohibit all multiple representations, a lawyer should not represent multiple clients where a possible conflict of interest may arise. See EC5-14, EC5-15, EC5-16, EC5-17 and DR5-105. While disclosure to the clients of the risk of conflict, and their subsequent consent to multiple representation, will often allow such an arrangement to proceed, the possibility of prejudice in the divorce situation is sufficiently great that ethics opinions generally advise that such multiple representation should be avoided regardless of the parties' consent. See W. Va. S. Bar Committee on Legal Ethics, Ethics Case 169 (1963) and N.Y. County Lawyers Opinion 265 (1928).

7. No. Yes.

As to the first question, see DR2-102(B) and N.Y.S.B.A. Opinion 233. The test for maintaining the names of part-time public officials is generally whether they practice "actively and regularly," a test apparently met here. Of course, local law regarding limitations of practice by part-time officials always must be considered.

8. No. Yes.

A lawyer is not ordinarily under an affirmative obligation to reveal such information to the government. He is so obligated if he received information "clearly establishing" that his client or another person has committed fraud. In this case, the receipt of evidence of deliberate failure to disclose the inheritance on the part of the beneficiary would bind the lawyer to inform the Welfare Department of this fact. See N.Y.S.B.A. Opinion 207 and DR7-102(B).

Quiz No. 2 — Criminal Defense
Questions

Mr. Stryver has been approached by Charles Darnay, recently indicted for armed robbery, who asks Mr. Stryver to represent him.

1. May Mr. Stryver work out an arrangement with Mr. Darnay under which he receives a thousand-dollar retainer and a thousand dollars if and when Mr. Darnay is acquitted?

2. Is Mr. Stryver justified in refusing to take the case because the community's reaction to Mr. Darnay's cause has been extremely adverse? What if Mr. Stryver himself feels a great deal of animosity towards Mr. Darnay?

3. Assuming Mr. Stryver takes the case, is the subsequent development, on his part, of a belief that Mr. Darnay is guilty, cause to withdraw from the case? If Mr. Darnay fails to pay his retainer after Mr. Stryver has informed the court that he has taken the case, may Mr. Stryver withdraw on his own initiative?

4. If Mr. Darnay informs Mr. Stryver that he committed the crime in question, must Mr. Stryver inform the court of this fact? Possessing such knowledge, may Mr. Stryver introduce testimony to the effect that Mr. Darnay was not at the scene of the crime at the time it occurred?

5. If a second party is charged with the same robbery as

is Mr. Darnay, may Mr. Stryver represent the codefendant as well?

6. May Mr. Stryver interview the prosecution's chief witness against Mr. Darnay after the D.A. has explicitly refused him permission to do so?

7. During Mr. Darnay's trial, may Mr. Stryver comment to the press on his opinion of the prosecution's witnesses? May he quote the testimony of those witnesses from the record?

8. If Mr. Darnay's trial ends in a hung jury, may Mr. Stryver interview the jurors to find out which of his trial tactics had been effective or ineffective?

Quiz No. 2
Answers

1. No.

A lawyer shall not enter into an arrangement for, charge or collect, a contingent fee for representing a defendant in a criminal case. See DR2-106(C).

2. No. Yes.

A lawyer should not refuse a case because of community reaction. See EC2-27. But a lawyer may refuse employment if his personal feelings would affect his ability to represent his client. See EC2-30.

3. No. No.

A belief in the defendant's guilt is, in itself, not grounds to refuse or withdraw from employment. See EC2-29. While failure to observe a fee arrangement is grounds for withdrawal from a case, a lawyer may not, when his case is pending before a tribunal, withdraw without obtaining that tribunal's permission. See N.Y.S.B.A. Opinion 187.

4. No. No.

Mr. Darnay's admission to Mr. Stryver is, of course, a privileged communication that Mr. Stryver could not reveal without Mr. Darnay's permission. But Mr. Stryver may not subsequently introduce evidence he knows to be perjured or false. See EC7-26, EC7-27 and DR7-102(A).

5. Yes, but only if both defendants consent after a full discussion in which the risks of possible conflicts are raised. If Mr. Stryver feels that he can effectively represent both defendants, and there has been informed consent by the clients, neither the Code, nor opinions of bar associations, preclude such representation. See EC5-14, EC5-15, EC5-16, EC5-17 and DR5-105.

6. Yes.

A defense lawyer has an obligation to prepare his case fully. A witness is not the client or property of the district attorney, so the strictures of DR7-104 do not apply.

7. No. Yes.

During trial, an attorney may not make *any* statements to the press concerning the evidence, except that he may quote or refer — without comment — to the record itself. See DR7-107(D).

8. Yes.

A lawyer may interview jurors after they have been discharged provided he does not do so in a vexatious or embarrassing manner. See DR 7-108.

Quiz No. 3 — Conduct of Public Officials
Questions

1. Is it proper for a lawyer who directed an antitrust suit against a computer corporation for the Justice Depart-

ment to accept private employment on an analagous suit brought by a competitor of the defendant corporation?

2. Is it proper for a district attorney, subsequent to the indictment of a person for a particular crime, to call a press conference to announce that the indicted person has confessed?

3. May a judge solicit funds for his or her favorite charity?

4. May the corporation counsel of a city permit the police to take statements from people injured in an accident involving a city bus when he knows these people plan to sue the city and have already retained counsel?

5. May a district attorney serve as a member of a state political committee?

6. May a judge, while remaining on the bench, run for the United States Senate?

7. May a former judge litigate a case arising out of the same facts as had a previous case, the merits of which he had decided as a judge several years before?

8. May a judge express an opinion publicly on the desirability of legislation which would change the rules of practice and procedure used in his or her courtroom?

Quiz No. 3
Answers

1. No.
"A lawyer shall not accept private employment in a matter in which he had substantial responsibility while he was a public employee." DR9-101(B). See also A.B.A. Informal Opinion 1182 (1971).

2. No.

Quiz No. 4—General

This would violate the explicit dictates of DR7-107(B).
3. No.
This is prohibited by Judicial Canon 25.
4. No.
Such a practice would violate DR7-104(A)(1). See A.B.A. Formal Opinion 95 (1933).
5. No.
It has been held that such a practice could undermine the public confidence in the impartiality of the criminal justice system. See N.Y.S.B.A. Opinion 241. This same prohibition is extended to judges by Judicial Canon 28.
6. No.
A judge must resign before running for any non-judicial office. See Judicial Canon 30 and N.Y.S.B.A. Opinion 197.
7. No.
See DR9-101.
8. Yes.
Since a judge has an "exceptional opportunity" to judge the effectiveness of laws relating to practice, he can and should express his opinion on how they can best be improved.

Quiz No. 4 — General
Questions

1. May a lawyer's fee agreement with an expert witness he plans to call include a bonus if the lawyer's client is granted judgment?

2. A lawyer is asked by a client to draft a will involving a series of complicated future interest provisions. The lawyer has had little experience in the area, and he fears he

may not be able to do the job correctly. May the lawyer accept the job after requiring the client to sign an agreement that he, the attorney, is liable to no one if the will fails? May the attorney take the case at all?

3. Mr. Walker is asked to represent a client in a complicated tax case. He does not feel capable of handling the litigation, and thus he simply refers it to another attorney with whom he is familiar. May he, without informing the client, accept twenty-five percent of the eventual fee from the lawyer to whom he referred the case? Would his informing the client of the split fee arrangement change the answer to the first question?

4. May the board of directors of a legal aid society give a directive to a staff attorney on the manner in which he should conduct the defense of a controversial black militant in a highly publicized "incitement to riot" case?

5. May a lawyer for a plaintiff, at the explicit request of a defendant, recommend a particular attorney for that defendant?

6. A local reporter writes an unsolicited article on the defense strategy used in a recent murder trial, which resulted in an acquittal. Though not uncritical, the article basically praised the work of the chief defense counsel. Would it be proper for the attorney in question to send the reporter a set of theatre tickets with a note simply stating, "Thanks for the objective coverage?"

7. In the course of handling an insolvent client's matters, an attorney, through his own efforts, discovers an asset to which his client's creditors have a right. Must he reveal the existence of the asset to the creditors if his client refuses to do so?

8. May an attorney accept employment offered because the prospective client is interested in using confidential

knowledge the attorney has gained from other clients? Does it make any difference that the attorney's relationship with these other clients has been satisfactorily terminated?

9. May a bar association recommend a minimum fee schedule?

Quiz No. 4
Answers

1. No.
This is explicitly prohibited by DR7-109.

2. No. No.
Attempting to limit liability for malpractice is explicitly forbidden by DR6-102(A). And if the attorney does not feel competent to handle a matter, he should not accept it at all, unless he associates with an attorney who is capable of doing an adequate job. See DR6-101(A)(1).

3. No. No.
A fee can never be divided without a client's knowledge and consent. See DR2-107. Even if such consent is given, however, ". . . the division is to be made in proportion to the services performed and responsibility assumed by each." Under such a rule, a seventy-five-twenty-five percent split is not justified on these facts.

4. No.
Such a board should limit itself to formulating broad policy, leaving the conducting of individual cases to the attorneys assigned to them. See DR2-103(D). For an extended discussion of this question, see A.B.A. Formal Opinion 324 (1970).

5. No.
Even at a defendant's request, an attorney cannot rec-

ommend particular counsel in this situation. See A.B.A. Formal Opinion 245 (1942).

6. No.

This is clearly prohibited by DR2-102(C).

7. Yes.

As the facts indicate unprivileged knowledge, the situation would be covered by DR7-102(B). An attorney must reveal such fraud if his client refuses to do so.

8. No. No.

An attorney may not use a confidence or secret of a client for the benefit of himself or a third party. See DR4-101(B)(3). "The obligation of a lawyer to preserve the confidences and secrets of his client continues after the termination of his employment." See EC4-6.

9. No. Such schedules were held to violate the Sherman Act. See *Goldfarb v. Virginia State Bar*, 421 U.S. 773 (1975).

Quiz No. 5 — Disclosure and Suppression of Evidence
Questions

Ms. Mason, an attorney, is contacted by Mr. Allen, who wishes her to defend him against a homicide charge.

1. Assume Mr. Allen is a fugitive at the time he contacts Ms. Mason, and that he reveals to her his whereabouts. She advises him to surrender, and he does so. Is she later permitted to reveal, upon police questioning, Mr. Allen's location at the time he contacted her? What if Mr. Allen had jumped bail and did not surrender after talking to Ms. Mason? Is she permitted, if asked, to reveal his present hiding place?

2. Mr. Allen informs Ms. Mason that the police are

Quiz No. 5—Disclosure and Suppression of Evidence

looking for a particular gun alleged to have been used in the crime, and that he has hidden that gun at his home. May Ms. Mason advise Mr. Allen to destroy the gun? May she take the gun and keep it in her possession?

3. In the course of investigating Mr. Allen's case, Ms. Mason discovers from Mr. Allen's elementary school teacher that he had once, in a fit of anger, severely beaten a classmate. The conversation with the teacher is not protected by the attorney-client privilege, under local law, but Mr. Allen asks Ms. Mason never to disclose it. Is Ms. Mason permitted voluntarily to reveal this information?

4. In the course of investigating Mr. Allen's case Ms. Mason interviews a number of his friends and acquaintances. From one of them Ms. Mason receives unprivileged information, which she is convinced is accurate, of an unrelated crime committed by two people, one of whom was an attorney. Her client was in no way involved in the offense. After consulting the relevant statutes, Ms. Mason finds she is under no binding legal obligation to notify the police of what she has learned. Does the Code impose any such obligation?

5. Ms. Mason files a motion to dismiss for a defective indictment. Recently another trial court in the same jurisdiction had denied a motion brought on precisely the same grounds by one of Ms. Mason's partners. The prosecutor neglects to brief or argue this precedent in opposing Ms. Mason's motion. Is Ms. Mason under any duty to disclose this precedent to the trial judge deciding her motion?

6. During Mr. Allen's sentencing, the clerk informs the judge that Mr. Allen has no previous record. Mr. Allen has in confidence told Ms. Mason of prior convictions. Is she bound to disclose this fact to the judge? May she disclose it? What if the judge asks her a direct question on the matter?

7. Suppose that Mr. Allen, feeling bitter toward Ms. Mason, writes to the local bar association from prison and charges Ms. Mason with advising him to destroy certain physical evidence. May Ms. Mason, in defending herself against the charge, reveal the nature of the advice she gave to her client concerning such evidence?

Quiz No. 5
Answers

1. No. Yes.

Any disclosure by Mr. Allen as to his whereabouts prior to surrender would be related to past criminal activity and hence privileged. Thus, Ms. Mason neither must, nor may, reveal it to the police. See DR4-101(B). Bailjumping, however, is a crime in itself. As long as Mr. Allen refuses to surrender, that crime continues, and any disclosure related to it is not privileged. See McCormick on Evidence, §95 and DR4-101(C)(3). Thus if Ms. Mason is asked to reveal Mr. Allen's whereabouts by proper authorities, she may not refuse to do so. Nor does the Code prevent her volunteering the information. (See Problems 9 and 20 which raise the difficult questions of the lawyer's *obligation* to reveal information concerning continuing, or future, crimes).

2. No. No.

The concealment or destruction of physical evidence is, at least in most jurisdictions, a crime in itself. While a lawyer may defend his or her client zealously, he or she must do so within the bounds of the law. See DR7-102. Thus Ms. Mason may not advise her client to engage in such conduct nor may she engage in it herself. As future criminal

Quiz No. 5—Disclosure and Suppression of Evidence

activity, such concealment or destruction of evidence would be in no way privileged.

3. No.

Even though the conversation with the teacher is not within the attorney-client privilege under applicable law, and is not, therefore, a "confidence" of the client, it would be a "secret," and DR4-101(B)(1) precludes a lawyer from knowingly revealing a "confidence" or "secret."

4. Yes.

Ms. Mason is under the same moral obligation to report crimes as any citizen. This would apply to the information Ms. Mason receives about the criminal activity of the layman. As to the lawyer, however, the Code imposes an additional ethical duty. A lawyer is bound to report the misconduct of other lawyers to the relevant authorities. See DR1-103. A.B.A. Informal Opinion 1210 (1972) states: ". . . The Code of Professional Responsibility through its Disciplinary Rules necessarily deals directly with reporting of lawyer misconduct or misconduct of others directly observed in the legal practice or the administration of justice. It, of course, was not intended to strip a lawyer of the other obligations imposed on him as a member of society."

5. Yes.

See DR7-106(B). The test to be used is whether the precedent is one that the court should clearly consider in deciding the case. See also A.B.A. Formal Opinion 280 (1949).

6. No. No. No.

Ms. Mason may not disclose her knowledge of Mr. Allen's record, since it is a privileged communication. If asked a direct question, she should withdraw from the case. See A.B.A. Formal Opinion 287 (1953).

7. Yes.

This situation is an exception to the obligation of the lawyer to preserve the confidences or secrets of the client. See DR4-101(C)(3).

APPENDIX
The Code of Professional Responsibility of the American Bar Association

© Copyright 1975, 1976 by American Bar Association

PREAMBLE AND PRELIMINARY STATEMENT

Preamble

The continued existence of a free and democratic society depends upon recognition of the concept that justice is based upon the rule of law grounded in respect for the dignity of the individual and his capacity through reason for enlightened self-government. Law so grounded makes justice possible, for only through such law does the dignity of the individual attain respect and protection. Without it, individual rights become subject to unrestrained power, respect for law is destroyed, and rational self-government is impossible.

Lawyers, as guardians of the law, play a vital role in the preservation of society. The fulfillment of this role requires an understanding by lawyers of their relationship with and function in our legal system. A consequent obligation of lawyers is to maintain the highest standards of ethical conduct.

In fulfilling his professional responsibilities, a lawyer necessarily assumes various roles that require the performance of many difficult tasks. Not every situation which he may encounter can be foreseen, but fundamental ethical principles are always present to guide him. Within the framework of these principles, a lawyer must with courage and foresight be able and ready to shape the body of the law to the ever-changing relationships of society.

The Code of Professional Responsibility points the way to the aspiring and provides standards by which to judge the transgressor. Each lawyer must find within his own conscience the touchstone against which to test the extent to which his actions should rise above minimum standards. But in the last analysis it is the desire for the respect and confidence of the members of his profession and of the society which he serves that should provide to a lawyer the incentive for the highest possible degree of ethical conduct. The possible loss of that respect and confidence is the ultimate sanction. So long as its practitioners are guided by these principles, the law will continue to be a noble profession. This is its greatness and its strength, which permit of no compromise.

Preliminary Statement

In furtherance of the principles stated in the Preamble, the American Bar Association has promulgated this Code of Professional Responsibility, consisting of three separate but interrelated parts: Canons, Ethical Considerations, and Disciplinary Rules. The Code is designed to be adopted by appropriate agencies both as an inspirational guide to the members of the profession and as a basis for disciplinary action when the conduct of a lawyer falls below the required minimum standards stated in the Disciplinary Rules.

Obviously the Canons, Ethical Considerations, and Disciplinary Rules cannot apply to non-lawyers; however, they do define the type of ethical conduct that the public has a right to expect not only of lawyers but also of their non-professional employees and associates in all matters pertaining to professional employment. A lawyer should ultimately be responsible for the conduct of his employees and associates in the course of the professional representation of the client.

The Canons are statements of axiomatic norms, expressing in general terms the standards of professional conduct expected of lawyers in their relationships with the public, with the legal system, and with the legal profession. They embody the general concepts from which the Ethical Consideration and the Disciplinary Rules are derived.

The Ethical Considerations are aspirational in character and represent the objectives toward which every member of the profession should strive. They constitute a body of principles upon which the lawyer can rely for guidance in many specific situations.

The Disciplinary Rules, unlike the Ethical Considerations, are mandatory in character. The Disciplinary Rules state the minimum level of conduct below which no lawyer can fall without being

Appendix

subject to disciplinary action. Within the framework of fair trial, the Disciplinary Rules should be uniformly applied to all lawyers, regardless of the nature of their professional activities. The Code makes no attempt to prescribe either disciplinary procedures or penalties for violation of a Disciplinary Rule, nor does it undertake to define standards for civil liability of lawyers for professional conduct. The severity of judgment against one found guilty of violating a Disciplinary Rule should be determined by the character of the offense and the attendant circumstances. An enforcing agency, in applying the Disciplinary Rules, may find interpretive guidance in the basic principles embodied in the Canons and in the objectives reflected in the Ethical Considerations.

CANON 1

A Lawyer Should Assist in Maintaining the Integrity and Competence of the Legal Profession

Ethical Considerations

EC 1-1 A basic tenet of the professional responsibility of lawyers is that every person in our society should have ready access to the independent professional services of a lawyer of integrity and competence. Maintaining the integrity and improving the competence of the bar to meet the highest standards is the ethical responsibility of every lawyer.

EC 1-2 The public should be protected from those who are not qualified to be lawyers by reason of a deficiency in education or moral standards or of other relevant factors but who nevertheless seek to practice law. To assure the maintenance of high moral and educational standards of the legal profession, lawyers should affirmatively assist courts and other appropriate bodies in promulgating, enforcing, and improving requirements for admission to the bar. In like manner, the bar has a positive obligation to aid in the continued improvement of all phases of pre-admission and post-admission legal education.

EC 1-3 Before recommending an applicant for admission, a lawyer should satisfy himself that the applicant is of good moral character. Although a lawyer should not become a self-appointed investigator or judge of applicants for admission, he should report to proper officials all unfavorable information he possesses relating to the character or other qualifications of an applicant.

EC 1-4 The integrity of the profession can be maintained only if conduct of lawyers in violation of the Disciplinary Rules is brought to the attention of the proper officials. A lawyer should reveal voluntarily to those officials all unprivileged knowledge of conduct of lawyers which he believes clearly to be in violation of the Disciplinary Rules. A lawyer should, upon request serve on and assist committees and boards having responsibility for the administration of the Disciplinary Rules.

EC 1-5 A lawyer should maintain high standards of professional conduct and should encourage fellow lawyers to do likewise. He should be temperate and dignified, and he should refrain from all illegal and morally reprehensible conduct. Because of his position in society, even minor violations of law by a lawyer may tend to lessen public confidence in the legal profession. Obedience to law exemplifies respect for law. To lawyers especially, respect for the law should be more than a platitude.

EC 1-6 An applicant for admission to the bar or a lawyer may be unqualified, temporarily or permanently, for other than moral and educational reasons, such as mental or emotional instability. Lawyers should be diligent in taking steps to see that during a period of disqualification such person is not granted a license or, if licensed, is not permitted to practice. In like manner, when the disqualification has terminated, members of the bar should assist such person in being licensed, or, if licensed, in being restored to his full right to practice.

Appendix

Disciplinary Rules

DR 1-101 Maintaining Integrity and Competence of the Legal Profession

(A) A lawyer is subject to discipline if he has made a materially false statement in, or if he has deliberately failed to disclose a material fact requested in connection with, his application for admission to the bar.

(B) A lawyer shall not further the application for admission to the bar of another person known by him to be unqualified in respect to character, education, or other relevant attribute.

DR 1-102 Misconduct

(A) A lawyer shall not:
   (1) Violate a Disciplinary Rule.
   (2) Circumvent a Disciplinary Rule through actions of another.
   (3) Engage in illegal conduct involving moral turpitude.
   (4) Engage in conduct involving dishonesty, fraud, deceit, or misrepresentation.
   (5) Engage in conduct that is prejudicial to the administration of justice.
   (6) Engage in any other conduct that adversely reflects on his fitness to practice law.

DR 1-103 Disclosure of Information to Authorities

(A) A lawyer possessing unprivileged knowledge of a violation of DR 1-102 shall report such knowledge to a tribunal or other authority empowered to investigate or act upon such violation.

(B) A lawyer possessing unprivileged knowledge or evidence concerning another lawyer or a judge shall reveal fully such knowledge or evidence upon proper request of a tribunal or other authority empowered to investigate or act upon the conduct of lawyers or judges.

CANON 2

A Lawyer Should Assist the Legal Profession in Fulfilling Its Duty to Make Legal Counsel Available

Ethical Considerations

EC 2-1   The need of members of the public for legal services is met only if they recognize their legal problems, appreciate the importance of seeking assistance, and are able to obtain the services of acceptable legal counsel. Hence, important functions of the legal profession are to educate laymen to recognize their problems, to facilitate the process of intelligent selection of lawyers, and to assist in making legal services fully available.

Recognition of Legal Problems

EC 2-2   The legal profession should assist laymen to recognize legal problems because such problems may not be self-revealing and often are not timely noticed. Therefore, lawyers acting under proper auspices should encourage and participate in educational and public relations programs concerning our legal system with particular reference to legal problems that frequently arise. Such educational programs should be motivated by a desire to benefit the public rather than to obtain publicity or employment for particular lawyers. Examples of permissible activities include preparation of institutional advertisements and professional articles for lay publications and participation in seminars, lectures, and civic programs. But a lawyer who participates in such activities should shun personal publicity.

EC 2-3   Whether a lawyer acts properly in volunteering advice to a layman to seek legal services depends upon the circumstances. The giving of advice that one should take legal action could well be in fulfillment of the duty of the legal profession to assist laymen in recognizing legal problems. The advice is proper only if motivated by a desire to protect one who does not recognize that he may have legal problems or who is ignorant of his legal rights or obligations. Hence, the advice is improper if motivated by a desire to obtain personal benefit, secure personal publicity, or cause litigation to be brought merely to harass or injure another. Obviously, a lawyer should not contact a non-client, directly or indirectly, for the purpose of being retained to represent him for compensation.

EC 2-4 Since motivation is subjective and often difficult to judge, the motives of a lawyer who volunteers advice likely to produce legal controversy may well be suspect if he receives professional employment or other benefits as a result. A lawyer who volunteers advice that one should obtain the services of a lawyer generally should not himself accept employment, compensation, or other benefit in connection with that matter. However, it is not improper for a lawyer to volunteer such advice and render resulting legal services to close friends, relatives, former clients (in regard to matters germane to former employment), and regular clients.

EC 2-5 A lawyer who writes or speaks for the purpose of educating members of the public to recognize their legal problems should carefully refrain from giving or appearing to give a general solution applicable to all apparently similar individual problems, since slight changes in fact situations may require a material variance in the applicable advice; otherwise, the public may be misled and misadvised. Talks and writings by lawyers for laymen should caution them not to attempt to solve individual problems upon the basis of the information contained therein.

Selection of a Lawyer: Generally

EC 2-6 Formerly a potential client usually knew the reputations of local lawyers for competency and integrity and therefore could select a practitioner in whom he had confidence. This traditional selection process worked well because it was initiated by the client and the choice was an informed one.

EC 2-7 Changed conditions, however, have seriously restricted the effectiveness of the traditional selection process. Often the reputations of lawyers are not sufficiently known to enable laymen to make intelligent choices. The law has become increasingly complex and specialized. Few lawyers are willing and competent to deal with every kind of legal matter, and many laymen have difficulty in determining the competence of lawyers to render different types of legal services. The selection of legal counsel is particularly difficult for transients, persons moving into new areas, persons of limited education or means, and others who have little or no contact with lawyers.

EC 2-8 Selection of a lawyer by a layman often is the result of the advice and recommendation of third parties — relatives, friends, acquaintances, business associates, or other lawyers. A layman is best served if the recommendation is disinterested and informed. In order that the recommendation be disinterested, a lawyer should not seek to influence another to recommend his employment. A lawyer should not compensate another person for recommending him, for influencing a prospective client to employ him, or to encourage future recommendations.

Selection of a Lawyer: Professional Notices and Listings

EC 2-9 The traditional ban against advertising by lawyers, which is subject to certain limited exceptions, is rooted in the public interest. Competitive advertising would encourage extravagant, artful, self-laudatory brashness in seeking business and thus could mislead the layman. Furthermore, it would inevitably produce unrealistic expectations in particular cases and bring about distrust of the law and lawyers. Thus, public confidence in our legal system would be impaired by such advertisements of professional services. The attorney-client relationship is personal and unique and should not be established as the result of pressures and deceptions. History has demonstrated that public confidence in the legal system is best preserved by strict, self-imposed controls over, rather than by unlimited, advertising.

EC 2-10 Methods of advertising that are subject to the objections stated above should be and are prohibited. However, the

Appendix

Disciplinary Rules recognize the value of giving assistance in the selection process through forms of advertising that furnish identification of a lawyer while avoiding such objections. For example, a lawyer may be identified in the classified section of the telephone directory, in the office building directory, and on his letterhead and professional card. But at all times the permitted notices should be dignified and accurate.

EC 2-11 The name under which a lawyer conducts his practice may be a factor in the selection process. The use of a trade name or an assumed name could mislead laymen concerning the identity, responsibility, and status of those practicing thereunder. Accordingly, a lawyer in private practice should practice only under his own name, the name of a lawyer employing him, a partnership name composed of the name of one or more of the lawyers practicing in a partnership, or, if permitted by law, in the name of a professional legal corporation, which should be clearly designated as such. For many years some law firms have used a firm name retaining one or more names of deceased or retired partners and such practice is not improper if the firm is a bona fide successor of a firm in which the deceased or retired person was a member, if the use of the name is authorized by law or by contract, and if the public is not misled thereby. However, the name of a partner who withdraws from a firm but continues to practice law should be omitted from the firm name in order to avoid misleading the public.

EC 2-12 A lawyer occupying a judicial, legislative, or public executive or administrative position who has the right to practice law concurrently may allow his name to remain in the name of the firm if he actively continues to practice law as a member thereof. Otherwise, his name should be removed from the firm name, and he should not be identified as a past or present member of the firm; and he should not hold himself out as being a practicing lawyer.

EC 2-13 In order to avoid the possibility of misleading persons with whom he deals, a lawyer should be scrupulous in the representation of his professional status. He should not hold himself out as being a partner or associate of a law firm if he is not one in fact, and thus should not hold himself out as a partner or associate if he only shares offices with another lawyer.

EC 2-14 In some instances a lawyer confines his practice to a particular field of law. In the absence of state controls to insure the existence of special competence, a lawyer should not be permitted to hold himself out as a specialist or as having special training or ability, other than in the historically excepted fields of admiralty, trademark, and patent law.

EC 2-15 The legal profession has developed lawyer referral systems designed to aid individuals who are able to pay fees but need assistance in locating lawyers competent to handle their particular problems. Use of a lawyer referral system enables a layman to avoid an uninformed selection of a lawyer because such a system makes possible the employment of competent lawyers who have indicated an interest in the subject matter involved. Lawyers should support the principle of lawyer referral systems and should encourage the evolution of other ethical plans which aid in the selection of qualified counsel.

Financial Ability to Employ Counsel: Generally

EC 2-16 The legal profession cannot remain a viable force in fulfilling its role in our society unless its members receive adequate compensation for services rendered, and reasonable fees should be charged in appropriate cases to clients able to pay them. Nevertheless, persons unable to pay all or a portion of a reasonable fee should be able to obtain necessary legal services, and lawyers should support and participate in ethical activities designed to achieve that objective.

Financial Ability to Employ Counsel: Persons Able to Pay Reasonable Fees

EC 2-17 The determination of a proper fee requires consideration of the interests of both client and lawyer. A lawyer should not charge more than a reasonable fee, for excessive cost of legal service would deter laymen from utilizing the legal system in pro-

Appendix

tection of their rights. Furthermore, an excessive charge abuses the professional relationship between lawyer and client. On the other hand, adequate compensation is necessary in order to enable the lawyer to serve his client effectively and to preserve the integrity and independence of the profession.

EC 2-18 The determination of the reasonableness of a fee requires consideration of all relevant circumstances, including those stated in the Disciplinary Rules. The fees of a lawyer will vary according to many factors, including the time required, his experience, ability, and reputation, the nature of the employment, the responsibility involved, and the results obtained. It is a commendable and long-standing tradition of the bar that special consideration is given in the fixing of any fee for services rendered a brother lawyer or a member of his immediate family.

EC 2-19 As soon as feasible after a lawyer has been employed, it is desirable that he reach a clear agreement with his client as to the basis of the fee charges to be made. Such a course will not only prevent later misunderstanding but will also work for good relations between the lawyer and the client. It is usually beneficial to reduce to writing the understanding of the parties regarding the fee, particularly when it is contingent. A lawyer should be mindful that many persons who desire to employ him may have had little or no experience with fee charges of lawyers, and for this reason he should explain fully to such persons the reasons for the particular fee arrangement he proposes.

EC 2-20 Contingent fee arrangements in civil cases have long been commonly accepted in the United States in proceedings to enforce claims. The historical bases of their acceptance are that (1) they often, and in a variety of circumstances, provide the only practical means by which one having a claim against another can economically afford, finance, and obtain the services of a competent lawyer to prosecute his claim, and (2) a successful prosecution of the claim produces a *res* out of which the fee can be paid. Although a lawyer generally should decline to accept employment on a contingent fee basis by one who is able to pay a reasonable fixed fee, it is not necessarily improper for a lawyer, where justified by the particular circumstances of a case, to enter into a contingent fee contract in a civil case with any client who, after being fully informed of all relevant factors, desires that arrangement. Because of the human relationships involved and the unique character of the proceedings, contingent fee arrangements in domestic relation cases are rarely justified. In administrative agency proceedings contingent fee contracts should be governed by the same consideration as in other civil cases. Public policy properly condemns contingent fee arrangements in criminal cases, largely on the ground that legal services in criminal cases do not produce a *res* with which to pay the fee.

EC 2-21 A lawyer should not accept compensation or any thing of value incident to his employment or services from one other than his client without the knowledge and consent of his client after full disclosure.

EC 2-22 Without the consent of his client, a lawyer should not associate in a particular matter another lawyer outside his firm. A fee may properly be divided between lawyers properly associated if the division is in proportion to the services performed and the responsibility assumed by each lawyer and if the total fee is reasonable.

EC 2-23 A lawyer should be zealous in his efforts to avoid controversies over fees with clients and should attempt to resolve amicably any differences on the subject. He should not sue a client for a fee unless necessary to prevent fraud or gross imposition by the client.

Financial Ability to Employ Counsel: Persons Unable to Pay Reasonable Fees

EC 2-24 A layman whose financial ability is not sufficient to permit payment of any fee cannot obtain legal services, other than in cases where a contingent fee is appropriate, unless the services are provided for him. Even a person of moderate means may be unable to pay a reasonable fee which is large because of the complexity, novelty, or difficulty of the problem or similar factors.

EC 2-25 Historically, the need for legal services of those

unable to pay reasonable fees has been met in part by lawyers who donated their services or accepted court appointments on behalf of such individuals. The basic responsibility for providing legal services for those unable to pay ultimately rests upon the individual lawyer, and personal involvement in the problems of the disadvantaged can be one of the most rewarding experiences in the life of a lawyer. Every lawyer, regardless of professional prominence or professional workload, should find time to participate in serving the disadvantaged. The rendition of free legal services to those unable to pay reasonable fees continues to be an obligation of each lawyer, but the efforts of individual lawyers are often not enough to meet the need. Thus it has been necessary for the profession to institute additional programs to provide legal services. Accordingly, legal aid offices, lawyer referral services, and other related programs have been developed, and others will be developed, by the profession. Every lawyer should support all proper efforts to meet this need for legal services.

Acceptance and Retention of Employment

EC 2-26 A lawyer is under no obligation to act as adviser or advocate for every person who may wish to become his client; but in furtherance of the objective of the bar to make legal services fully available, a lawyer should not lightly decline proffered employment. The fulfillment of this objective requires acceptance by a lawyer of his share of tendered employment which may be unattractive both to him and the bar generally.

EC 2-27 History is replete with instances of distinguished and sacrificial services by lawyers who have represented unpopular clients and causes. Regardless of his personal feelings, a lawyer should not decline representation because a client or a cause is unpopular or community reaction is adverse.

EC 2-28 The personal preference of a lawyer to avoid adversary alignment against judges, other lawyers, public officials, or influential members of the community does not justify his rejection of tendered employment.

EC 2-29 When a lawyer is appointed by a court or requested

by a bar association to undertake representation of a person unable to obtain counsel, whether for financial or other reasons, he should not seek to be excused from undertaking the representation except for compelling reasons. Compelling reasons do not include such factors as the repugnance of the subject matter of the proceeding, the identity or position of a person involved in the case, the belief of the lawyer that the defendant in a criminal proceeding is guilty, or the belief of the lawyer regarding the merits of the civil case.

EC 2-30 Employment should not be accepted by a lawyer when he is unable to render competent service or when he knows or it is obvious that the person seeking to employ him desires to institute or maintain an action merely for the purpose of harassing or maliciously injuring another. Likewise, a lawyer should decline employment if the intensity of his personal feeling, as distinguished from a community attitude, may impair his effective representation of a prospective client. If a lawyer knows a client has previously obtained counsel, he should not accept employment in the matter unless the other counsel approves or withdraws, or the client terminates the prior employment.

EC 2-31 Full availability of legal counsel requires both that persons be able to obtain counsel and that lawyers who undertake representation complete the work involved. Trial counsel for a convicted defendant should continue to represent his client by advising whether to take an appeal and, if the appeal is prosecuted, by representing him through the appeal unless new counsel is substituted or withdrawal is permitted by the appropriate court.

EC 2-32 A decision by a lawyer to withdraw should be made only on the basis of compelling circumstances, and in a matter pending before a tribunal he must comply with the rules of the tribunal regarding withdrawal. A lawyer should not withdraw without considering carefully and endeavoring to minimize the possible adverse effect on the rights of his client and the possibility of prejudice to his client as a result of his withdrawal. Even when he justifiably withdraws, a lawyer should protect the welfare of his client by giving due notice of his withdrawal, suggesting employment of other counsel, delivering to the client all papers and prop-

Appendix

erty to which the client is entitled, cooperating with counsel subsequently employed, and otherwise endeavoring to minimize the possibility of harm. Further, he should refund to the client any compensation not earned during the employment.

EC 2-33   As a part of the legal profession's commitment to the principle that high quality legal services should be available to all, attorneys are encouraged to cooperate with qualified legal assistance organizations providing prepaid legal services. Such participation should at all times be in accordance with the basic tenets of the profession: independence, integrity, competence and devotion to the interests of individual clients. An attorney so participating should make certain that his relationship with a qualified legal assistance organization in no way interferes with his independent, professional representation of the interests of the individual client. An attorney should avoid situations in which officials of the organization who are not lawyers attempt to direct attorneys concerning the manner in which legal services are performed for individual members, and should also avoid situations in which considerations of economy are given undue weight in determining the attorneys employed by an organization or the legal services to be performed for the member or beneficiary rather than competence and quality of service. An attorney interested in maintaining the historic traditions of the profession and preserving the function of a lawyer as a trusted and independent advisor to individual members of society should carefully assess such factors when accepting employment by, or otherwise participating in, a particular qualified legal assistance organization, and while so participating should adhere to the highest professional standards of effort and competence.

Disciplinary Rules

DR 2-101   Publicity in General

(A) A lawyer shall not prepare, cause to be prepared, use, or participate in the use of, any form of public communication that contains professionally self-laudatory statements calculated to attract lay clients; as used herein, "public communication" includes, but is not limited to, communication by means of television, radio, motion picture, newspaper, magazine, or book.

(B) A lawyer shall not publicize himself, or his partner, or associate, or any other lawyer affiliated with him or his firm, as a lawyer through newspaper or magazine advertisements, radio or television announcements, display advertisements in city or telephone directories, or other means of commercial publicity, nor shall he authorize or permit others to do so in his behalf. However, a lawyer recommended by, paid by or whose legal services are furnished by, a qualified legal assistance organization may authorize or permit or assist such organization to use means of dignified commercial publicity, which does not identify any lawyer by name, to describe the availability or nature of its legal services or legal service benefits. This rule does not prohibit limited and dignified identification of a lawyer as a lawyer as well as by name:

    (1) In political advertisements when his professional status is germane to the political campaign or to a political issue.

    (2) In public notices when the name and profession of a lawyer are required or authorized by law or are reasonably pertinent for a purpose other than the attraction of potential clients.

    (3) In routine reports and announcements of a bona fide business, civic, professional, or political organization in which he serves as a director or officer.

    (4) In and on legal documents prepared by him.

    (5) In and on legal textbooks, treatises, and other legal publications, and in dignified advertisements thereof.

    (6) In communications by a qualified legal assistance organization, along with the biographical information permitted under DR 2-102(A) (6), directed to a member or beneficiary of such organization.

(C) A lawyer shall not compensate or give any thing of value to representatives of the press, radio, television, or other communication medium in anticipation of or in return for professional publicity in a news item.

DR 2-102 Professional Notices, Letterheads, Offices, and Law Lists

(A) A lawyer or law firm shall not use or participate in the use of professional cards, professional announcement cards, office signs, letterheads, telephone directory listings, law lists, legal directory listings, or similar professional notices or devices, except that the following may be used if they are in dignified form:

(1) A professional card of a lawyer identifying him by name and as a lawyer, and giving his addresses, telephone numbers, the name of his law firm, and any information permitted under DR 2-105. A professional card of a law firm may also give the names of members and associates. Such cards may be used for identification but may not be published in periodicals, magazines, newspapers, or other media.

(2) A brief professional announcement card stating new or changed associations or addresses, change of firm name, or similar matters pertaining to the professional office of a lawyer or law firm, which may be mailed to lawyers, clients, former clients, personal friends, and relatives. It shall not state biographical data except to the extent reasonably necessary to identify the lawyer or to explain the change in his association, but it may state the immediate past position of the lawyer. It may give the names and dates of predecessor firms in a continuing line of succession. It shall not state the nature of the practice except as permitted under DR 2-105.

(3) A sign on or near the door of the office and in the building directory identifying the law office. The sign shall not state the nature of the practice, except as permitted under DR 2-105.

(4) A letterhead of a lawyer identifying him by name and

as a lawyer, and giving his addresses, telephone numbers, the name of his law firm, associates and any information permitted under DR 2-105. A letterhead of a law firm may also give the names of members and associates, and names and dates relating to deceased and retired members. A lawyer may be designated "Of Counsel" on a letterhead if he has a continuing relationship with a lawyer or law firm, other than as a partner or associate. A lawyer or law firm may be designated as "General Counsel" or by similar professional reference on stationery of a client if he or the firm devotes a substantial amount of professional time in the representation of that client. The letterhead of a law firm may give the names and dates of predecessor firms in a continuing line of succession.

(5) A listing of the office of a lawyer or law firm in the alphabetical and classified sections of the telephone directory or directories for the geographical area or areas in which the lawyer resides or maintains offices or in which a significant part of his clientele resides and in the city directory of the city in which his or the firm's office is located; but the listing in the alphabetical section may give only the name of the lawyer or law firm, the fact he is a lawyer, addresses, and telephone numbers, and the listing in the classified section must comply with the provisions of DR 2-102 (A) (6). The listing shall not be in distinctive form or type. A law firm may have a listing in the firm name separate from that of its members and associates. The listing in the classified section shall not be under a heading or classification other than "Attorneys" or "Lawyers," except that additional headings or classifications descriptive of the types of practice referred to in DR 2-105 are permitted.

(6) A listing in a reputable law list, legal directory, a directory published by a state, county or local bar

association, or the classified section of telephone company directories giving brief biographical and other informative data. A law list or any directory is not reputable if its management or contents are likely to be misleading or injurious to the public or to the profession. A law list or any directory is conclusively established to be reputable if it is certified by the American Bar Association as being in compliance with its rules and standards. The published data may include only the following: name, including name of law firm and names of professional associates; addresses and telephone numbers; one or more fields of law in which the lawyer or law firm concentrates, a statement that practice is limited to one or more fields of law, or a statement that the lawyer or law firm specializes in a particular field of law or law practice, to the extent permitted by the authority having jurisdiction under state law over the subject and in accordance with rules prescribed by that authority; date and place of birth; date and place of admission to the bar of state and federal courts; schools attended, with dates of graduation, degrees, and other scholastic distinctions; public or quasi-public offices; military service; posts of honor; legal authorships; legal teaching positions; memberships, offices, committee assignments, and section memberships in bar associations; memberships and offices in legal fraternities and legal societies; technical and professional licenses; memberships in scientific, technical and professional associations and societies; foreign language ability; names and addresses of references, and, with their consent, names of clients regularly represented; whether credit cards or other credit arrangements are accepted; office and other hours of availability; a statement of legal fees for an initial consultation or the availability upon request of a written schedule of fees or an estimate of the fee to be charged for the specific services; provided, all such published data shall be disseminated only to the extent and in such format and language uniformly applicable to all lawyers, as prescribed by the authority having jurisdiction by state law over the subject.

(B) A lawyer in private practice shall not practice under a trade name, a name that is misleading as to the identity of the lawyer or lawyers practicing under such name, or a firm name containing names other than those of one or more of the lawyers in the firm, except that the name of a professional corporation or professional association may contain "P.C." or "P.A." or similar symbols indicating the nature of the organization, and if otherwise lawful a firm may use as, or continue to include in, its name the name or names of one or more deceased or retired members of the firm or of a predecessor firm in a continuing line of succession. A lawyer who assumes a judicial, legislative, or public executive or administrative post or office shall not permit his name to remain in the name of a law firm or to be used in professional notices of the firm during any significant period in which he is not actively and regularly practicing law as a member of the firm, and during such period other members of the firm shall not use his name in the firm name or in professional notices of the firm.

(C) A lawyer shall not hold himself out as having a partnership with one or more other lawyers unless they are in fact partners.

(D) A partnership shall not be formed or continued between or among lawyers licensed in different jurisdictions unless all enumerations of the members and associates of the firm on its letterhead and in other permissible listings make clear the jurisdictional limitations on those members and associates of the firm not licensed to practice in all listed jurisdictions; however, the same firm name may be used in each jurisdiction.

(E) A lawyer who is engaged both in the practice of law and another profession or business shall not so indicate on his letterhead, office sign, or professional card, nor shall he identify himself as a lawyer in any publication in connection with his other profession or business.

(F) Nothing contained herein shall prohibit a lawyer from using or permitting the use of, in connection with his name, an earned degree or title derived therefrom indicating his training in the law.

DR 2-103 Recommendation of Professional Employment

(A) A lawyer shall not recommend employment, as a private practitioner, of himself, his partner, or associate to a non-lawyer who has not sought his advice regarding employment of a lawyer.

(B) A lawyer shall not compensate or give anything of value to a person or organization to recommend or secure his employment by a client, or as a reward for having made a recommendation resulting in his employment by a client, except that he may pay the usual and reasonable fees or dues charged by any of the organizations listed in DR 2-103(D).

(C) A lawyer shall not request a person or organization to recommend or promote the use of his services or those of his partner or associate, or any other lawyer affiliated with him or his firm, as a private practitioner, except that

> (1) He may request referrals from a lawyer referral service operated, sponsored, or approved by a bar association and may pay its fees incident thereto.
> (2) He may cooperate with the legal service activities of any of the offices or organizations enumerated in DR 2-103 (D) (1) through (4) and may perform legal services for those to whom he was recommended by it to do such work if:
> > (a) The person to whom the recommendation is made is a member or beneficiary of such office or organization; and
> > (b) The lawyer remains free to exercise his independent professional judgment on behalf of his client.

(D) A lawyer shall not knowingly assist a person or organization that furnishes or pays for legal services to others to promote the use of his services or those of his partner or associate or any other lawyer affiliated with him or his firm except as permitted in DR 2-101(B). However, this does not prohibit a lawyer or his partner or associate or any other lawyer affiliated with him or his firm from being recommended, employed or paid by, or cooperating with, one of the following offices or organizations that promote the use of his services or those of his partner or associate or any other lawyer affiliated with him or his firm if there is no interference with the exercise of independent professional judgment in behalf of his client:

(1) A legal aid office or public defender office:
   (a) Operated or sponsored by a duly accredited law school.
   (b) Operated or sponsored by a bona fide nonprofit community organization.
   (c) Operated or sponsored by a governmental agency.
   (d) Operated, sponsored, or approved by a bar association.
(2) A military legal assistance office.
(3) A lawyer referral service operated, sponsored, or approved by a bar association.
(4) Any bona fide organization that recommends, furnishes or pays for legal services to its members or beneficiaries provided the following conditions are satisfied:
   (a) Such organization, including any affiliate, is so organized and operated that no profit is derived by it from the rendition of legal services by lawyers, and that, if the organization is organized for profit, the legal services are not rendered by lawyers employed, directed, supervised or selected by it except in connection with matters where such organization bears ultimate liability of its member or beneficiary.

Appendix

(b) Neither the lawyer, nor his partner, nor associate, nor any other lawyer affiliated with him or his firm, nor any non-lawyer, shall have initiated or promoted such organization for the primary purpose of providing financial or other benefit to such lawyer, partner, associate or affiliated lawyer.

(c) Such organization is not operated for the purpose of procuring legal work or financial benefit for any lawyer as a private practitioner outside of the legal services program of the organization.

(d) The member or beneficiary to whom the legal services are furnished, and not such organization, is recognized as the client of the lawyer in the matter.

(e) Any member or beneficiary who is entitled to have legal services furnished or paid for by the organization may, if such member or beneficiary so desires, select counsel other than that furnished, selected or approved by the organization for the particular matter involved; and the legal service plan of such organization provides appropriate relief for any member or beneficiary who asserts a claim that representation by counsel furnished, selected or approved would be unethical, improper or inadequate under the circumstances of the matter involved and the plan provides an appropriate procedure for seeking such relief.

(f) The lawyer does not know or have cause to know that such organization is in violation of applicable laws, rules of court and other legal requirements that govern its legal service operations.

(g) Such organization has filed with the appropriate disciplinary authority at least annually a report with respect to its legal service plan, if any, showing its terms, its schedule of benefits, its subscription charges, agreements with counsel, and financial results of its legal service activities or, if it has failed to do so, the lawyer does not know or have cause to know of such failure.

(E) A lawyer shall not accept employment when he knows or it is obvious that the person who seeks his services does so as a result of conduct prohibited under this Disciplinary Rule.

DR 2-104 Suggestion of Need of Legal Services

(A) A lawyer who has given unsolicited advice to a layman that he should obtain counsel or take legal action shall not accept employment resulting from that advice, except that:

(1) A lawyer may accept employment by a close friend, relative, former client (if the advice is germane to the former employment), or one whom the lawyer reasonably believes to be a client.

(2) A lawyer may accept employment that results from his participation in activities designed to educate laymen to recognize legal problems, to make intelligent selection of counsel, or to utilize available legal services if such activities are conducted or sponsored by a qualified legal assistance organization.

(3) A lawyer who is recommended, furnished or paid by a qualified legal assistance organization enumerated in DR 2-103 (D) (1) through (4) may represent a member or beneficiary thereof, to the extent and under the conditions prescribed therein.

(4) Without affecting his right to accept employment, a lawyer may speak publicly or write for publication on legal topics so long as he does not emphasize his own professional experience or reputation and does not undertake to give individual advice.

(5) If success in asserting rights or defenses of his client in litigation in the nature of a class action is dependent upon the joinder of others, a lawyer may accept,

Appendix

but shall not seek, employment from those contacted for the purpose of obtaining their joinder.

DR 2-105 Limitation of Practice

(A) A lawyer shall not hold himself out publicly as a specialist or as limiting his practice, except as permitted under DR 2-102 (A)(6) or as follows:

    (1) A lawyer admitted to practice before the United States Patent Office may use the designation "Patents," "Patent Attorney," or "Patent Lawyer," or any combination of those terms, on his letterhead and office sign. A lawyer engaged in the trademark practice may use the designation "Trademarks," "Trademark Attorney," or "Trademark Lawyer," or any combination of those terms, on his letterhead and office sign, and a lawyer engaged in the admiralty practice may use the designation "Admiralty," "Proctor in Admiralty," or "Admiralty Lawyer," or any combination of those terms, on his letterhead and office sign.

    (2) A lawyer may permit his name to be listed in lawyer referral service offices according to the fields of law in which he will accept referrals.

    (3) A lawyer available to act as a consultant to or as an associate of other lawyers in a particular branch of law or legal service may distribute to other lawyers and publish in legal journals a dignified announcement of such availability, but the announcement shall not contain a representation of special competence or experience. The announcement shall not be distributed to lawyers more frequently than once in a calendar year, but it may be published periodically in legal journals.

    (4) A lawyer who is certified as a specialist in a particular field of law or law practice by the authority having jurisdiction under state law over the subject of spe-

cialization by lawyers may hold himself out as such specialist but only in accordance with the rules prescribed by that authority.

DR 2-106 Fees for Legal Services

(A) A lawyer shall not enter into an agreement for, charge, or collect an illegal or clearly excessive fee.

(B) A fee is clearly excessive when, after a review of the facts, a lawyer of ordinary prudence would be left with a definite and firm conviction that the fee is in excess of a reasonable fee. Factors to be considered as guides in determining the reasonableness of a fee include the following:

> (1) The time and labor required, the novelty and difficulty of the questions involved, and the skill requisite to perform the legal service properly.
> (2) The likelihood, if apparent to the client, that the acceptance of the particular employment will preclude other employment by the lawyer.
> (3) The fee customarily charged in the locality for similar legal services.
> (4) The amount involved and the results obtained.
> (5) The time limitations imposed by the client or by the circumstances.
> (6) The nature and length of the professional relationship with the client.
> (7) The experience, reputation, and ability of the lawyer or lawyers performing the services.
> (8) Whether the fee is fixed or contingent.

(C) A lawyer shall not enter into an arrangement for, charge, or collect a contingent fee for representing a defendant in a criminal case.

DR 2-107 Division of Fees Among Lawyers

(A) A lawyer shall not divide a fee for legal services with another lawyer who is not a partner in or associate of his law firm or law office, unless:

> (1) The client consents to employment of the other law-

Appendix

yer after a full disclosure that a division of fees will be made.
   (2) The division is made in proportion to the services performed and responsibility assumed by each.
   (3) The total fee of the lawyers does not clearly exceed reasonable compensation for all legal services they rendered the client.

(B) This Disciplinary Rule does not prohibit payment to a former partner or associate pursuant to a separation or retirement agreement.

DR 2-108 Agreements Restricting the Practice of a Lawyer

(A) A lawyer shall not be a party to or participate in a partnership or employment agreement with another lawyer that restricts the right of a lawyer to practice law after the termination of a relationship created by the agreement, except as a condition to payment of retirement benefits.

(B) In connection with the settlement of a controversy or suit, a lawyer shall not enter into an agreement that restricts his right to practice law.

DR 2-109 Acceptance of Employment

(A) A lawyer shall not accept employment on behalf of a person if he knows or it is obvious that such person wishes to:
   (1) Bring a legal action, conduct a defense, or assert a position in litigation, or otherwise have steps taken for him, merely for the purpose of harassing or maliciously injuring any person.
   (2) Present a claim or defense in litigation that is not warranted under existing law, unless it can be supported by good faith argument for an extension, modification, or reversal of existing law.

DR 2-110 Withdrawal from Employment

(A) In general.
   (1) If permission for withdrawal from employment is required by the rules of a tribunal, a lawyer shall not

withdraw from employment in a proceeding before that tribunal without its permission.

(2) In any event, a lawyer shall not withdraw from employment until he has taken reasonable steps to avoid foreseeable prejudice to the rights of his client, including giving due notice to his client, allowing time for employment of other counsel, delivering to the client all papers and property to which the client is entitled, and complying with applicable laws and rules.

(3) A lawyer who withdraws from employment shall refund promptly any part of a fee paid in advance that has not been earned.

(B) Mandatory withdrawal.

A lawyer representing a client before a tribunal, with its permission if required by its rules, shall withdraw from employment, and a lawyer representing a client in other matters shall withdraw from employment, if:

(1) He knows or it is obvious that his client is bringing the legal action, conducting the defense, or asserting a position in the litigation, or is otherwise having steps taken for him, merely for the purpose of harassing or maliciously injuring any person.

(2) He knows or it is obvious that his continued employment will result in violation of a Disciplinary Rule.

(3) His mental or physical condition renders it unreasonably difficult for him to carry out the employment effectively.

(4) He is discharged by his client.

(C) Permissive withdrawal.

If DR 2-110 (B) is not applicable, a lawyer may not request permission to withdraw in matters pending before a tribunal, and may not withdraw in other matters, unless such request or such withdrawal is because:

(1) His client:

(a) Insists upon presenting a claim or defense that is

not warranted under existing law and cannot be supported by good faith argument for an extension, modification, or reversal of existing law.
- (b) Personally seeks to pursue an illegal course of conduct.
- (c) Insist that the lawyer pursue a course of conduct that is illegal or that is prohibited under the Disciplinary Rules.
- (d) By other conduct renders it unreasonably difficult for the lawyer to carry out his employment effectively.
- (e) Insists, in a matter not pending before a tribunal, that the lawyer engage in conduct that is contrary to the judgment and advice of the lawyer but not prohibited under the Disciplinary Rules.
- (f) Deliberately disregards an agreement or obligation to the lawyer as to expenses or fees.

(2) His continued employment is likely to result in a violation of a Disciplinary Rule.

(3) His inability to work with co-counsel indicates that the best interests of the client likely will be served by withdrawal.

(4) His mental or physical condition renders it difficult for him to carry out the employment effectively.

(5) His client knowingly and freely assents to termination of his employment.

(6) He believes in good faith, in a proceeding pending before a tribunal, that the tribunal will find the existence of other good cause for withdrawal.

CANON 3

A Lawyer Should Assist in Preventing the Unauthorized Practice of Law

Ethical Considerations

EC 3-1   The prohibition against the practice of law by a layman is grounded in the need of the public for integrity and competence of those who undertake to render legal services. Because of the fiduciary and personal character of the lawyer-client relationship and the inherently complex nature of our legal system, the public can better be assured of the requisite responsibility and competence if the practice of law is confined to those who are subject to the requirements and regulations imposed upon members of the legal profession.

EC 3-2   The sensitive variations in the considerations that bear on legal determinations often make it difficult even for a lawyer to exercise appropriate professional judgment, and it is therefore essential that the personal nature of the relationship of client and lawyer be preserved. Competent professional judgment is the product of a trained familiarity with law and legal processes, a disciplined, analytical approach to legal problems, and a firm ethical commitment.

EC 3-3   A non-lawyer who undertakes to handle legal matters is not governed as to integrity or legal competence by the same rules that govern the conduct of a lawyer. A lawyer is not only subject to that regulation but also is committed to high standards of ethical conduct. The public interest is best served in legal matters by a regulated profession committed to such standards. The Disciplinary Rules protect the public in that they prohibit a lawyer from seeking employment by improper overtures, from acting in cases of divided loyalties, and from submitting to the control of others in the exercise of his judgment. Moreover, a person who entrusts legal matters to a lawyer is protected by the attorney-client privilege and by the duty of the lawyer to hold inviolate the confidences and secrets of his client.

EC 3-4 A layman who seeks legal services often is not in a position to judge whether he will receive proper professional attention. The entrustment of a legal matter may well involve the confidences, the reputation, the property, the freedom, or even the life of the client. Proper protection of members of the public demands that no person be permitted to act in the confidential and demanding capacity of a lawyer unless he is subject to the regulations of the legal profession.

EC 3-5 It is neither necessary nor desirable to attempt the formulation of a single, specific definition of what constitutes the practice of law. Functionally, the practice of law relates to the rendition of services for others that call for the professional judgment of a lawyer. The essence of the professional judgment of the lawyer is his educated ability to relate the general body and philosophy of law to a specific legal problem of a client; and thus, the public interest will be better served if only lawyers are permitted to act in matters involving professional judgment. Where this professional judgment is not involved, non-lawyers, such as court clerks, police officers, abstracters, and many governmental employees, may engage in occupations that require a special knowledge of law in certain areas. But the services of a lawyer are essential in the public interest whenever the exercise of professional legal judgment is required.

EC 3-6 A lawyer often delegates tasks to clerks, secretaries, and other lay persons. Such delegation is proper if the lawyer maintains a direct relationship with his client, supervises the delegated work, and has complete professional responsibility for the work product. This delegation enables a lawyer to render legal service more economically and efficiently.

EC 3-7 The prohibition against a non-lawyer practicing law does not prevent a layman from representing himself, for then he is ordinarily exposing only himself to possible injury. The purpose of the legal profession is to make educated legal representation available to the public; but anyone who does not wish to avail himself of such representation is not required to do so. Even so, the legal profession should help members of the public to recognize legal problems and to understand why it may be unwise for them to act for themselves in matters having legal consequences.

EC 3-8 Since a lawyer should not aid or encourage a layman to practice law, he should not practice law in association with a layman or otherwise share legal fees with a layman. This does not mean, however, that the pecuniary value of the interest of a deceased lawyer in his firm or practice may not be paid to his estate or specified persons such as his widow or heirs. In like manner, profit-sharing retirement plans of a lawyer or law firm which include non-lawyer office employees are not improper. These limited exceptions to the rule against sharing legal fees with laymen are permissible since they do not aid or encourage laymen to practice law.

EC 3-9 Regulation of the practice of law is accomplished principally by the respective states. Authority to engage in the practice of law conferred in any jurisdiction is not per se a grant of the right to practice elsewhere, and it is improper for a lawyer to engage in practice where he is not permitted by law or by court order to do so. However, the demands of business and the mobility of our society pose distinct problems in the regulation of the practice of law by the states. In furtherance of the public interest, the legal profession should discourage regulation that unreasonably imposes territorial limitations upon the right of a lawyer to handle the legal affairs of his client or upon the opportunity of a client to obtain the services of a lawyer of his choice in all matters including the presentation of a contested matter in a tribunal before which the lawyer is not permanently admitted to practice.

Disciplinary Rules

DR 3-101 Aiding Unauthorized Practice of Law

(A) A lawyer shall not aid a non-lawyer in the unauthorized practice of law.

Appendix

(B) A lawyer shall not practice law in a jurisdiction where to do so would be in violation of regulations of the profession in that jurisdiction.

DR 3-102 Dividing Legal Fees with a Non-Lawyer

(A) A lawyer or law firm shall not share legal fees with a non-lawyer, except that:

> (1) An agreement by a lawyer with his firm, partner, or associate may provide for the payment of money, over a reasonable period of time after his death, to his estate or to one or more specified persons.
>
> (2) A lawyer who undertakes to complete unfinished legal business of a deceased lawyer may pay to the estate of the deceased lawyer that proportion of the total compensation which fairly represents the services rendered by the deceased lawyer.
>
> (3) A lawyer or law firm may include non-lawyer employees in a retirement plan, even though the plan is based in whole or in part on a profit-sharing arrangement.

DR 3-103 Forming a Partnership with a Non-Lawyer

(A) A lawyer shall not form a partnership with a non-lawyer if any of the activities of the partnership consist of the practice of law.

CANON 4

A Lawyer Should Preserve the Confidences and Secrets of a Client

Ethical Considerations

EC 4-1 Both the fiduciary relationship existing between lawyer and client and the proper functioning of the legal system require the preservation by the lawyer of confidences and secrets of one who has employed or sought to employ him. A client must feel free to discuss whatever he wishes with his lawyer and a lawyer must be equally free to obtain information beyond that volunteered by his client. A lawyer should be fully informed of all the facts of the matter he is handling in order for his client to obtain the full advantage of our legal system. It is for the lawyer in the exercise of his independent professional judgment to separate the relevant and important from the irrelevant and unimportant. The observance of the ethical obligation of a lawyer to hold inviolate the confidences and secrets of his client not only facilitates the full development of facts essential to proper representation of the client but also encourages laymen to seek early legal assistance.

EC 4-2 The obligation to protect confidences and secrets obviously does not preclude a lawyer from revealing information when his client consents after full disclosure, when necessary to perform his professional employment, when permitted by a Disciplinary Rule, or when required by law. Unless the client otherwise directs, a lawyer may disclose the affairs of his client to partners or associates of his firm. It is a matter of common knowledge that the normal operation of a law office exposes confidential professional information to non-lawyer employees of the office, particularly secretaries and those having access to the files; and this obligates a lawyer to exercise care in selecting and training his employees so that the sanctity of all confidences and secrets of his clients may be preserved. If the obligation extends to two or more clients as to the same information, a lawyer should obtain the permission of all before revealing the information. A lawyer must always be sensitive to the rights and wishes of his client and act scrupulously in the making of decisions which may involve the disclosure of information obtained in his professional relationship. Thus, in the absence of consent of his client after full disclosure, a lawyer should not associate another lawyer in the handling of a matter; nor should he, in the absence of consent, seek counsel from another lawyer if there is a reasonable possibility that the identity of the client or his confidences or secrets would be revealed to such lawyer. Both

Appendix

social amenities and professional duty should cause a lawyer to shun indiscreet conversations concerning his clients.

EC 4-3 Unless the client otherwise directs, it is not improper for a lawyer to give limited information from his files to an outside agency necessary for statistical, bookkeeping, accounting, data processing, banking, printing, or other legitimate purposes, provided he exercises due care in the selection of the agency and warns the agency that the information must be kept confidential.

EC 4-4 The attorney-client privilege is more limited than the ethical obligation of a lawyer to guard the confidences and secrets of his client. This ethical precept, unlike the evidentiary privilege, exists without regard to the nature or source of information or the fact that others share the knowledge. A lawyer should endeavor to act in a manner which preserves the evidentiary privilege; for example, he should avoid professional discussions in the presence of persons to whom the privilege does not extend. A lawyer owes an obligation to advise the client of the attorney-client privilege and timely to assert the privilege unless it is waived by the client.

EC 4-5 A lawyer should not use information acquired in the course of the representation of a client to the disadvantage of the client and a lawyer should not use, except with the consent of his client after full disclosure, such information for his own purposes. Likewise, a lawyer should be diligent in his efforts to prevent the misuse of such information by his employees and associates. Care should be exercised by a lawyer to prevent the disclosure of the confidences and secrets of one client to another, and no employment should be accepted that might require such disclosure.

EC 4-6 The obligation of a lawyer to preserve the confidences and secrets of his client continues after the termination of his employment. Thus a lawyer should not attempt to sell a law practice as a going business because, among other reasons, to do so would involve the disclosure of confidences and secrets. A lawyer should also provide for the protection of the confidences and secrets of his client following the termination of the practice of the lawyer, whether termination is due to death, disability, or retirement. For example, a lawyer might provide for the personal papers of the client to be returned to him and for the papers of the lawyer to be delivered to another lawyer or to be destroyed. In determining the method of disposition, the instructions and wishes of the client should be a dominant consideration.

Disciplinary Rules

DR 4-101 Preservation of Confidences and Secrets of a Client

(A) "Confidence" refers to information protected by the attorney-client privilege under applicable law, and "secret" refers to other information gained in the professional relationship that the client has requested be held inviolate or the disclosure of which would be embarrassing or would be likely to be detrimental to the client.

(B) Except when permitted under DR 4-101 (C), a lawyer shall not knowingly:
    (1) Reveal a confidence or secret of his client.
    (2) Use a confidence or secret of his client to the disadvantage of the client.
    (3) Use a confidence or secret of his client for the advantage of himself or of a third person, unless the client consents after full disclosure.

(C) A lawyer may reveal:
    (1) Confidences or secrets with the consent of the client or clients affected, but only after a full disclosure to them.
    (2) Confidences or secrets when permitted under Disciplinary Rules or required by law or court order.
    (3) The intention of his client to commit a crime and the information necessary to prevent the crime.
    (4) Confidences or secrets necessary to establish or collect his fee or to defend himself or his employees or associates against an accusation of wrongful conduct.

Appendix

(D) A lawyer shall exercise reasonable care to prevent his employees, associates, and others whose services are utilized by him from disclosing or using confidences or secrets of a client, except that a lawyer may reveal the information allowed by DR 4-101 (C) through an employee.

CANON 5

A Lawyer Should Exercise Independent Professional Judgment on Behalf of a Client

Ethical Considerations

EC 5-1 The professional judgment of a lawyer should be exercised, within the bounds of the law, solely for the benefit of his client and free of compromising influences and loyalties. Neither his personal interests, the interests of other clients, nor the desires of third persons should be permitted to dilute his loyalty to his client.

Interests of a Lawyer That May Affect His Judgment

EC 5-2 A lawyer should not accept proffered employment if his personal interests or desires will, or there is a reasonable probability that they will, affect adversely the advice to be given or services to be rendered the prospective client. After accepting employment, a lawyer carefully should refrain from acquiring a property right or assuming a position that would tend to make his judgment less protective of the interests of his client.

EC 5-3 The self-interest of a lawyer resulting from his ownership of property in which his client also has an interest or which may affect property of his client may interfere with the exercise of free judgment on behalf of his client. If such interference would occur with respect to a prospective client, a lawyer should decline employment proffered by him. After accepting employment, a lawyer should not acquire property rights that would adversely affect his professional judgment in the representation of his client. Even if the property interests of a lawyer do not presently interfere with the exercise of his independent judgment, but the likelihood of interference can reasonably be foreseen by him, a lawyer should explain the situation to his client and should decline employment or withdraw unless the client consents to the continuance of the relationship after full disclosure. A lawyer should not seek to persuade his client to permit him to invest in an undertaking of his client nor make improper use of his professional relationship to influence his client to invest in an enterprise in which the lawyer is interested.

EC 5-4 If, in the course of his representation of a client, a lawyer is permitted to receive from his client a beneficial ownership in publication rights relating to the subject matter of the employment, he may be tempted to subordinate the interests of his client to his own anticipated pecuniary gain. For example, a lawyer in a criminal case who obtains from his client television, radio, motion picture, newspaper, magazine, book, or other publication rights with respect to the case may be influenced, consciously or unconsciously, to a course of conduct that will enhance the value of his publication rights to the prejudice of his client. To prevent these potentially differing interests, such arrangements should be scrupulously avoided prior to the termination of all aspects of the matter giving rise to the employment, even though his employment has previously ended.

EC 5-5 A lawyer should not suggest to his client that a gift be made to himself or for his benefit. If a lawyer accepts a gift from his client, he is peculiarly susceptible to the charge that he unduly influenced or over-reached the client. If a client voluntarily offers to make a gift to his lawyer, the lawyer may accept the gift, but before doing so, he should urge that his client secure disinterested advice from an independent, competent person who is cognizant of all the circumstances. Other than in exceptional circumstances, a lawyer should insist that an instrument in which his client desires to name him beneficially be prepared by another lawyer selected by the client.

Appendix

EC 5-6 A lawyer should not consciously influence a client to name him as executor, trustee, or lawyer in an instrument. In those cases where a client wishes to name his lawyer as such, care should be taken by the lawyer to avoid even the appearance of impropriety.

EC 5-7 The possibility of an adverse effect upon the exercise of free judgment by a lawyer on behalf of his client during litigation generally makes it undesirable for the lawyer to acquire a proprietary interest in the case of his client or otherwise to become financially interested in the outcome of the litigation. However, it is not improper for a lawyer to protect his right to collect a fee for his services by the assertion of legally permissible liens, even though by doing so he may acquire an interest in the outcome of litigation. Although a contingent fee arrangement gives a lawyer a financial interest in the outcome of litigation, a reasonable contingent fee is permissible in civil cases because it may be the only means by which a layman can obtain the services of a lawyer of his choice. But a lawyer, because he is in a better position to evaluate a cause of action, should enter into a contingent fee arrangement only in those instances where the arrangement will be beneficial to the client.

EC 5-8 A financial interest in the outcome of litigation also results if monetary advances are made by the lawyer to his client. Although this assistance generally is not encouraged, there are instances when it is not improper to make loans to a client. For example, the advancing or guaranteeing of payment of the costs and expenses of litigation by a lawyer may be the only way a client can enforce his cause of action, but the ultimate liability for such costs and expenses must be that of the client.

EC 5-9 Occasionally a lawyer is called upon to decide in a particular case whether he will be a witness or an advocate. If a lawyer is both counsel and witness, he becomes more easily impeachable for interest and thus may be a less effective witness. Conversely, the opposing counsel may be handicapped in challenging the credibility of the lawyer when the lawyer also appears as an advocate in the case. An advocate who becomes a witness is in the unseemly and ineffective position of arguing his own credibility.

The roles of an advocate and of a witness are inconsistent; the function of an advocate is to advance or argue the cause of another, while that of a witness is to state facts objectively.

EC 5-10 Problems incident to the lawyer-witness relationship arise at different stages; they relate either to whether a lawyer should accept employment or should withdraw from employment. Regardless of when the problem arises, his decision is to be governed by the same basic considerations. It is not objectionable for a lawyer who is a potential witness to be an advocate if it is unlikely that he will be called as a witness because his testimony would be merely cumulative or if his testimony will relate only to an uncontested issue. In the exceptional situation where it will be manifestly unfair to the client for the lawyer to refuse employment or to withdraw when he will likely be a witness on a contested issue, he may serve as advocate even though he may be a witness. In making such decision, he should determine the personal or financial sacrifice of the client that may result from his refusal of employment or withdrawal therefrom, the materiality of his testimony, and the effectiveness of his representation in view of his personal involvement. In weighing these factors, it should be clear that refusal or withdrawal will impose an unreasonable hardship upon the client before the lawyer accepts or continues the employment. Where the question arises, doubts should be resolved in favor of the lawyer testifying and against his becoming or continuing as an advocate.

EC 5-11 A lawyer should not permit his personal interests to influence his advice relative to a suggestion by his client that additional counsel be employed. In like manner, his personal interests should not deter him from suggesting that additional counsel be employed; on the contrary, he should be alert to the desirability of recommending additional counsel when, in his judgment, the proper representation of his client requires it. However, a lawyer should advise his client not to employ additional counsel suggested by the client if the lawyer believes that such employment would be a disservice to the client, and he should disclose the reasons for his belief.

EC 5-12 Inability of co-counsel to agree on a matter vital to the representation of their client requires that their disagreement be submitted by them jointly to their client for his resolution, and the decision of the client shall control the action to be taken.

EC 5-13 A lawyer should not maintain membership in or be influenced by any organization of employees that undertakes to prescribe, direct, or suggest when or how he should fulfill his professional obligations to a person or organization that employs him as a lawyer. Although it is not necessarily improper for a lawyer employed by a corporation or similar entity to be a member of an organization of employees, he should be vigilant to safeguard his fidelity as a lawyer to his employer, free from outside influences.

Interests of Multiple Clients

EC 5-14 Maintaining the independence of professional judgment required of a lawyer precludes his acceptance or continuation of employment that will adversely affect his judgment on behalf of or dilute his loyalty to a client. This problem arises whenever a lawyer is asked to represent two or more clients who may have differing interests, whether such interests be conflicting, inconsistent, diverse, or otherwise discordant.

EC 5-15 If a lawyer is requested to undertake or to continue representation of multiple clients having potentially differing interests, he must weigh carefully the possibility that his judgment may be impaired or his loyalty divided if he accepts or continues the employment. He should resolve all doubts against the propriety of the representation. A lawyer should never represent in litigation multiple clients with differing interests; and there are few situations in which he would be justified in representing in litigation multiple clients with potentially differing interests. If a lawyer accepted such employment and the interests did become actually differing, he would have to withdraw from employment with likelihood of resulting hardship on the clients; and for this reason it is preferable that he refuse the employment initially. On the other hand, there are many instances in which a lawyer may properly serve multiple clients having potentially differing interests in matters not involving litigation. If the interests vary only slightly, it is generally likely that the lawyer will not be subjected to an adverse influence and that he can retain his independent judgment on behalf of each client; and if the interests become differing, withdrawal is less likely to have a disruptive effect upon the causes of his clients.

EC 5-16 In those instances in which a lawyer is justified in representing two or more clients having differing interests, it is nevertheless essential that each client be given the opportunity to evaluate his need for representation free of any potential conflict and to obtain other counsel if he so desires. Thus before a lawyer may represent multiple clients, he should explain fully to each client the implications of the common representation and should accept or continue employment only if the clients consent. If there are present other circumstances that might cause any of the multiple clients to question the undivided loyalty of the lawyer, he should also advise all of the clients of those circumstances.

EC 5-17 Typically recurring situations involving potentially differing interests are those in which a lawyer is asked to represent co-defendants in a criminal case, co-plaintiffs in a personal injury case, an insured and his insurer, and beneficiaries of the estate of a decedent. Whether a lawyer can fairly and adequately protect the interests of multiple clients in these and similar situations depends upon an analysis of each case. In certain circumstances, there may exist little chance of the judgment of the lawyer being adversely affected by the slight possibility that the interests will become actually differing; in other circumstances, the chance of adverse effect upon his judgment is not unlikely.

EC 5-18 A lawyer employed or retained by a corporation or similar entity owes his allegiance to the entity and not to a stockholder, director, officer, employee, representative, or other person connected with the entity. In advising the entity, a lawyer should keep paramount its interests and his professional judgment should not be influenced by the personal desires of any person or organization. Occasionally a lawyer for an entity is requested by a stockholder, director, officer, employee, representative, or other person connected with the entity to represent him in an individual capac-

Appendix

ity; in such case the lawyer may serve the individual only if the lawyer is convinced that differing interests are not present.

EC 5-19 A lawyer may represent several clients whose interests are not actually or potentially differing. Nevertheless, he should explain any circumstances that might cause a client to question his undivided loyalty. Regardless of the belief of a lawyer that he may properly represent multiple clients, he must defer to a client who holds the contrary belief and withdraw from representation of that client.

EC 5-20 A lawyer is often asked to serve as an impartial arbitrator or mediator in matters which involve present or former clients. He may serve in either capacity if he first discloses such present or former relationships. After a lawyer has undertaken to act as an impartial arbitrator or mediator, he should not thereafter represent in the dispute any of the parties involved.

Desires of Third Persons

EC 5-21 The obligation of a lawyer to exercise professional judgment solely on behalf of his client requires that he disregard the desires of others that might impair his free judgment. The desires of a third person will seldom adversely affect a lawyer unless that person is in a position to exert strong economic, political, or social pressures upon the lawyer. These influences are often subtle, and a lawyer must be alert to their existence. A lawyer subjected to outside pressures should make full disclosure of them to his client; and if he or his client believes that the effectiveness of his representation has been or will be impaired thereby, the lawyer should take proper steps to withdraw from representation of his client.

EC 5-22 Economic, political, or social pressures by third persons are less likely to impinge upon the independent judgment of a lawyer in a matter in which he is compensated directly by his client and his professional work is exclusively with his client. On the other hand, if a lawyer is compensated from a source other than his client, he may feel a sense of responsibility to someone other than his client.

EC 5-23 A person or organization that pays or furnishes lawyers to represent others possesses a potential power to exert strong pressures against the independent judgment of those lawyers. Some employers may be interested in furthering their own economic, political, or social goals without regard to the professional responsibility of the lawyer to his individual client. Others may be far more concerned with establishment or extension of legal principles than in the immediate protection of the rights of the lawyer's individual client. On some occasions, decisions on priority of work may be made by the employer rather than the lawyer with the result that prosecution of work already undertaken for clients is postponed to their detriment. Similarly, an employer may seek, consciously or unconsciously, to further its own economic interests through the action of the lawyers employed by it. Since a lawyer must always be free to exercise his professional judgment without regard to the interests or motives of a third person, the lawyer who is employed by one to represent another must constantly guard against erosion of his professional freedom.

EC 5-24 To assist a lawyer in preserving his professional independence, a number of courses are available to him. For example, a lawyer should not practice with or in the form of a professional legal corporation, even though the corporate form is permitted by law, if any director, officer, or stockholder of it is a non-lawyer. Although a lawyer may be employed by a business corporation with non-lawyers serving as directors or officers, and they necessarily have the right to make decisions of business policy, a lawyer must decline to accept direction of his professional judgment from any layman. Various types of legal aid offices are administered by boards of directors composed of lawyers and laymen. A lawyer should not accept employment from such an organization unless the board sets only broad policies and there is no interference in the relationship of the lawyer and the individual client he serves. Where a lawyer is employed by an organization, a written agreement that defines the relationship between him and the organization and provides for his independence is desirable since it may serve to prevent misunderstanding as to their respective roles. Although other innovations in the means of supplying legal counsel may develop, the responsibility of the lawyer to maintain his

Appendix

professional independence remains constant, and the legal profession must insure that changing circumstances do not result in loss of the professional independence of the lawyer.

Disciplinary Rules

DR 5-101 Refusing Employment When the Interests of the Lawyer May Impair His Independent Professional Judgment

(A) Except with the consent of his client after full disclosure, a lawyer shall not accept employment if the exercise of his professional judgment on behalf of his client will be or reasonably may be affected by his own financial, business, property, or personal interests.

(B) A lawyer shall not accept employment in contemplated or pending litigation if he knows or it is obvious that he or a lawyer in his firm ought to be called as a witness, except that he may undertake the employment and he or a lawyer in his firm may testify:

> (1) If the testimony will relate solely to an uncontested matter.
>
> (2) If the testimony will relate solely to a matter of formality and there is no reason to believe that substantial evidence will be offered in opposition to the testimony.
>
> (3) If the testimony will relate solely to the nature and value of legal services rendered in the case by the lawyer or his firm to the client.
>
> (4) As to any matter, if refusal would work a substantial hardship on the client because of the distinctive value of the lawyer or his firm as counsel in the particular case.

DR 5-102 Withdrawal as Counsel When the Lawyer Becomes a Witness

(A) If, after undertaking employment in contemplated or pending litigation, a lawyer learns or it is obvious that he or a lawyer in his firm ought to be called as a witness on behalf of his client, he shall withdraw from the conduct of the trial and his firm, if any, shall not continue representation in the trial, except that he may continue the representation and he or a lawyer in his firm may testify in the circumstances enumerated in DR 5-101(B) (1) through (4).

(B) If, after undertaking employment in contemplated or pending litigation, a lawyer learns or it is obvious that he or a lawyer in his firm may be called as a witness other than on behalf of his client, he may continue the representation until it is apparent that his testimony is or may be prejudicial to his client.

DR 5-103 Avoiding Acquisition of Interest in Litigation

(A) A lawyer shall not acquire a proprietary interest in the cause of action or subject matter of litigation he is conducting for a client, except that he may:

    (1) Acquire a lien granted by law to secure his fee or expenses.

    (2) Contract with a client for a reasonable contingent fee in a civil case.

(B) While representing a client in connection with contemplated or pending litigation, a lawyer shall not advance or guarantee financial assistance to his client, except that a lawyer may advance or guarantee the expenses of litigation, including court costs, expenses of investigation, expenses of medical examination, and costs of obtaining and presenting evidence, provided the client remains ultimately liable for such expenses.

DR 5-104 Limiting Business Relations with a Client

(A) A lawyer shall not enter into a business transaction with a client if they have differing interests therein and if the client expects the lawyer to exercise his professional judgment therein for the protection of the client, unless the client has consented after full disclosure.

(B) Prior to conclusion of all aspects of the matter giving rise to his employment, a lawyer shall not enter into any arrangement or understanding with a client or a prospective client by which he

Appendix

acquires an interest in publication rights with respect to the subject matter of his employment or proposed employment.

DR 5-105 Refusing to Accept or Continue Employment if the Interests of Another Client May Impair the Independent Professional Judgment of the Lawyer

(A) A lawyer shall decline proffered employment if the exercise of his independent professional judgment in behalf of a client will be or is likely to be adversely affected by the acceptance of the proffered employment, or if it would be likely to involve him in representing differing interests, except to the extent permitted under DR 5-105(C).

(B) A lawyer shall not continue multiple employment if the exercise of his independent professional judgment in behalf of a client will be or is likely to be adversely affected by his representation of another client, or if it would be likely to involve him in representing differing interests, except to the extent permitted under DR5-105(C).

(C) In the situations covered by DR 5-105 (A) and (B), a lawyer may represent multiple clients if it is obvious that he can adequately represent the interest of each and if each consents to the representation after full disclosure of the possible effect of such representation on the exercise of his independent professional judgment on behalf of each.

(D) If a lawyer is required to decline employment or to withdraw from employment under a Disciplinary Rule, no partner, or associate, or any other lawyer affiliated with him or his firm, may accept or continue such employment.

DR 5-106 Settling Similar Claims of Clients

(A) A lawyer who represents two or more clients shall not make or participate in the making of an aggregate settlement of the claims of or against his clients, unless each client has consented to the settlement after being advised of the existence and nature of all the claims involved in the proposed settlement, of the total amount of the settlement, and of the participation of each person in the settlement.

DR 5-107 Avoiding Influence by Others Than the Client

(A) Except with the consent of his client after full disclosure, a lawyer shall not:

> (1) Accept compensation for his legal services from one other than his client.
>
> (2) Accept from one other than his client any thing of value related to his representation of or his employment by his client.

(B) A lawyer shall not permit a person who recommends, employs, or pays him to render legal services for another to direct or regulate his professional judgment in rendering such legal services.

(C) A lawyer shall not practice with or in the form of a professional corporation or association authorized to practice law for a profit, if:

> (1) A non-lawyer owns any interest therein, except that a fiduciary representative of the estate of a lawyer may hold the stock or interest of the lawyer for a reasonable time during administration;
>
> (2) A non-lawyer is a corporate director or officer thereof; or
>
> (3) A non-lawyer has the right to direct or control the professional judgment of a lawyer.

CANON 6

A Lawyer Should Represent a Client Competently

Ethical Considerations

EC 6-1 Because of his vital role in the legal process, a lawyer should act with competence and proper care in representing clients. He should strive to become and remain proficient in his practice and should accept employment only in matters which he is or intends to become competent to handle.

EC 6-2 A lawyer is aided in attaining and maintaining his

Appendix

competence by keeping abreast of current legal literature and developments, participating in continuing legal education programs, concentrating in particular areas of the law, and by utilizing other available means. He has the additional ethical obligation to assist in improving the legal profession, and he may do so by participating in bar activities intended to advance the quality and standards of members of the profession. Of particular importance is the careful training of his younger associates and the giving of sound guidance to all lawyers who consult him. In short, a lawyer should strive at all levels to aid the legal profession in advancing the highest possible standards of integrity and competence and to meet those standards himself.

EC 6-3   While the licensing of a lawyer is evidence that he has met the standards then prevailing for admission to the bar, a lawyer generally should not accept employment in any area of the law in which he is not qualified. However, he may accept such employment if in good faith he expects to become qualified through study and investigation, as long as such preparation would not result in unreasonable delay or expense to his client. Proper preparation and representation may require the association by the lawyer of professionals in other disciplines. A lawyer offered employment in a matter in which he is not and does not expect to become so qualified should either decline the employment or, with the consent of his client, accept the employment and associate a lawyer who is competent in the matter.

EC 6-4   Having undertaken representation, a lawyer should use proper care to safeguard the interests of his client. If a lawyer has accepted employment in a matter beyond his competence but in which he expected to become competent, he should diligently undertake the work and study necessary to qualify himself. In addition to being qualified to handle a particular matter, his obligation to his client requires him to prepare adequately for and give appropriate attention to his legal work.

EC 6-5   A lawyer should have pride in his professional endeavors. His obligation to act competently calls for higher motivation than that arising from fear of civil liability or disciplinary penalty.

EC 6-6 A lawyer should not seek, by contract or other means, to limit his individual liability to his client for his malpractice. A lawyer who handles the affairs of his client properly has no need to attempt to limit his liability for his professional activities and one who does not handle the affairs of his client properly should not be permitted to do so. A lawyer who is a stockholder in or is associated with a professional legal corporation may, however, limit his liability for malpractice of his associates in the corporation, but only to the extent permitted by law.

Disciplinary Rules

DR 6-101 Failing to Act Competently
(A) A lawyer shall not:
 (1) Handle a legal matter which he knows or should know that he is not competent to handle, without associating with him a lawyer who is competent to handle it.
 (2) Handle a legal matter without preparation adequate in the circumstances.
 (3) Neglect a legal matter entrusted to him.

DR 6-102 Limiting Liability to Client
(A) A lawyer shall not attempt to exonerate himself from or limit his liability to his client for his personal malpractice.

CANON 7

A Lawyer Should Represent a Client Zealously Within the Bounds of the Law

Ethical Considerations

EC 7-1 The duty of a lawyer, both to his client and to the legal system, is to represent his client zealously within the bounds of the law, which includes Disciplinary Rules and enforceable professional regulations. The professional responsibility of a lawyer derives from his membership in a profession which has the duty of assisting members of the public to secure and protect available legal rights and benefits. In our government of laws and not of men, each member of our society is entitled to have his conduct judged and regulated in accordance with the law, to seek any lawful objective through legally permissible means; and to present for adjudication any lawful claim, issue, or defense.

EC 7-2 The bounds of the law in a given case are often difficult to ascertain. The language of legislative enactments and judicial opinions may be uncertain as applied to varying factual situations. The limits and specific meaning of apparently relevant law may be made doubtful by changing or developing constitutional interpretations, inadequately expressed statutes or judicial opinions, and changing public and judicial attitudes. Certainty of law ranges from well-settled rules through areas of conflicting authority to areas without precedent.

EC 7-3 Where the bounds of law are uncertain, the action of a lawyer may depend on whether he is serving as advocate or adviser. A lawyer may serve simultaneously as both advocate and adviser, but the two roles are essentially different. In asserting a position on behalf of his client, and advocate for the most part deals with past conduct and must take the facts as he finds them. By contrast, a lawyer serving as adviser primarily assists his client in determining the course of future conduct and relationships. While serving as advocate, a lawyer should resolve in favor of his client doubts as to the bounds of the law. In serving a client as adviser, a lawyer in appropriate circumstances should give his professional opinion as to what the ultimate decisions of the courts would likely be as to the applicable law.

Duty of the Lawyer to a Client

EC 7-4 The advocate may urge any permissible construction of the law favorable to his client, without regard to his professional opinion as to the likelihood that the construction will ultimately prevail. His conduct is within the bounds of the law, and therefore permissible, if the position taken is supported by the law or is supportable by a good faith argument for an extension, modification, or reversal of the law. However, a lawyer is not justified in asserting a position in litigation that is frivolous.

EC 7-5 A lawyer as adviser furthers the interest of his client by giving his professional opinion as to what he believes would likely be the ultimate decision of the courts on the matter at hand and by informing his client of the practical effect of such decision. He may continue in the representation of his client even though his client has elected to pursue a course of conduct contrary to the advice of the lawyer so long as he does not thereby knowingly assist the client to engage in illegal conduct or to take a frivolous legal position. A lawyer should never encourage or aid his client to commit criminal acts or counsel his client on how to violate the law and avoid punishment therefor.

EC 7-6 Whether the proposed action of a lawyer is within the bounds of the law may be a perplexing question when his client is contemplating a course of conduct having legal consequences that vary according to the client's intent, motive, or desires at the time of the action. Often a lawyer is asked to assist his client in developing evidence relevant to the state of mind of the client at a particular time. He may properly assist his client in the development and preservation of evidence of existing motive, intent, or desire; obviously, he may not do anything furthering the creation or preservation of false evidence. In many cases a lawyer may not be certain as to the state of mind of his client, and in those situations he should resolve reasonable doubts in favor of his client.

EC 7-7 In certain areas of legal representation not affecting the merits of the cause or substantially prejudicing the rights of a client, a lawyer is entitled to make decisions on his own. But otherwise the authority to make decisions is exclusively that of the client and, if made within the framework of the law, such decisions are binding on his lawyer. As typical examples in civil cases, it is for the client to decide whether he will accept a settlement offer or whether he will waive his right to plead an affirmative defense. A defense lawyer in a criminal case has the duty to advise his client fully on whether a particular plea to a charge appears to be desirable and as to the prospects of success on appeal, but it is for the client to decide what plea should be entered and whether an appeal should be taken.

EC 7-8 A lawyer should exert his best efforts to insure that decisions of his client are made only after the client has been informed of relevant considerations. A lawyer ought to initiate this decision-making process if the client does not do so. Advice of a lawyer to his client need not be confined to purely legal considerations. A lawyer should advise his client of the possible effect of each legal alternative. A lawyer should bring to bear upon this decision-making process the fullness of his experience as well as his objective viewpoint. In assisting his client to reach a proper decision, it is often desirable for a lawyer to point out those factors which may lead to a decision that is morally just as well as legally permissible. He may emphasize the possibility of harsh consequences that might result from assertion of legally permissible positions. In the final analysis, however, the lawyer should always remember that the decision whether to forego legally available objectives or methods because of non-legal factors is ultimately for the client and not for himself. In the event that the client in a non-adjudicatory matter insists upon a course of conduct that is contrary to the judgment and advice of the lawyer but not prohibited by Disciplinary Rules, the lawyer may withdraw from the employment.

EC 7-9 In the exercise of his professional judgment on those decisions which are for his determination in the handling of a legal matter, a lawyer should always act in a manner consistent with the best interests of his client. However, when an action in the best interest of his client seems to him to be unjust, he may ask his client for permission to forego such action.

EC 7-10 The duty of a lawyer to represent his client with zeal does not militate against his concurrent obligation to treat with consideration all persons involved in the legal process and to avoid the infliction of needless harm.

EC 7-11 The responsibilities of a lawyer may vary according to the intelligence, experience, mental condition or age of a client, the obligation of a public officer, or the nature of a particular proceeding. Examples include the representation of an illiterate or an incompetent, service as a public prosecutor or other government lawyer, and appearances before administrative and legislative bodies.

EC 7-12 Any mental or physical condition of a client that renders him incapable of making a considered judgment on his own behalf casts additional responsibilities upon his lawyer. Where an incompetent is acting through a guardian or other legal representative, a lawyer must look to such representative for those decisions which are normally the prerogative of the client to make. If a client under disability has no legal representative, his lawyer may be compelled in court proceedings to make decisions on behalf of the client. If the client is capable of understanding the matter in question or of contributing to the advancement of his interests, regardless of whether he is legally disqualified from performing certain acts, the lawyer should obtain from him all possible aid. If the disability of a client and the lack of a legal representative compel the lawyer to make decisions for his client, the lawyer should consider all circumstances then prevailing and act with care to safeguard and advance the interests of his client. But obviously a lawyer cannot perform any act or make any decision which the law requires his client to perform or make, either acting for himself if competent, or by a duly constituted representative if legally incompetent.

EC 7-13 The responsibility of a public prosecutor differs from that of the usual advocate; his duty is to seek justice, not merely to convict. This special duty exists because: (1) the prosecutor represents the sovereign and therefore should use restraint in the discretionary exercise of governmental powers, such as in the selection of cases to prosecute; (2) during trial the prosecutor is not only an advocate but he also may make decisions normally made by an individual client, and those affecting the public interest should be fair to all; and (3) in our system of criminal justice the accused is to be given the benefit of all reasonable doubts. With respect to evidence and witnesses, the prosecutor has responsibilities different from those of a lawyer in private practice: the prosecutor should make timely disclosure to the defense of available evidence, known to him, that tends to negate the guilt of the accused, mitigate the degree of the offense, or reduce the punishment. Further, a prosecutor should not intentionally avoid pursuit of evidence merely because he believes it will damage the prosecutor's case or aid the accused.

EC 7-14 A government lawyer who has discretionary power relative to litigation should refrain from instituting or continuing litigation that is obviously unfair. A government lawyer not having such discretionary power who believes there is lack of merit in a controversy submitted to him should so advise his superiors and recommend the avoidance of unfair litigation. A government lawyer in a civil action or administrative proceeding has the responsibility to seek justice and to develop a full and fair record, and he should not use his position or the economic power of the government to harass parties or to bring about unjust settlements or results.

EC 7-15 The nature and purpose of proceedings before administrative agencies vary widely. The proceedings may be legislative or quasi-judicial, or a combination of both. They may be *ex parte* in character, in which event they may originate either at the instance of the agency or upon motion of an interested party. The scope of an inquiry may be purely investigative or it may be truly adversary looking toward the adjudication of specific rights of a party or of classes of parties. The foregoing are but examples of some of the types of proceedings conducted by administrative agencies. A lawyer appearing before an administrative agency, regardless of the nature of the proceeding it is conducting, has the continuing duty to advance the cause of his client within the bounds of the law. Where the applicable rules of the agency impose specific obligations upon a lawyer, it is his duty to comply therewith, unless the lawyer has a legitimate basis for challenging the validity thereof. In all appearances before administrative agencies, a lawyer should identify himself, his client if identity of his client is not privileged, and the representative nature of his appearance. It is not improper, however, for a lawyer to seek from an agency information available to the public without identifying his client.

EC 7-16 The primary business of a legislative body is to enact laws rather than to adjudicate controversies, although on occasion the activities of a legislative body may take on the characteristics of an adversary proceeding, particularly in investigative and impeachment matters. The role of a lawyer supporting or opposing proposed legislation normally is quite different from his role in representing a person under investigation or on trial by a legislative body. When a lawyer appears in connection with proposed legislation, he seeks to affect the lawmaking process, but when he appears on behalf of a client in investigatory or impeachment proceedings, he is concerned with the protection of the rights of his client. In either event, he should identify himself and his client, if identity of his client is not privileged, and should comply with applicable laws and legislative rules.

EC 7-17 The obligation of loyalty to his client applies only to a lawyer in the discharge of his professional duties and implies no obligation to adopt a personal viewpoint favorable to the interests or desires of his client. While a lawyer must act always with circumspection in order that his conduct will not adversely affect the rights of a client in a matter he is then handling, he may take positions on public issues and espouse legal reforms he favors without regard to the individual views of any client.

EC 7-18 The legal system in its broadest sense functions best when persons in need of legal advice or assistance are represented by their own counsel. For this reason a lawyer should not communicate on the subject matter of the representation of his client with a person he knows to be represented in the matter by a lawyer, unless pursuant to law or rule of court or unless he has the consent of the lawyer for that person. If one is not represented by

Appendix

counsel, a lawyer representing another may have to deal directly with the unrepresented person; in such an instance, a lawyer should not undertake to give advice to the person who is attempting to represent himself, except that he may advise him to obtain a lawyer.

Duty of the Lawyer to the Adversary System of Justice

EC 7-19 Our legal system provides for the adjudication of disputes governed by the rules of substantive, evidentiary, and procedural law. An adversary presentation counters the natural human tendency to judge too swiftly in terms of the familiar that which is not yet fully known, the advocate, by his zealous preparation and presentation of facts and law, enables the tribunal to come to the hearing with an open and neutral mind and to render impartial judgments. The duty of a lawyer to his client and his duty to the legal system are the same: to represent his client zealously within the bounds of the law.

EC 7-20 In order to function properly, our adjudicative process requires an informed, impartial tribunal capable of administering justice promptly and efficiently according to procedures that command public confidence and respect. Not only must there be competent, adverse presentation of evidence and issues, but a tribunal must be aided by rules appropriate to an effective and dignified process. The procedures under which tribunals operate in our adversary system have been prescribed largely by legislative enactments, court rules and decisions, and administrative rules. Through the years certain concepts of proper professional conduct have become rules of law applicable to the adversary adjudicative process. Many of these concepts are the bases for standards of professional conduct set forth in the Disciplinary Rules.

EC 7-21 The civil adjudicative process is primarily designed for the settlement of disputes between parties, while the criminal process is designed for the protection of society as a whole. Threatening to use, or using, the criminal process to coerce adjustment of private civil claims or controversies is a subversion of that process; further, the person against whom the criminal process is so misused may be deterred from asserting his legal rights and thus the usefulness of the civil process in settling private disputes is impaired. As in all cases of abuse of judicial process, the improper use of criminal process tends to diminish public confidence in our legal system.

EC 7-22 Respect for judicial rulings is essential to the proper administration of justice; however, a litigant or his lawyer may, in good faith and within the framework of the law, take steps to test the correctness of a ruling of a tribunal.

EC 7-23 The complexity of law often makes it difficult for a tribunal to be fully informed unless the pertinent law is presented by the lawyers in the cause. A tribunal that is fully informed on the applicable law is better able to make a fair and accurate determination of the matter before it. The adversary system contemplates that each lawyer will present and argue the existing law in the light most favorable to his client. Where a lawyer knows of legal authority in the controlling jurisdiction directly adverse to the position of his client, he should inform the tribunal of its existence unless his adversary has done so; but, having made such disclosure, he may challenge its soundness in whole or in part.

EC 7-24 In order to bring about just and informed decisions, evidentiary and procedural rules have been established by tribunals to permit the inclusion of relevant evidence and argument and the exclusion of all other considerations. The expression by a lawyer of his personal opinion as to the justness of a cause, as to the credibility of a witness, as to the culpability of a civil litigant, or as to the guilt or innocence of an accused is not a proper subject for argument to the trier of fact. It is improper as to factual matters because admissible evidence possessed by a lawyer should be presented only as sworn testimony. It is improper as to all other matters because, were the rule otherwise, the silence of a lawyer on a given occasion could be construed unfavorably to his client. However, a lawyer may argue, on his analysis of the evidence, for any position or conclusion with respect to any of the foregoing matters.

Appendix

EC 7-25 Rules of evidence and procedure are designed to lead to just decisions and are part of the framework of the law. Thus while a lawyer may take steps in good faith and within the framework of the law to test the validity of rules, he is not justified in consciously violating such rules and he should be diligent in his efforts to guard against his unintentional violation of them. As examples, a lawyer should subscribe to or verify only those pleadings that he believes are in compliance with applicable law and rules; a lawyer should not make any prefatory statement before a tribunal in regard to the purported facts of the case on trial unless he believes that his statement will be supported by admissible evidence; a lawyer should not ask a witness a question solely for the purpose of harassing or embarrassing him; and a lawyer should not by subterfuge put before a jury matters which it cannot properly consider.

EC 7-26 The law and Disciplinary Rules prohibit the use of fraudulent, false, or perjured testimony or evidence. A lawyer who knowingly participates in introduction of such testimony or evidence is subject to discipline. A lawyer should, however, present any admissible evidence his client desires to have presented unless he knows, or from facts within his knowledge should know, that such testimony or evidence is false, fraudulent, or perjured.

EC 7-27 Because it interferes with the proper administration of justice, a lawyer should not suppress evidence that he or his client has a legal obligation to reveal or produce. In like manner, a lawyer should not advise or cause a person to secrete himself or to leave the jurisdiction of a tribunal for the purpose of making him unavailable as a witness therein.

EC 7-28 Witnesses should always testify truthfully and should be free from any financial inducements that might tempt them to do otherwise. A lawyer should not pay or agree to pay a non-expert witness an amount in excess of reimbursement for expenses and financial loss incident to his being a witness; however, a lawyer may pay or agree to pay an expert witness a reasonable fee for his services as an expert. But in no event should a lawyer pay or agree to pay a contingent fee to any witness. A lawyer should exercise reasonable diligence to see that his client and lay associates conform to these standards.

EC 7-29 To safeguard the impartiality that is essential to the judicial process, veniremen and jurors should be protected against extraneous influences. When impartiality is present, public confidence in the judicial system is enhanced. There should be no extrajudicial communication with veniremen prior to trial or with jurors during trial by or on behalf of a lawyer connected with the case. Furthermore, a lawyer who is not connected with the case should not communicate with or cause another to communicate with a venireman or a juror about the case. After the trial, communication by a lawyer with jurors is permitted so long as he refrains from asking questions or making comments that tend to harass or embarrass the juror or to influence actions of the juror in future cases. Were a lawyer to be prohibited from communicating after trial with a juror, he could not ascertain if the verdict might be subject to legal challenge, in which event the invalidity of a verdict might go undetected. When an extrajudicial communication by a lawyer with a juror is permitted by law, it should be made considerately and with deference to the personal feelings of the juror.

EC 7-30 Vexatious or harassing investigations of veniremen or jurors seriously impair the effectiveness of our jury system. For this reason, a lawyer or anyone on his behalf who conducts an investigation of veniremen or jurors should act with circumspection and restraint.

EC 7-31 Communications with or investigations of members of families of veniremen or jurors by a lawyer or by anyone on his behalf are subject to the restrictions imposed upon the lawyer with respect to his communications with or investigations of veniremen and jurors.

EC 7-32 Because of his duty to aid in preserving the integrity of the jury system, a lawyer who learns of improper conduct by or towards a venireman, a juror, or a member of the family of either should make a prompt report to the court regarding such conduct.

EC 7-33 A goal of our legal system is that each party shall have his case, criminal or civil, adjudicated by an impartial tribu-

Appendix

nal. The attainment of this goal may be defeated by dissemination of news or comments which tend to influence judge or jury. Such news or comments may prevent prospective jurors from being impartial at the outset of the trial and may also interfere with the obligation of jurors to base their verdict solely upon the evidence admitted in the trial. The release by a lawyer of out-of-court statements regarding an anticipated or pending trial may improperly affect the impartiality of the tribunal. For these reasons, standards for permissible and prohibited conduct of a lawyer with respect to trial publicity have been established.

EC 7-34 The impartiality of a public servant in our legal system may be impaired by the receipt of gifts or loans. A lawyer, therefore, is never justified in making a gift or a loan to a judge, a hearing officer, or an official or employee of a tribunal except as permitted by Section C(4) of Canon 5 of the Code of Judicial Conduct, but a lawyer may make a contribution to the campaign fund of a candidate for judicial office in conformity with Section B(2) under Canon 7 of the Code of Judicial Conduct.

EC 7-35 All litigants and lawyers should have access to tribunals on an equal basis. Generally, in adversary proceedings a lawyer should not communicate with a judge relative to a matter pending before, or which is to be brought before, a tribunal over which he presides in circumstances which might have the effect or give the appearance of granting undue advantage to one party. For example, a lawyer should not communicate with a tribunal by a writing unless a copy thereof is promptly delivered to opposing counsel or to the adverse party if he is not represented by a lawyer. Ordinarily an oral communication by a lawyer with a judge or hearing officer should be made only upon adequate notice to opposing counsel, or, if there is none, to the opposing party. A lawyer should not condone or lend himself to private importunities by another with a judge or hearing officer on behalf of himself or his client.

EC 7-36 Judicial hearings ought to be conducted through dignified and orderly procedures designed to protect the rights of all parties. Although a lawyer has the duty to represent his client zealously, he should not engage in any conduct that offends the dignity and decorum of proceedings. While maintaining his independence, a lawyer should be respectful, courteous, and aboveboard in his relations with a judge or hearing officer before whom he appears. He should avoid undue solicitude for the comfort or convenience of judge or jury and should avoid any other conduct calculated to gain special consideration.

EC 7-37 In adversary proceedings, clients are litigants and though ill feeling may exist between clients, such ill feeling should not influence a lawyer in his conduct, attitude, and demeanor towards opposing lawyers. A lawyer should not make unfair or derogatory personal reference to opposing counsel. Haranguing and offensive tactics by lawyers interfere with the orderly administration of justice and have no proper place in our legal system.

EC 7-38 A lawyer should be courteous to opposing counsel and should accede to reasonable requests regarding court proceedings, settings, continuances, waiver of procedural formalities, and similar matters which do not prejudice the rights of his client. He should follow local customs of courtesy or practice, unless he gives timely notice to opposing counsel of his intention not to do so. A lawyer should be punctual in fulfilling all professional commitments.

EC 7-39 In the final analysis, proper functioning of the adversary system depends upon cooperation between lawyers and tribunals in utilizing procedures which will preserve the impartiality of tribunals and make their decisional processes prompt and just, without impinging upon the obligation of lawyers to represent their clients zealously within the framework of the law.

Disciplinary Rules

DR 7-101 Representing a Client Zealously
(A) A lawyer shall not intentionally:
    (1) Fail to seek the lawful objectives of his client through reasonably available means permitted by law and the

Appendix

Disciplinary Rules, except as provided by DR 7-101(B). A lawyer does not violate this Disciplinary Rule, however, by acceding to reasonable requests of opposing counsel which do not prejudice the rights of his client, by being punctual in fulfilling all professional commitments, by avoiding offensive tactics, or by treating with courtesy and consideration all persons involved in the legal process.

(2) Fail to carry out a contract of employment entered into with a client for professional services, but he may withdraw as permitted under DR2-110, DR5-102, and DR5-105.

(3) Prejudice or damage his client during the course of the professional relationship, except as required under DR7-102(B).

(B) In his representation of a client, a lawyer may:

(1) Where permissible, exercise his professional judgment to waive or fail to assert a right or position of his client.

(2) Refuse to aid or participate in conduct that he believes to be unlawful, even though there is some support for an argument that the conduct is legal.

DR 7-102 Representing a Client Within the Bounds of the Law

(A) In his representation of a client, a lawyer shall not:

(1) File a suit, assert a position, conduct a defense, delay a trial, or take other action on behalf of his client when he knows or when it is obvious that such action would serve merely to harass or maliciously injure another.

(2) Knowingly advance a claim or defense that is unwarranted under existing law, except that he may advance such claim or defense if it can be supported by good faith argument for an extension, modification, or reversal of existing law.

(3) Conceal or knowingly fail to disclose that which he is required by law to reveal.

(4) Knowingly use perjured testimony or false evidence.
(5) Knowingly make a false statement of law or fact.
(6) Participate in the creation or preservation of evidence when he knows or it is obvious that the evidence is false.
(7) Counsel or assist his client in conduct that the lawyer knows to be illegal or fraudulent.
(8) Knowingly engage in other illegal conduct or conduct contrary to a Disciplinary Rule.

(B) A lawyer who receives information clearly establishing that:

(1) His client has, in the course of the representation, perpetrated a fraud upon a person or tribunal shall promptly call upon his client to rectify the same, and if his client refuses or is unable to do so, he shall reveal the fraud to the affected person or tribunal, except when the information is protected as a privileged communication.
(2) A person other than his client has perpetrated a fraud upon a tribunal shall promptly reveal the fraud to the tribunal.

DR 7-103 Performing the Duty of Public Prosecutor or Other Government Lawyer

(A) A public prosecutor or other government lawyer shall not institute or cause to be instituted criminal charges when he knows or it is obvious that the charges are not supported by probable cause.

(B) A public prosecutor or other government lawyer in criminal litigation shall make timely disclosure to counsel for the defendant, or to the defendant if he has no counsel, of the existence of evidence, known to the prosecutor or other government lawyer, that tends to negate the guilt of the accused, mitigate the degree of the offense, or reduce the punishment.

DR 7-104 Communicating With One of Adverse Interest

(A) During the course of his representation of a client a lawyer shall not:

Appendix

(1) Communicate or cause another to communicate on the subject of the representation with a party he knows to be represented by a lawyer in that matter unless he has the prior consent of the lawyer representing such other party or is authorized by law to do so.

(2) Give advice to a person who is not represented by a lawyer, other than the advice to secure counsel, if the interests of such person are or have a reasonable possibility of being in conflict with the interests of his client.

DR 7-105 Threatening Criminal Prosecution

(A) A lawyer shall not present, participate in presenting, or threaten to present criminal charges solely to obtain an advantage in a civil matter.

DR 7-106 Trial Conduct

(A) A lawyer shall not disregard or advise his client to disregard a standing rule of a tribunal or a ruling of a tribunal made in the course of a proceeding, but he may take appropriate steps in good faith to test the validity of such rule or ruling.

(B) In presenting a matter to a tribunal, a lawyer shall disclose:

(1) Legal authority in the controlling jurisdiction known to him to be directly adverse to the position of his client and which is not disclosed by opposing counsel.

(2) Unless privileged or irrelevant, the identities of the clients he represents and of the persons who employed him.

(C) In appearing in his professional capacity before a tribunal, a lawyer shall not:

(1) State or allude to any matter that he has no reasonable basis to believe is relevant to the case or that will not be supported by admissible evidence.

(2) Ask any question that he has no reasonable basis to

believe is relevant to the case and that is intended to degrade a witness or other person.
(3) Assert his personal knowledge of the facts in issue, except when testifying as a witness.
(4) Assert his personal opinion as to the justness of a cause, as to the credibility of a witness, as to the culpability of a civil litigant, or as to the guilt or innocence of an accused; but he may argue, on his analysis of the evidence, for any position or conclusion with respect to the matters stated herein.
(5) Fail to comply with known local customs of courtesy or practice of the bar or a particular tribunal without giving to opposing counsel timely notice of his intent not to comply.
(6) Engage in undignified or discourteous conduct which is degrading to a tribunal.
(7) Intentionally or habitually violate any established rule of procedure or of evidence.

DR 7-107 Trial Publicity

(A) A lawyer participating in or associated with the investigation of a criminal matter shall not make or participate in making an extrajudicial statement that a reasonable person would expect to be disseminated by means of public communication and that does more than state without elaboration:
(1) Information contained in a public record.
(2) That the investigation is in progress.
(3) The general scope of the investigation including a description of the offense and, if permitted by law, the identity of the victim.
(4) A request for assistance in apprehending a suspect or assistance in other matters and the information necessary thereto.
(5) A warning to the public of any dangers.

(B) A lawyer or law firm associated with the prosecution or defense of a criminal matter shall not, from the time of the filing of a

Appendix

complaint, information, or indictment, the issuance of an arrest warrant, or arrest until the commencement of the trial or disposition without trial, make or participate in making an extrajudicial statement that a reasonable person would expect to be disseminated by means of public communication and that relates to:

(1) The character, reputation, or prior criminal record (including arrests, indictments, or other charges of crime) of the accused.

(2) The possibility of a plea of guilty to the offense charged or to a lesser offense.

(3) The existence or contents of any confession, admission, or statement given by the accused or his refusal or failure to make a statement.

(4) The performance or results of any examinations or test or the refusal or failure of the accused to submit to examinations or tests.

(5) The identity, testimony, or credibility of a prospective witness.

(6) Any opinion as to the guilt or innocence of the accused, the evidence, or the merits of the case.

(C) DR 7-107(B) does not preclude a lawyer during such period from announcing:

(1) The name, age, residence, occupation, and family status of the accused.

(2) If the accused has not been apprehended, any information necessary to aid in his apprehension or to warn the public of any dangers he may present.

(3) A request for assistance in obtaining evidence.

(4) The identity of the victim of the crime.

(5) The fact, time, and place of arrest, resistance, pursuit, and use of weapons.

(6) The identity of investigating and arresting officers or agencies and the length of the investigation.

(7) At the time of seizure, a description of the physical evidence seized, other than a confession, admission, or statement.

>   (8) The nature, substance, or text of the charge.
>   (9) Quotations from or references to public records of the court in the case.
>   (10) The scheduling or result of any step in the judicial proceedings.
>   (11) That the accused denies the charges made against him.

(D) During the selection of a jury or the trial of a criminal matter, a lawyer or law firm associated with the prosecution or defense of a criminal matter shall not make or participate in making an extra-judicial statement that a reasonable person would expect to be disseminated by means of public communication and that relates to the trial, parties, or issues in the trial or other matters that are reasonably likely to interfere with a fair trial, except that he may quote from or refer without comment to public records of the court in the case.

(E) After the completion of a trial or disposition without trial of a criminal matter and prior to the imposition of sentence, a lawyer or law firm associated with the prosecution or defense shall not make or participate in making an extrajudicial statement that a reasonable person would expect to be disseminated by public communication and that is reasonably likely to affect the imposition of sentence.

(F) The foregoing provisions of DR 7-107 also apply to professional disciplinary proceedings and juvenile disciplinary proceedings when pertinent and consistent with other law applicable to such proceedings.

(G) A lawyer or law firm associated with a civil action shall not during its investigation or litigation make or participate in making an extra-judicial statement, other than a quotation from or reference to public records, that a reasonable person would expect to be disseminated by means of public communication and that relates to:

>   (1) Evidence regarding the occurrence or transaction involved.

Appendix

    (2) The character, credibility, or criminal record of a party, witness, or prospective witness.

    (3) The performance or results of any examinations or tests or the refusal or failure of a party to submit to such.

    (4) His opinion as to the merits of the claims or defenses of a party, except as required by law or administrative rule.

    (5) Any other matter reasonably likely to interfere with a fair trial of the action.

(H) During the pendency of an administrative proceeding, a lawyer or law firm associated therewith shall not make or participate in making a statement, other than a quotation from or reference to public records, that a reasonable person would expect to be disseminated by means of public communication if it is made outside the official course of the proceeding and relates to:

    (1) Evidence regarding the occurrence or transaction involved.

    (2) The character, credibility, or criminal record of a party, witness, or prospective witness.

    (3) Physical evidence or the performance or results of any examinations or tests or the refusal or failure of a party to submit to such.

    (4) His opinion as to the merits of the claims, defenses, or positions of an interested person.

    (5) Any other matter reasonably likely to interfere with a fair hearing.

(I) The foregoing provisions of DR 7-107 do not preclude a lawyer from replying to charges of misconduct publicly made against him or from participating in the proceedings of legislative, administrative, or other investigative bodies.

(J) A lawyer shall exercise reasonable care to prevent his employees and associates from making an extrajudicial statement that he would be prohibited from making under DR7-107.

DR 7-108 Communication with or Investigation of Jurors

(A) Before the trial of a case a lawyer connected therewith shall not communicate with or cause another to communicate with anyone he knows to be a member of the venire from which the jury will be selected for the trial of the case.

(B) During the trial of a case:

    (1) A lawyer connected therewith shall not communicate with or cause another to communicate with any member of the jury.

    (2) A lawyer who is not connected therewith shall not communicate with or cause another to communicate with a juror concerning the case.

(C) DR 7-108 (A) and (B) do not prohibit a lawyer from communicating with veniremen or jurors in the course of official proceedings.

(D) After discharge of the jury from further consideration of a case with which the lawyer was connected, the lawyer shall not ask questions of or make comments to a member of that jury that are calculated merely to harass or embarrass the juror or to influence his actions in future jury service.

(E) A lawyer shall not conduct or cause, by financial support or otherwise, another to conduct a vexatious or harassing investigation of either a venireman or a juror.

(F) All restrictions imposed by DR7-108 upon a lawyer also apply to communications with or investigations of members of a family of a venireman or a juror.

(G) A lawyer shall reveal promptly to the court improper conduct by a venireman or a juror, or by another toward a venireman or a juror or a member of his family, of which the lawyer has knowledge.

DR 7-109 Contact with Witnesses

(A) A lawyer shall not suppress any evidence that he or his client has a legal obligation to reveal or produce.

(B) A lawyer shall not advise or cause a person to secrete

Appendix

himself or to leave the jurisdiction of a tribunal for the purpose of making him unavailable as a witness therein.

(C) A lawyer shall not pay, offer to pay, or acquiesce in the payment of compensation to a witness contingent upon the content of his testimony or the outcome of the case. But a lawyer may advance, guarantee, or acquiesce in the payment of:

>   (1) Expenses reasonably incurred by a witness in attending or testifying.
>   (2) Reasonable compensation to a witness for his loss of time in attending or testifying.
>   (3) A reasonable fee for the professional services of an expert witness.

DR 7-110 Contact with Officials

(A) A lawyer shall not give or lend any thing of value to a judge, official, or employee of a tribunal except as permitted by Section C(4) of Canon 5 of the Code of Judicial Conduct, but a lawyer may make a contribution to the campaign fund of a candidate for judicial office in conformity with Section B(2) under Canon 7 of the Code of Judicial Conduct.

(B) In an adversary proceeding, a lawyer shall not communicate, or cause another to communicate, as to the merits of the cause with a judge or an official before whom the proceeding is pending, except:

>   (1) In the course of official proceedings in the cause.
>   (2) In writing if he promptly delivers a copy of the writing to opposing counsel or to the adverse party if he is not represented by a lawyer.
>   (3) Orally upon adequate notice to opposing counsel or to the adverse party if he is not represented by a lawyer.
>   (4) As otherwise authorized by law, or by Section A(4) under Canon 3 of the Code of Judicial Conduct.

CANON 8

A Lawyer Should Assist in Improving the Legal System

Ethical Considerations

EC 8-1 Changes in human affairs and imperfections in human institutions make necessary constant efforts to maintain and improve our legal system. This system should function in a manner that commands public respect and fosters the use of legal remedies to achieve redress of grievances. By reason of education and experience, lawyers are especially qualified to recognize deficiencies in the legal system and to initiate corrective measures therein. Thus they should participate in proposing and supporting legislation and programs to improve the system, without regard to the general interests or desires of clients or former clients.

EC 8-2 Rules of law are deficient if they are not just, understandable, and responsive to the needs of society. If a lawyer believes that the existence or absence of a rule of law, substantive or procedural, causes or contributes to an unjust result, he should endeavor by lawful means to obtain appropriate changes in the law. He should encourage the simplification of laws and the repeal or amendment of laws that are outmoded. Likewise, legal procedures should be improved whenever experience indicates a change is needed.

EC 8-3 The fair administration of justice requires the availability of competent lawyers. Members of the public should be educated to recognize the existence of legal problems and the resultant need for legal services, and should be provided methods for intelligent selection of counsel. Those persons unable to pay for legal services should be provided needed services. Clients and lawyers should not be penalized by undue geographical restraints upon representation in legal matters, and the bar should address itself to improvements in licensing, reciprocity, and admission procedures consistent with the needs of modern commerce.

EC 8-4 Whenever a lawyer seeks legislative or administrative changes, he should identify the capacity in which he appears, whether on behalf of himself, a client, or the public. A lawyer may advocate such changes on behalf of a client even though he does not agree with them. But when a lawyer purports to act on behalf of the public, he should espouse only those changes which he conscientiously believes to be in the public interest.

EC 8-5 Fraudulent, deceptive, or otherwise illegal conduct by a participant in a proceeding before a tribunal or legislative body is inconsistent with fair administration of justice, and it should never be participated in or condoned by lawyers. Unless constrained by his obligation to preserve the confidences and secrets of his client, a lawyer should reveal to appropriate authorities any knowledge he may have of such improper conduct.

EC 8-6 Judges and administrative officials having adjudicatory powers ought to be persons of integrity, competence, and suitable temperament. Generally, lawyers are qualified, by personal observation or investigation, to evaluate the qualifications of persons seeking or being considered for such public offices, and for this reason they have a special responsibility to aid in the selection of only those who are qualified. It is the duty of lawyers to endeavor to prevent political considerations from outweighing judicial fitness in the selection of judges. Lawyers should protest earnestly against the appointment or election of those who are unsuited for the bench and should strive to have elected or appointed thereto only those who are willing to forego pursuits, whether of a business, political, or other nature, that may interfere with the free and fair consideration of questions presented for adjudication. Adjudicatory officials, not being wholly free to defend themselves, are entitled to receive the support of the bar against unjust criticism. While a lawyer as a citizen has a right to criticize such officials publicly, he should be certain of the merit of his complaint, use appropriate language, and avoid petty criticisms, for unrestrained and intemperate statements tend to lessen public confidence in our legal system. Criticisms motivated by reasons other than a desire to improve the legal system are not justified.

EC 8-7 Since lawyers are a vital part of the legal system, they should be persons of integrity, of professional skill, and of dedication to the improvement of the system. Thus a lawyer should aid in establishing, as well as enforcing, standards of conduct adequate to protect the public by insuring that those who practice law are qualified to do so.

EC 8-8 Lawyers often serve as legislators or as holders of other public offices. This is highly desirable, as lawyers are uniquely qualified to make significant contributions to the improvement of the legal system. A lawyer who is a public officer, whether full or part-time, should not engage in activities in which his personal or professional interests are or foreseeably may be in conflict with his official duties.

EC 8-9 The advancement of our legal system is of vital importance in maintaining the rule of law and in facilitating orderly changes; therefore, lawyers should encourage, and should aid in making, needed changes and improvements.

Disciplinary Rules

    DR 8-101 Action as a Public Official
(A) A lawyer who holds public office shall not:
    (1) Use his public position to obtain, or attempt to obtain, a special advantage in legislative matters for himself or for a client under circumstances where he knows or it is obvious that such action is not in the public interest.
    (2) Use his public position to influence, or attempt to influence, a tribunal to act in favor of himself or of a client.
    (3) Accept any thing of value from any person when the lawyer knows or it is obvious that the offer is for the purpose of influencing his action as a public official.

DR 8-102 Statements Concerning Judges and Other Adjudicatory Officers

(A) A lawyer shall not knowingly make false statements of fact concerning the qualifications of a candidate for election or appointment to a judicial office.

(B) A lawyer shall not knowingly make false accusations against a judge or other adjudicatory officer.

DR 8-103 Lawyer Candidate for Judicial Office

(A) A lawyer who is a candidate for judicial office shall comply with the applicable provisions of Canon 7 of the Code of Judicial Conduct.

CANON 9

A Lawyer Should Avoid Even the Appearance of Professional Impropriety

Ethical Considerations

EC 9-1 Continuation of the American concept that we are to be governed by rules of law requires that the people have faith that justice can be obtained through our legal system. A lawyer should promote public confidence in our system and in the legal profession.

EC 9-2 Public confidence in law and lawyers may be eroded by irresponsible or improper conduct of a lawyer. On occasion, ethical conduct of a lawyer may appear to laymen to be unethical. In order to avoid misunderstandings and hence to maintain confidence, a lawyer should fully and promptly inform his client of material developments in the matters being handled for the client. While a lawyer should guard against otherwise proper conduct that has a tendency to diminish public confidence in the legal system or in the legal profession, his duty to clients or to the public should never be subordinate merely because the full discharge of his obligation may be misunderstood or may tend to subject him or the legal profession to criticism. When explicit ethical guidance does not exist, a lawyer should determine his conduct by acting in a manner that promotes public confidence in the integrity and efficiency of the legal system and the legal profession.

EC 9-3 After a lawyer leaves judicial office or other public employment, he should not accept employment in connection with any matter in which he had substantial responsibility prior to his leaving, since to accept employment would give the appearance of impropriety even if none exists.

EC 9-4 Because the very essence of the legal system is to provide procedures by which matters can be presented in an impartial manner so that they may be decided solely upon the merits, any statement or suggestion by a lawyer that he can or would attempt to circumvent those procedures is detrimental to the legal system and tends to undermine public confidence in it.

ED 9-5 Separation of the funds of a client from those of his lawyer not only serves to protect the client but also avoids even the appearance of impropriety, and therefore commingling of such funds should be avoided.

EC 9-6 Every lawyer owes a solemn duty to uphold the integrity and honor of his profession; to encourage respect for the law and for the courts and the judges thereof; to observe the Code of Professional Responsibility; to act as a member of a learned profession, one dedicated to public service; to cooperate with his brother lawyers in supporting the organized bar through the devoting of his time, efforts, and financial support as his professional standing and ability reasonably permit; to conduct himself so as to reflect credit on the legal profession and to inspire the confidence, respect, and trust of his clients and of the public; and to strive to avoid not only professional impropriety but also the appearance of impropriety.

Appendix

Disciplinary Rules

DR 9-101 Avoiding Even the Appearance of Impropriety

(A) A lawyer shall not accept private employment in a matter upon the merits of which he has acted in a judicial capacity.

(B) A lawyer shall not accept private employment in a matter in which he had substantial responsibility while he was a public employee.

(C) A lawyer shall not state or imply that he is able to influence improperly or upon irrelevant grounds any tribunal, legislative body, or public official.

DR 9-102 Preserving Identity of Funds and Property of a Client

(A) All funds of clients paid to a lawyer or law firm, other than advances for costs and expenses, shall be deposited in one or more identifiable bank accounts maintained in the state in which the law office is situated and no funds belonging to the lawyer or law firm shall be deposited therein except as follows:

> (1) Funds reasonably sufficient to pay bank charges may be deposited therein.
>
> (2) Funds belonging in part to a client and in part presently or potentially to the lawyer or law firm must be deposited therein, but the portion belonging to the lawyer or law firm may be withdrawn when due unless the right of the lawyer or law firm to receive it is disputed by the client, in which event the disputed portion shall not be withdrawn until the dispute is finally resolved.

(B) A lawyer shall:

> (1) Promptly notify a client of the receipt of his funds, securities, or other properties.
>
> (2) Identify and label securities and properties of a client promptly upon receipt and place them in a safe deposit box or other place of safekeeping as soon as practicable.

(3) Maintain complete records of all funds, securities, and other properties of a client coming into the possession of the lawyer and render appropriate accounts to his client regarding them.
(4) Promptly pay or deliver to the client as requested by a client the funds, securities, or other properties in the possession of the lawyer which the client is entitled to receive.

Definitions*

As used in the Disciplinary Rules of the Code of Professional Responsibility:
(1) "Differing interests" include every interest that will adversely affect either the judgment or the loyalty of a lawyer to a client, whether it be a conflicting, inconsistent, diverse, or other interest.
(2) "Law firm" includes a professional legal corporation.
(3) "Person" includes a corporation, an association, a trust, a partnership, and any other organization or legal entity.
(4) "Professional legal corporation" means a corporation, or an association treated as a corporation, authorized by law to practice law for profit.
(5) "State" includes the District of Columbia, Puerto Rico, and other federal territories and possessions.
(6) "Tribunal" includes all courts and all other adjudicatory bodies.
(7) "A Bar association" includes a bar association of specialists as referred to in DR2-105 (A)(1) or (4).
(8) "Qualified legal assistance organization" means an office or organization of one of the four types listed in DR2-103(D)(1)-(4), inclusive that meets all the requirements thereof.

*"Confidence" and "secret" are defined in DR4-101(A).

Table of References to the
ABA Code of Professional Responsibility

Canon	Page
Canon 1	67
EC 1-2	88
DR 1-102(A)(3), (4), (5), (6)	67, 86, 87, 88
DR 1-103	198, 245
Canon 2	4, 24
EC 2-1	4
EC 2-20	30
EC 2-26	4
EC 2-27	4, 236
EC 2-28	4
EC 2-29	4, 236
EC 2-30	4, 24, 38, 236
EC 2-31	24
EC 2-32	24
DR 2-102(B)	234
DR 2-102(C)	242
DR 2-103(D)	241
DR 2-104(A)	233
DR 2-106(C)	236
DR 2-107	241
DR 2-109	4, 24
DR 2-110	24

References to ABA Code

Canon	Page
DR 2-110(B)	4
DR 2-110(C)	4
DR 2-110(C)(1)(a), (c), (d), (e)	38
Canon 4	9, 43, 56, 59, 95, 108, 124, 155, 196
EC 4-1	9, 43, 56, 59, 95, 124, 155, 196
EC 4-2	95, 124, 155, 196
EC 4-3	196
EC 4-4	43, 56, 59, 95, 108, 124, 155, 196
EC 4-5	9, 43, 56, 59, 95, 108, 155, 196
EC 4-6	9, 95, 108, 155, 242
DR 4-101	9, 124
DR 4-101(A)	43, 56, 59, 155, 196
DR 4-101(B)	43, 56, 155, 196
DR 4-101(B)(1), (2), (3)	59, 242, 244, 245
DR 4-101(C)	196
DR 4-101(C)(3)	43, 244, 246
Canon 5	9, 30, 93, 95, 124, 141
EC 5-1	30
EC 5-2	30
EC 5-3	30
EC 5-7	30, 234
EC 5-8	234
EC 5-14	30, 93, 95, 234, 237
EC 5-15	30, 93, 95, 141, 234, 237
EC 5-16	30, 93, 234, 237
EC 5-17	93, 124, 234, 237
EC 5-18	9, 93, 124, 141

References to ABA Code

Canon	Page
EC 5-19	30, 93, 124
EC 5-21	141
EC 5-22	141
DR 5-101	198, 234
DR 5-103(A)	30, 234
DR 5-103(B)	234
DR 5-105	124, 234, 237
DR 5-105(A)	93
DR 5-105(B)	93
DR 5-105(C)	93
Canon 6	196
EC 6-2	27
EC 6-4	196
EC 6-5	196
DR 6-101(A)	196
DR 6-101(A)(1)	241
DR 6-102(A)	241
Canon 7	9, 24, 38, 43, 56, 59, 124, 141, 192
EC 7-1	24
EC 7-3	9, 24, 38
EC 7-4	9, 24, 38, 141
EC 7-5	9, 24, 141
EC 7-6	192
EC 7-7	24, 38, 141
EC 7-8	9, 24, 38, 124, 141
EC 7-9	9, 38, 43, 56, 141
EC 7-10	56
EC 7-12	9
EC 7-13	147, 150
EC 7-14	141

Canon	Page
EC 7-17	27
EC 7-19	38, 56
EC 7-22	67
EC 7-23	38, 59
EC 7-24	56
EC 7-26	43, 56, 59, 237
EC 7-27	9, 59, 237
EC 7-33	67
EC 7-36	67
DR 7-101(A)(1)	24, 38
DR 7-101(B)(1)	24, 38, 59
DR 7-102	244
DR 7-102(A)	237
DR 7-102(A)(1), (2), (4), (5), (6), (7)	24, 38, 43, 56, 192
DR 7-102(B)	196, 197 et seq., 235, 242
DR 7-102(B)(1), (2)	9, 43, 64, 197 et seq.
DR 7-103(A)	150
DR 7-104	237
DR 7-104(A)(1)	239
DR 7-106	87
DR 7-106(B)	245
DR 7-106(B)(1)	59
DR 7-107(B)	239
DR 7-107(D)	237
DR 7-107(G)	67
DR 7-108	237
DR 7-108(G)	198
DR 7-109	241
Canon 8	67
EC 8-6	67

References to ABA Code

Canon	Page
DR 8-101	234
DR 8-102(A)	87
DR 8-102(B)	67, 87
Canon 9	67, 93, 95, 108, 155, 233, 234
EC 9-1	67, 95, 108
EC 9-2	95, 108
EC 9-3	155
EC 9-4	67
EC 9-6	27, 67, 93
DR 9-101	239
DR 9-101(B)	155, 182, 183, 185, 186, 238